New Hampshire 1742 Estate List

Pauline Johnson Oesterlin

	Name										
	Rob[t] Cort	J	D	2	6		J	2	3	5	10	J
	James Calswell	2	J	2	3	3			3	6		J	J
	W[m] Adams	2	J	2	3	3			3	6		J	J
Deecon	John Moore	J	D	1	2	3			3	3		J	J
	Patrick Douglass	J	D	1	2	5	2	1		4	8		J
	John Hunter	1	D	1	2	2	3	1	1	6	2	J	J
	Widdow M[c] Murphy	J	D	1	1	1		2	2	4	1		
	John Brown	J	1		1	1		2	2	2			J
	Hugh Brown					1				2	2		
	James Adams, Weaver	1	1		1					2	2		
	Widdow Archibald		1		2			4		2	2		
	W[m] Addison	J	1							2	2		
	Alex[r] Ashpin	J				2				3	3		J	J
	James Gillmore	J	D	1	2	3		2		2	3		J	J
	William Gillmore	2	D	1			2			3	3		J	J
	John French	J	J		J					2	2		
	Widdow Moore	J	D	1	2	3		2		2	2		
	Peter Custy	J	J	1	2			2		2	2		
	Robert Gillmore	J	J		J		J		J	J	J		J
	James Ewing	J	J	1					J	3	3		J	J
	Arch[d] Miller	2	1		2	J			J	2	6	2	J
	Sam[l] Peterson	1	1		2				J	2	2		
	William Chambers	1	1		2			J		2	3		
	Thomas Custy	J	D	1	2	2		J	8	J	2	4	2	J
	Robert M[c]Cardy	J	D	1		J	8	J	2	2		
	Michail Gordon		1		2			J		2	2		
	William Kelso	3	J		2	J				J	3	2	J	J
	Alex[r] Kelso	J	J		2	2		2		2	5	1		J
	Thomas Horner	J	J	1	2	4		2	2	J	6	7	2	J	J
	William Hogg	J	J		2	4		2	J	3	3		J	J
	William M[c]Master	2	J	1	2	4	1			2	8		
	Arthur Boyd	1	1		J			J	J			
	Archibald Cunningham	1	1		1			J	2	J		
	Archibald M[c]Intosh							J	2	2	J		
	Walter M[c]Farland	1	1		J					2	2		
	John Stinson		J	1	2			J	3	J	J		J
	Nathan M[c]Farland	1	J		4	1	3	J	J			
	David M[c]Duffee	3	D	1	2	4	3	2		5	5		
Deecon	James Adams	2	D	1	2	4	8	3		4	8	2	8	J
	William Willson	J	1	F	J	2		17	12	2	12	J
	Gabriel Bar							J	4		J
	James Bar	J	D	1	2	6	2	2	2	6	4	J	J
	John Stewart	J	J	D	1	2	1	1	1	1	9	

NEW HAMPSHIRE 1742 ESTATE LIST

New Hampshire Society
of Genealogists

Special Publication
No. 1

Pauline Johnson Oesterlin

HERITAGE BOOKS
2012

HERITAGE BOOKS
AN IMPRINT OF HERITAGE BOOKS, INC.

Books, CDs, and more—Worldwide

For our listing of thousands of titles see our website at
www.HeritageBooks.com

Published 2012 by
HERITAGE BOOKS, INC.
Publishing Division
100 Railroad Ave. #104
Westminster, Maryland 21157

Copyright © 1994 Pauline Johnson Oesterlin

Other Heritage Books by the author:
Hillsborough County, New Hampshire Court Records, 1772–1799
Hopkinton, New Hampshire Vital Records: Volumes 1 and 2
New Hampshire 1742 Estate List
New Hampshire Marriage Licenses and Intentions, 1709–1961
Rockingham County, New Hampshire Paupers
Surname Guide to Massachusetts Town Histories
Pauline J. Oesterlin and Phyllis O. Longver

All rights reserved. No part of this book may be reproduced or transmitted in any form or by any means, electronic or mechanical, including photocopying, recording or by any information storage and retrieval system without written permission from the author, except for the inclusion of brief quotations in a review.

International Standard Book Numbers
Paperbound: 978-0-7884-0129-9
Clothbound: 978-0-7884-9304-1

For Jeff

TABLE OF CONTENTS

Frontispiece	ii
Acknowledgements	ix
Preface	xi
Introduction	xiii
Dunstable	1
Durham	15
Exeter	47
Greenland	53
Hampton	57
Hampton Falls	91
Haverhill	121
Kensington	145
Kingston	161
Litchfield	177
Londonderry	187
Methuen-Dracut	223
New Castle	237
Newington	253
Newmarket	261
Nottingham	279
Portsmouth	283
Rochester	289
Rumford	303
Rye	315
South Hampton	333
Amesbury	334
Byfield	356
Stratham	365
Windham	391

ACKNOWLEDGEMENTS

The support and encouragement of the staff at the Division of Records Management and Archives for the State of New Hampshire is warmly acknowledged. State Archivist Frank Mevers and State Records Manager Andrew Taylor were both instrumental in making materials available for this project.

Special appreciation is extended to Jeffrey Houston of Hampton, New Hampshire, who took the challenge of formatting this material for camera-ready presentation after several of the country's best-known typesetters turned the project down as too complicated. Without the dozens of extra hours he freely contributed, this publication would not have been possible.

PREFACE

Any government should base its operations upon a fairly accurate census of individuals as well as of taxable property. This was as true in the developing American colonies as it is today. On December 13, 1741 Benning Wentworth assumed the governorship of the province of New Hampshire to which he had been appointed earlier in the year by King George II with the concurrence of his councilors. Up to this point New Hampshire had shared a royal governor with Massachusetts with executive duties in New Hampshire actually performed by lieutenant governors, one of whom had been Benning's father, John Wentworth.

Each royal govenor in the American colonies functioned under a commission and a set of accompanying instructions from the King in Council plus another set of instructions from the Board of Trade. The King's instructions set forth the same policy as the commission but were more inclusive in content and more specific in direction. Of the 86 numbered paragraphs, number 61 directs the new governor to submit a population count.

> 61. You shall send to His Majesty and to his Commissioners for Trade & Plantations by the first Conveyance An Account of the present Number of Planters and Inhabitants, Men, Women, and Children, as well as Masters as Servants, free and unfree, and of the Slaves in the said Province, as also a Yearly Account of the Increase or Decrease of them; and how many of them are fit to bear Arms in the Militia of the said Province.

It is interesting to note that this is placed well toward the end of the instructions, following items such as whale fishing, mast trees, oaths, and liberty of conscience but preceding the several paragraphs bearing on the military establishment for defense of the Province.

To carry out this inventory (as well as all parts of his instructions) the new governor required the support of the populace. Thus, with the concurrence of his provincial council, whose members had likewise been designated by the King in Council, Wentworth called together the General Assembly whose twenty-one elected members met in Portsmouth in March 1742. Among the nineteen acts that they passed in the session, Chapter 7 directed clerks of towns and unchartered districts to take an inventory of all rateable estates. This act was passed on March 18, 1742. Most of the inventories were taken by early June, signed by the selectmen, and sent to the Secretary of State who would have forwarded a copy to the Board of Trade in London.

Establishment of the New Hampshire boundary in 1741 coupled with increasing confidence of the people in the government to defend the frontiers served to increase the value of the land and thus to increase the need for such inventories. Simultaneously, there was recognition of the increasing value of the products of the land, particularly of the mast trees and other timber products for the royal navy and fleets of trading vessels.

The records from which the following publication is presented certainly do not appear to fulfill the letter of the King's instructions although they do answer to the New Hampshire law of March 18th. While they reveal the number of heads of households and rateable property (which apparently included "Negroes" in certain towns) they do not reveal the number of children, indentured servants, or other individuals. Apparently no record of the total population was made. When Jeremy Belknap requested a population figure of 1742 from Secretary of State Joseph Pearson in 1792 the Secretary answered giving the number of ratable polls as 5,172, excluding several towns that had not reported, and only hazarding a guess that a multiplication by 5 or 6 of that might give the true population figure (*New Hampshire State Papers*, 7:723). Nor is there any indication that there is any other population figure for 1742 among the British archives. Based upon other estimates made at the time, historians generally use the figure 24,000 as the estimated population of 1742 (Green and Harrington, *American Population Before the Federal Census of 1790* [1932], 72).

These original documents were kept by the Provincial Secretary in Portsmouth and Exeter and then by the Secretary of State in Exeter. Since about 1808 they have been in Concord, in the State House from its completion in 1820 and at the State Archives since the mid-1960s.

Frank C. Mevers   September 1994
State Archivist

INTRODUCTION

Some significant changes occurred in New Hampshire between 1732 and 1742, the dates of its two surviving colonial estate lists. The infant sons of the 1710s had come of age in the interim and become voters and land owners. The men born in the 1670s and 1680s had begun to drop from the ranks or were being absorbed into the households of their sons or daughters. Over one thousand persons, mostly children, had died in the late 1730s when the dreaded throat distemper swept through the colonies. Some families buried all their children; in Hampton Falls, more than one sixth of the inhabitants died. The grim reaper in another guise hovered in the wings, awaiting the start of the first French and Indian War.

In the 1742 New Hampshire Estate List we find over seven hundred different surnames, many with only one or two representatives. Surnames with roots particular to New Hampshire included Colbath, Cram, Dearborn, Fogg, Keniston, Lamprey, Philbrick, Rand, Sanborn, Sherburne and Towle. Surnames with more than thirty heads of household included Batchelder, Brown, Dow, Page, Sanborn and Smith.

These totals are drawn from surviving records which lack individual submissions from many of the early towns, most noticeably Portsmouth, Exeter, Chester, and Greenland.

The orthography in this text varied greatly from town to town, and often within the town itself. Few hands were as clear and consistent as that of Hampton's clerk and fortunately not many were as bad as Methuen-Dracut's, which gave us the unforgettable "John Muglady," (perhaps this is really "McGillicuddy?"). The only practical approach we could devise under these circumstances was to enter the names as they were written in the text and to index them as we believed them to be.

Much useful information can be gleaned from the statistical presentations for individual households. The number of polls is of considerable interest, being evidence for the likely presence of adult sons or brothers in a household when the number is more than one. Over 2,800 individuals in nineteen towns are named here.

NH 1742 ESTATE LIST

Entries in the pasture, plowing, and mowing columns indicate ownership of land. If no deeds can be found for this head of household, the researcher is alerted to search for available proprietors' records where grants may have been made, or probate records where the land may have been inherited. A third option might be the town's selectmen's minutes where grants were sometimes made directly.

Since many New Hampshire families perpetuated given names with very little variation, it is sometimes difficult to determine which individual is represented in these lists. Occasionally it is possible to discriminate between generations by noting the number of animals and their ages, as well as the amount of land in the man's estate. The more land and animals, the closer to middle age the householder will likely prove to be.

A few border and name changes can be noted here. The usage of the archaic term "doom'd" can be understood to mean "assessed." Single houses and double houses were appraised at different rates, but only a few towns indicated any double houses.

The entries in this list for Haverhill and Methuen-Dracut evidently stemmed from the continuing border confusion between Massachusetts and New Hampshire. Salem, N.H. was originally part of Methuen, however. In 1742, Byfield was part of Salisbury, Mass., and ultimately became Seabrook. Dunstable not only was the parent town of Nashua, but supplied portions of Hollis, Hudson, Litchfield, Merrimack, and Tyngsborough. Likewise, in South Hampton, Amesbury parish is now in Massachusetts. Rumford is now known as Concord. Most of the maps included here date from 1805, over sixty years after this list was taken. By and large, the extant, contemporary maps contained very little detail and were not considered informative enough for use here.

Nashua (Dunstable)

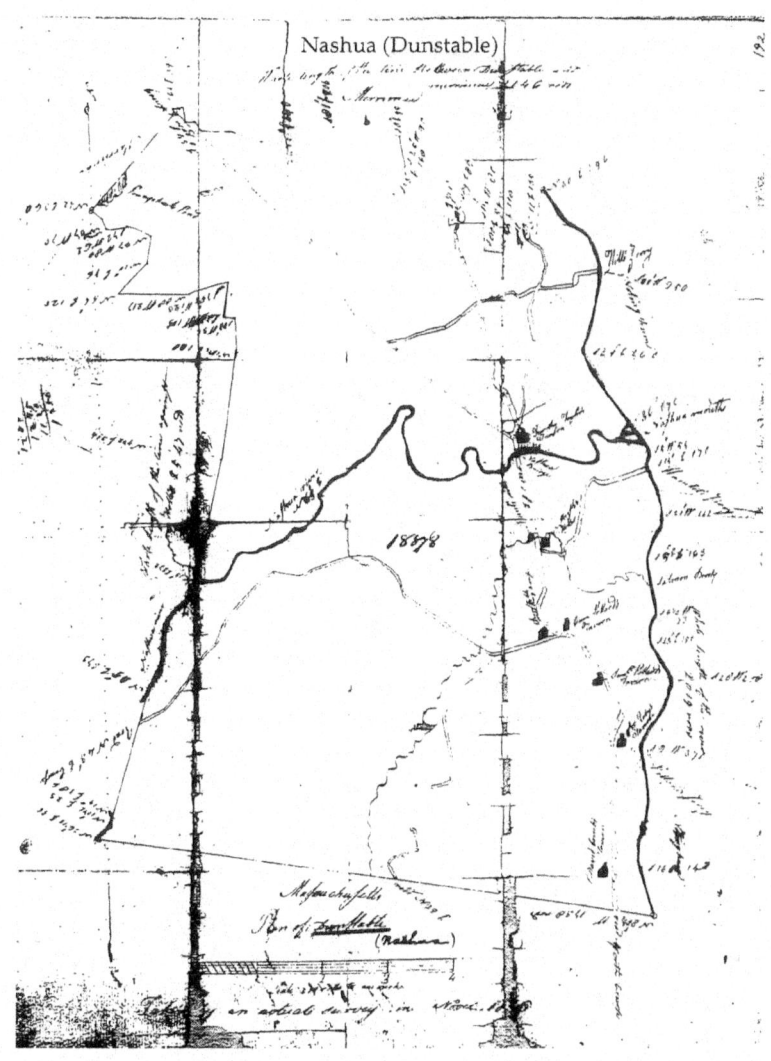

The Old Parish

Names	POLS	HOUSES	HORSES	OXEN	COWS	3 YEARS OLD
Joseph Blanchard Esq.	1	4	3	2	5	2
Isaac Farwell	1	1	1	4	3	0
Joseph French	1	1	1	2	2	0
Sampson French	1	1	1	0	2	0
Thomas Blanchard	2	1	1	2	4	0
Thomas Adams	2	1	1	2	5	2
Ephriam Adams	1	1	1	2	4	1
Zachariah Adams	1	0	1	2	2	0
Samuel Searls	1	1	1	0	2	0
Benj.a Eaton	1	1	0	2	3	0
Henry Parker	1	1	0	2	2	1
Daniel Searls	1	1	0	0	2	0
John Searls	1	0	1	0	1	0
Henry Adams	1	1	1	2	5	1
Tho.s Harwood	1	1	2	4	3	2
Isaac Cumings	1	2	1	2	5	0
Thomas Lund	1	1	1	0	2	0
Jonathan Lund	1	0	0	0	2	0

2 YEARS OLD	YEARLINGS	SWINE	MEADOW	MOWING	PASTURE
0	0	2	0	60	60
0	0	0	0	20	0
0	4	2	0	13	4
2	2	1	0	12	4
2	0	1	0	8	0
2	2	1	0	40	3
1	0	1	0	17	0
0	1	0	0	0	0
1	1	0	0	12	0
0	0	0	0	12	0
1	0	0	0	0	0
0	0	2	0	15	3
1	0	1	0	12	0
1	3	0	0	20	3
4	3	0	0	30	5
3	0	0	0	12	0
2	2	0	0	7	3
0	0	0	0	3	0

NH 1742 ESTATE TAX

Names	POLS	HOUSES	HORSES	OXEN	COWS	3 YEARS OLD
Ephriam Lund	1	0	0	0	0	0
William Lund	1	1	0	0	3	0
Phinehas Lund	1	1	0	2	0	0
Samuel Whiting	1	0	1	2	1	0
Jon^a French	1	1	1	2	2	0
Jon^a Lovewell	2	1	1	2	2	1
John Lovewell	1	1	0	2	2	0
Jonathan Combs	2	0	0	2	0	0
William Jonson	1	1	1	2	1	0
Josiah Butterfield	1	1	0	0	1	0
Thomas Chamberlain	1	0	0	0	3	0
Jabez Davise	2	1	1	0	3	0
Ben^a Richardson	1	0	1	0	2	0
John Alld	1	0	1	0	3	0
William Glin	1	0	1	2	2	1
Thomas Heall	2	1	0	2	1	0
Samuel Murder	2	1	1	0	2	0
Thomas Cowen	1	1	1	2	4	0

2 YEARS OLD	YEARLINGS	SWINE	MEADOW	MOWING	PASTURE
0	0	0	0	0	0
0	0	0	0	23	0
0	0	0	0	0	0
0	0	0	0	11	0
1	2	0	0	12	0
0	0	0	0	17	0
0	0	0	0	15	0
0	0	0	0	2	0
0	0	0	0	3	0
0	0	0	0	30	0
0	0	0	0	0	0
0	0	0	0	12	0
0	1	0	0	0	0
0	2	0	0	0	0
1	0	0	0	0	0
1	0	0	0	0	0
1	0	0	0	9	0
0	6	0	0	0	0

Names	POLS	HOUSES	HORSES	OXEN	COWS	3 YEARS OLD
Nath^{ll} Jewell	1	0	0	0	0	0
Thomas Jewell	1	0	1	4	0	0
John Buck	1	0	0	0	0	0
Gedion Behoney	1	0	0	0	0	0
Richard Temple	1	0	0	0	0	0
Salveirus Witney	1	1	0	0	3	0

New Parish

Names	POLS	HOUSES	HORSES	OXEN	COWS	3 YEARS OLD
Samuel Brown	1	1	1	2	5	1
Abraham Taylor	1	1	1	3	4	0
Peter Power	1	1	1	2	4	0
Elea^{zr} Flagg	1	1	1	5	5	0

2 YEARS OLD	YEARLINGS	SWINE	MEADOW	MOWING	PASTURE
0	0	0	0	4	0
0	0	0	0	0	0
0	0	0	0	0	0
0	0	0	0	0	0
0	0	0	0	0	0
0	0	0	0	6	0

2 YEARS OLD	YEARLINGS	SWINE	MEADOW	MOWING	PASTURE
1	1	1	0	20	3
0	0	1	0	30	0
0	0	2	0	10	0
0	0	1	0	30	2

New Parish

Names	POLS	HOUSES	HORSES	OXEN	COWS	3 YEARS OLD
Enoch Hunt	1	1	1	2	5	1
Stephen Harris	1	1	1	3	6	1
William Colburn	1	1	0	2	2	0
Samuel Cummings	1	1	1	0	2	0
Benja Farley	1	1	1	2	3	1
Jerah{ll} Cumings	1	1	0	0	2	0
William Blanchard	1	1	1	0	2	0
Josiah Wright	1	1	1	0	1	0
Josiah Blood	1	1	1	2	2	0
Jospeh Farley	1	1	0	4	2	1
Daniel Kendall	1	0	0	2	0	0
Samuel Farley	1	1	0	2	1	0
Josiah Brown	1	0	0	0	1	0
John Butterfield	1	1	1	0	2	0
Robert Blood	1	0	0	0	2	1
Benja Parker	1	1	0	0	0	0
Elnathan Blood	1	1	1	0	1	0
Thomas Patch	1	0	0	0	0	0

2 YEARS OLD	YEARLINGS	SWINE	MEADOW	MOWING	PASTURE
1	4	2	0	30	6
2	0	3	0	19	1
0	0	0	0	8	0
0	0	0	0	7	0
1	1	0	0	17	0
0	0	1	0	6	0
0	0	0	0	4	0
0	0	0	0	3	0
1	0	1	0	9	0
2	1	1	0	11	0
0	0	0	0	0	0
0	0	0	0	13	0
0	0	0	0	0	0
3	0	2	0	8	0
1	1	0	0	3	1
0	0	0	0	2	1
0	0	0	0	3	0
0	0	0	0	0	0

New Parish

Names	POLS	HOUSES	HORSES	OXEN	COWS	3 YEARS OLD
Amos Phillips	1	0	0	0	0	0
Benj[a] Blood	1	0	0	0	0	0
William Shattuck	1	1	1	1	2	0
David Nevins	2	1	1	3	1	0
William Nevins	1	0	0	0	0	0
Thomas Nevins	1	1	0	2	0	1
Robert Colburn	1	0	0	0	0	0
Peter Wheeler	1	0	0	0	1	1
Moses Proctor	1	1	0	4	2	0
James M[c]donnel	3	1	1	2	5	0
Jonathan Malven	1	0	0	0	2	1
Henry Barton	1	0	1	0	2	1
Nath[ll] Blood	1	1	0	2	1	0
William Adams	1	1	0	0	0	0
Jonathan Danforth	1	0	0	0	0	0
Stphen Ames	1	0	1	2	3	0
Phillip Woolerick	1	0	0	0	0	0
John Beard	1	0	0	0	0	0

2 YEARS OLD	YEARLINGS	SWINE	MEADOW	MOWING	PASTURE
0	0	0	0	0	0
0	0	0	0	0	0
1	0	0	0	10	0
0	0	2	0	3	0
0	0	0	0	5	0
1	1	0	0	7	0
0	0	0	0	0	0
0	0	0	0	0	0
2	0	0	0	12	0
1	1	0	0	7	0
0	0	0	0	4	0
0	0	2	0	8	0
0	0	1	0	7	0
0	0	0	0	7	0
0	0	0	0	0	0
0	0	0	3	0	0
0	0	0	0	0	0
0	0	0	0	0	0

New Parish

Names	POLS	HOUSES	HORSES	OXEN	COWS	3 YEARS OLD
Daniel Nutting	1	0	0	0	0	0
Nicklas French	1	0	0	2	0	0

This is a True and an Exact account of the Number of Rateable Poles and of ye Estates Real and Personall within Dunstable District (So Called) Taken agreeable To the Directions I Rec^d per the Com:^{tee} of the Grate and Genl Court of the Province of Newhampshire

Attested per Abr: Taylor Clerk

May the 20th 1742

2 YEARS OLD	YEARLINGS	SWINE	MEADOW	MOWING	PASTURE
0	0	0	0	0	0
0	0	3	0	3	0

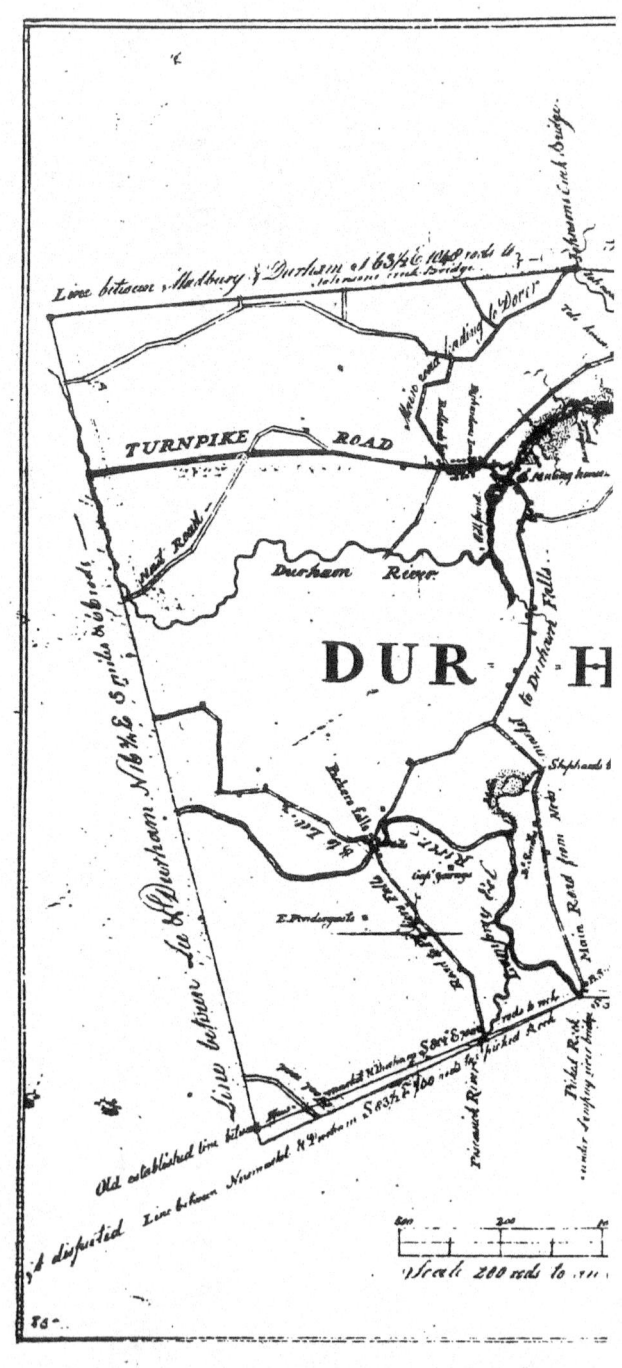

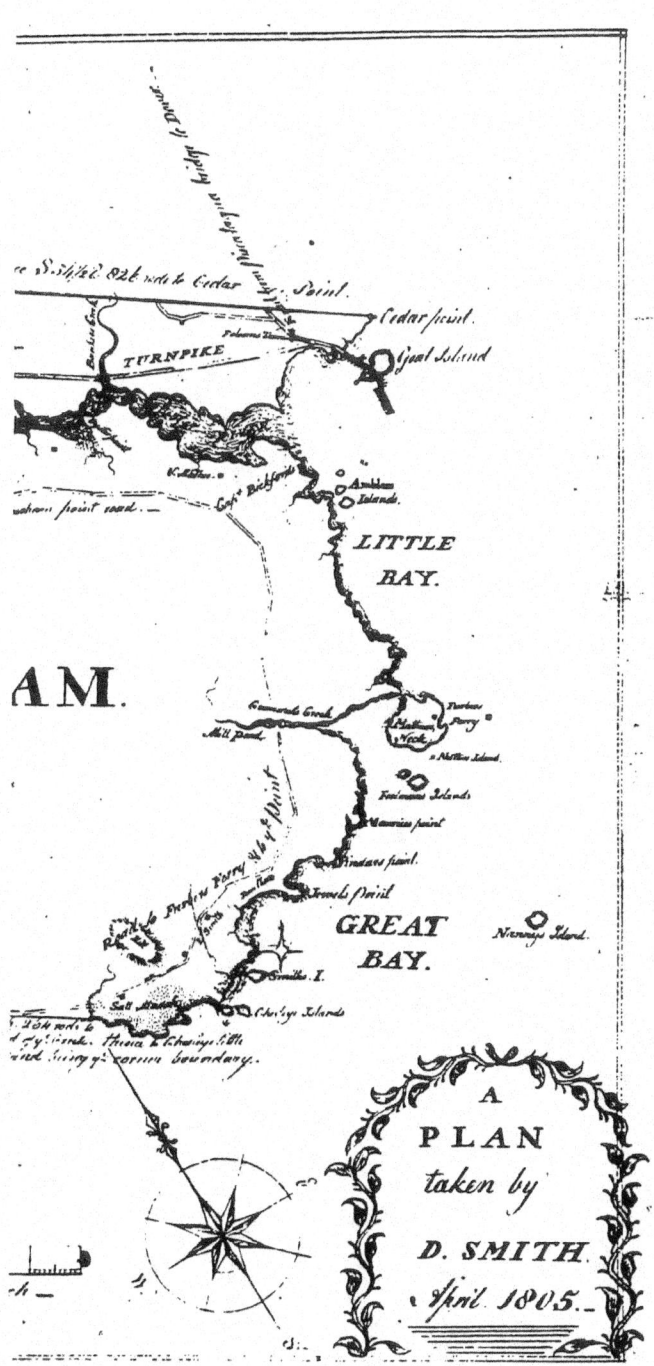

NH 1742 ESTATE TAX

Names	POLS	D/HOUSES	SINGLE HOUSE	PLANTING	PASTURE	HORSES
John Daniel	0		0	0	0	0
Eliphalet Daniel	1		1	3	3	0
Rheuben Daniel	1		0	0	0	0
Francis Drew	1		0	0	0	0
Benjamin Durgin	1	1	0	2	0	0
John Kent	1	1	0	15	10	0
Abraham Matthes	1	1	0	10	10	1
Thomas Drew	1		0	0	0	0
Joseph Drew	1	1	0	10	4	1
John Drew	1		0	0	0	0
Joseph Wheeler	1	1	0	8	20	0
John Edgerley	1	1	0	6	3	1
Joseph Edgerley	1		1	12	6	1
John Bickford	1	1	0	10	5	1
Thomas Langley	1	1	0	8	4	1
Robert Kent	1		1	10	7	0
William Lord	1		0	0	0	0
John Jenkes	1		1	2	2	1
Stephen Wille	1		1	6	6	0

DURHAM

OXEN	COWS	3 YEAR OLD	2 YEAR OLD	1 YEAR OLD	SWINE
0	0	0	0	0	0
0	2	0	0	0	0
0	0	0	0	0	0
0	0	0	0	0	0
0	2	1	0	0	0
2	5	0	1	0	0
0	1	0	0	0	0
0	0	0	0	0	0
2	5	4	1	2	2
2	0	0	0	0	0
0	4	0	4	4	1
0	1	0	1	1	1
0	2	1	0	1	0
2	3	0	2	1	1
6	5	2	2	1	1
0	6	4	2	1	
0	1	3	0	0	0
0	0	1	0	2	1
2	4	2	1	0	0

NH 1742 ESTATE TAX

Names	POLS	D/HOUSES	SINGLE HOUSE	PLANTING	PASTURE	HORSES
Cp.ᵗ Francis Matthes	2	1	0	25	25	1
Caleb Wakeham	1		1	9	3	1
Joseph Stevenson	1		1	10	10	0
Abraham Stevenson	1		1	6	6	1
Francis Footman	1		1	0	0	0
Thomas Bickford	1		1	2	6	0
William Wormwood	1	0	0	0	0	0
Daniel Davis	1	1	0	17	0	1
Stephen Jenknes	1	1	0	15	15	0
Robert Burnum	1	1	0	10	10	1
John Burnum	2	1	0	10	10	2
Peter Mason	1	1	0	10	15	0
Daniel Rogers	1	1	0	2	0	0
Stephen Glazier	1		0	0	0	0
Samuel Adams	1	1	0	1	0	1
John Buss	1		1	2	4	0
John Wille Jun.ʳ	1	1	0	0	0	0
Theodorus Wille	1		1	0	0	0
David Davis	2	1	0	14	5	0

DURHAM

OXEN	COWS	3 YEAR OLD	2 YEAR OLD	1 YEAR OLD	SWINE
0	5	3	3	3	1
2	4	0	4	0	1
0	2	2	0	1	0
4	3	0	2	0	0
0	1	0	0	0	0
0	1	2	1	0	1
0	0	0	0	0	0
2	3	1	2	0	0
2	3	0	0	0	1
2	5	0	3	0	0
4	4	2	2	0	1
4	3	0	2	0	0
0	2	0	0	0	0
0	0	0	0	0	0
0	1	0	0	0	0
0	2	0	0	0	0
0	2	0	0	0	0
1	2	0	0	0	0
3	0	2	4	0	1

NH 1742 ESTATE TAX

Names	POLS	D/HOUSES	SINGLE HOUSE	PLANTING	PASTURE	HORSES
Abraham Benneck	1		0	0	0	0
Benjamin Benneck	1		0	0	0	0
John Critchet	1		0	0	0	0
Samuel Watson	1		1	0	0	1
Isaac Mason	1		1	0	0	0
Elijah Drew	1		0	0	0	0
Nathaniel Frost	1		1	0	0	0
Nathanel Watson	1		0	0	0	0
Benjamin Matthes	1		1	0	30	1
Benjⁿ Benneck Junr			0	0	0	0
Joshua Cromet	1		1	10	10	1
Samuel Joy	1	1	0	10	0	1
Joseph Dudy Junr	1		0	0	0	0
Stephen Pendergast	1		1	10	10	2
Dennis Pendergast	1		0	0	0	0
Robert Burnum Junr	1		0	0	0	1
Joseph Baker	1		0	0	0	0
John Kelley	0		0	0	0	0
Samuel Burnum	1		0	0	0	0

DURHAM

OXEN	COWS	3 YEAR OLD	2 YEAR OLD	1 YEAR OLD	SWINE
0	0	0	0	0	0
0	0	0	0	0	0
0	0	0	0	0	0
0	1	0	0	0	0
0	1	0	0	0	0
0	0	0	0	0	0
2	1	0	0	0	0
0	1	0	0	0	0
4	0	4	0	0	0
0	0	0	0	0	0
0	3	2	1	2	0
4	3	0	2	0	1
0	1	0	0	0	0
4	4	0	5	0	0
0	0	0	0	0	0
2	1	0	0	0	0
0	0	0	0	0	0
0	0	0	0	0	0
0	0	0	0	0	0

NH 1742 ESTATE TAX

Names	POLS	D/HOUSES	SINGLE HOUSE	PLANTING	PASTURE	HORSES
Thomas York	1		1	0	0	0
Nathanl Stevens	1		1	0	0	0
Jabez Davis	1		1	5	0	1
Joseph Davis	1		1	2	4	0
Joseph Davis Jun*	1		0	4	4	0
William Everson	1		0	0	0	0
Joseph Bickford	1	1	0	10	10	1
Richard Densmore	1		1	16	10	1
Samuel Wille	1		1	4	0	3
Samuel Daniel	1		0	0	0	0
Benjamin Pindar	1		1	6	12	0
Benjamn Durgin Jun*	1		0	0	0	0
Benjamin Doe	1		0	0	0	0
John Wille	1	1	0	0	0	0
John Wille 3^{Tius}	1		0	0	0	0
Joseph Stevenson Jun*	1		0	0	0	0
William Davis	1		0	0	0	0
Jacob Sash	2		1	8	12	1

DURHAM

OXEN	COWS	3 YEAR OLD	2 YEAR OLD	1 YEAR OLD	SWINE
0	1	0	0	0	0
0	1	0	0	0	0
0	2	1	1	0	0
0	1	0	0	0	0
0	1	0	0	0	0
0	0	0	0	0	0
2	4	0	2	2	1
0	2	0	0	1	1
0	0	1	2	0	0
0	0	0	0	0	0
2	2	0	0	2	1
0	0	0	0	0	0
0	1	0	0	0	0
0	2	0	0	0	0
0	1	0	0	0	0
0	0	0	0	0	0
0	0	0	0	0	0
2	2	1	0	0	1

Durham June 9ᵗ 1742

Benjamin Smith   Selᵗman

June 9ᵗʰ 1742 Benjᵃ Smith made oath that the within accᵗ is a True & Exact List of all the Poles & Rateable Estates taken by him in that part of Durham, allottᵈ him to take the List of according to the Vote of the Genˡˡ Assembly Last Sessions according to the best of his Judgement

Sworn before Samˡˡ Gilman Jus of Peace

NH 1742 ESTATE TAX

Names	POLS	D/HOUSES	SINGLE HOUSE	PLANTING	PASTURE	HORSES
Thomas Wille	1		0	0	0	0
William Wille	1		1	2	3	0
Jonathan Durgin	1		1	1	3	1
William Shepherd	1		1	2	0	0
Eliezar Bickford	1		0	0	10	0
Benjamin Davis	0	1	0	0	10	0
Ebenez[r] Davis	1		1	0	0	0
Solomon Davis	1		1	4	4	0
John York	1	1	0	12	12	0
Daniel Doe	1		1	5	3	0
John Doe	1		0	0	0	0
Pumfret Whitehouse	1		0	0	0	0
Ezekiel Leathers	1		0	0	0	0
John Smith Jun[r]	1	1	0	10	15	1
Francis Durgin	1		0	0	1	0
John Dursin	1	0	1	5	2	0
John Footman	1	0	1	10	3	0
Benjamin Smith	1	1	0	20	20	1
John Smith	1		0	0	0	0
Ebenezer Smith	1	1	0	20	30	1

DURHAM

OXEN	COWS	3 YEAR OLD	2 YEAR OLD	1 YEAR OLD	SWINE
0	1	0	0	0	0
0	1	1	0	0	0
0	0	1	1	1	0
0	0	0	0	0	0
0	0	0	0	0	0
0	1	0	0	0	0
0	1	0	0	0	0
2	2	0	0	1	0
0	2	3	0	3	0
0	1	0	1	0	0
0	0	0	0	0	0
0	0	0	0	0	0
0	0	0	0	0	0
4	4	0	5	0	1
0	1	0	0	0	0
2	2	1	0	0	0
2	1	0	0	0	0
2	4	4	2	2	1
0	0	0	0	0	0
6	4	3	3	1	1

NH 1742 ESTATE TAX

Names	POLS	D/HOUSES	SINGLE HOUSE	PLANTING	PASTURE	HORSES
Samuel Smith	1		1	10	10	1
Joseph Chesle	1	1	0	10	15	1
David Hoeg	1		1	0	0	1
Joseph Thomas	1	0	1	10	4	0
Lt Abraham Bennecky	1		1	0	3	1
James Durgin +		0	0	0	0	0
Troworthy Durgin	1		0	0	0	0
William Durgin	1		1	6	10	1
James Durgin Jun" +	0		0	0	0	0
John Cromett	1		1	8	4	0
Joseph Dudy	1	1	0	12	15	0
James Burnum	1		0	0	0	1
Joseph Wormwood	1		0	0	0	0
James Davis	1		0	0	0	0
Joshua Woodman	1		1	5	0	1
Abraham Scales	1		0	0	0	0
Joseph Smith	1		1	2	4	0
Elias Critchet	1		1	2	0	0
James Smith	1		1	8	10	0
Philip Cromett	1		1	5	4	0

DURHAM

OXEN	COWS	3 YEAR OLD	2 YEAR OLD	1 YEAR OLD	SWINE
4	3	2	3	1	0
4	1	2	0	0	0
2	2	0	0	0	0
2	3	0	0	0	1
2	2	0	1	0	0
0	0	0	0	0	0
0	0	0	0	0	0
0	2	0	0	0	0
0	0	0	0	0	0
0	2	0	4	0	0
0	3	3	0	0	0
0	2	0	0	0	0
0	0	0	0	0	0
0	0	0	0	0	0
2	3	0	0	0	0
0	0	0	0	0	0
0	2	0	0	0	0
0	0	0	0	0	0
2	3	0	0	1	0
0	1	0	0	0	0

NH 1742 ESTATE TAX

Names	POLS	D/HOUSES	SINGLE HOUSE	PLANTING	PASTURE	HORSES
John Andrews	1		0	0	1	0
Joseph Williams	1		0	0	0	0
John Mason	1		0	0	0	0
Benjamin Jenknes	1		0	0	0	0
Joshua Durgin	1		1	5	4	0
Joseph Glidden	1		1	2	0	0
John Smart	1		1	8	5	1
Benjamin Glidden	1		1	7	7	0
James Davis Esqr	3	1	0	30	20	2
Nathaniel Randol	4	1	0	25	10	2
Joseph Atkinson	1		0	5	0	2
Samuel Perkins	1	1	0	12	5	1
Timothy Emerson	3		1	6	10	1
William Leathers	1	1	0	10	4	0
Philip Cheslee	3	1	0	20	20	2
Nathaniel Meder	1		1	12	4	1
Jonathan Woodman	1	1	0	20	20	0
John Woodman	1		0	5	10	1
Jonathan Woodman Junr	1	1	0	10	8	1
Archelaus Woodman	1		1	8	5	0

DURHAM

OXEN	COWS	3 YEAR OLD	2 YEAR OLD	1 YEAR OLD	SWINE
0	0	2	0	0	1
0	0	0	0	0	0
0	0	0	0	0	0
2	1	0	0	0	0
2	2	0	0	1	0
2	2	0	0	0	0
0	3	3	4	1	0
0	2	2	0	1	0
4	7	2	5	3	0
8	7	3	5	4	0
0	0	0	0	0	0
2	3	0	2	0	1
0	3	7	0	2	0
2	2	0	1	1	1
4	4	2	2	2	1
0	5	0	5	0	1
2	2	1	3	0	1
2	3	4	1	0	0
0	4	4	2	0	0
0	1	2	1	1	1

NH 1742 ESTATE TAX

Names	POLS	D/HOUSES	SINGLE HOUSE	PLANTING	PASTURE	HORSES
Edward Woodman	1		1	0	0	0
James Hall	1		0	0	0	1
John Tompson	2		1	10	6	1
Cap Samuel Emerson	2	1	0	20	10	1
Thomas Hall	1		1	3	2	1
Robert Huckins	1		1	10	5	1
Soloman Sias	1		1	3	0	1
Thomas Leathers	1	1	0	6	2	1
Volentine Hill	1	1	0	20	10	0
George Cheslee	1	1	0	15	6	0
William Clay	2		1	3	0	1
Cap Stephen Jones	2	1	0	15	10	0
Lt Stephen Jones	1		0	15	10	0
Ebenezer Jones	1	1	0	8	0	1
William Jackson	1	1	0	10	6	0
William Jackson Jun*	1		0	0	0	1
William Drew	1	1	0	6	0	1
Eli Clark	2		1	14	0	1
Joseph Huckins	1		0	0	0	0
Richard Glovier	2		0	0	0	0

DURHAM

OXEN	COWS	3 YEAR OLD	2 YEAR OLD	1 YEAR OLD	SWINE
0	1	0	1	0	0
0	1	1	0	0	0
2	3	0	0	0	0
2	3	3	1	1	1
0	0	0	0	0	0
2	1	0	4	0	1
2	2	2	0	1	1
4	1	1	1	0	0
0	0	0	0	0	0
4	3	5	1	1	2
4	3	0	0	1	1
4	1	0	3	0	1
4	3	3	1	0	0
2	2	0	0	0	1
2	2	0	1	1	1
0	2	1	0	1	1
2	2	0	0	0	0
2	2	1	1	1	0
0	2	0	0	0	0
0	0	0	0	0	0

NH 1742 ESTATE TAX

Names	POLS	D/HOUSES	SINGLE HOUSE	PLANTING	PASTURE	HORSES
Edward Leathers	1		0	4	0	1
John Jenknes	1		1	8	5	1
Jonathan Cheslee	2	0	1	20	15	3
Joshua Cheslee	1		1	5	0	0
Stephen Leathers	1		0	0	0	0
Daniel Meder	1	1	0	20	12	0
Nicholas Meder	1		1	15	15	1
Joseph Meder Jun"	1		1	0	0	0
Jn^a Welch	1		0	0	0	0
William Brown	1		0	0	0	0
James Bunker	1	1	0	12	7	1
Joseph Bunker	1	1	0	8	3	0
Clement Bunker	1		0	6	2	0
William Hill	1	1	0	10	5	0
John Williams	1	1	0	20	10	0
John Williams Jun"	1	0	0	0	4	1
Hubbard Stevens	1	1	0	6	0	2
Lt Samuel Smith	3	2	0	40	20	2
Robert Tompson	2	1	0	15	10	2
Job Runnals	1	1	0	20	8	1

DURHAM

OXEN	COWS	3 YEAR OLD	2 YEAR OLD	1 YEAR OLD	SWINE
4	3	1	1	0	1
0	2	1	0	0	0
8	4	2	0	2	0
0	1	0	2	2	0
2	1	0	0	0	1
2	6	4	2	5	1
2	3	1	0	3	0
0	0	0	0	0	0
0	0	0	0	0	0
0	0	0	0	0	0
0	2	1	0	1	0
2	2	0	0	1	0
2	2	0	0	0	0
0	2	0	0	1	0
0	3	1	2	0	0
2	3	0	1	2	0
0	4	0	3	3	1
8	7	8	8	7	2
4	9	4	4	2	1
2	5	2	6	1	0

NH 1742 ESTATE TAX

Names	POLS	D/HOUSES	SINGLE HOUSE	PLANTING	PASTURE	HORSES
Samuel Hill	3	1	0	16	5	2
John Monssy	2	1	0	8	2	0
Ichabod Folliott	2		1	12	6	1
John Sias	1	1	0	5	0	1
Ichabod Cheslee	1	1	0	10	8	1
John Pitman	2	1	0	3	0	1
John Davis	1	1	0	2	0	1
John Runnals	1		1	8	2	1
William Jenknes	2		1	10	10	2
William Randol	1		1	4	0	1
Abednego Leathers	1		1	0	0	0
Lt Jonathan Tompson	4	1	1	20	15	2
Ebenezer Spencer	1		0	0	0	0
Thomas Huckins	2	1		3	0	1
John Langley	1		1	3	0	0
Benjamin Bickford	1		1	6	0	1
Joseph Sias	1	1	0	6	5	1
Henery Hill	1		1	2	0	0
En^n Joseph Jones	1	1	0	6	0	1
John Jones	1		0	6	3	1

DURHAM

OXEN	COWS	3 YEAR OLD	2 YEAR OLD	1 YEAR OLD	SWINE
4	4	3	3	0	1
4	3	1	0	2	0
2	3	2	2	0	1
0	2	0	0	0	0
4	4	0	0	2	1
2	0	0	0	0	0
2	2	0	0	0	0
2	3	0	0	3	1
4	1	1	2	9	1
2	2	0	0	0	1
0	0	0	0	0	1
6	7	3	3	9	1
0	0	0	0	0	0
0	3	0	0	0	1
2	2	0	0	0	0
4	3	2	2	1	5
4	2	0	2	0	0
2	1	0	0	1	0
2	1	1	2	0	1
4	1	0	1	1	1

NH 1742 ESTATE TAX

Names	POLS	D/HOUSES	SINGLE HOUSE	PLANTING	PASTURE	HORSES
Benjamin Jones	1		1	6	7	1
John Laskey	1		1	6	2	1
Richard Kenney	1		0	0	0	0
James Tompson	1	0	1	0	0	0
Robert Tompson Jun*	1		0	0	0	0
Samuel Sias	1		1	0	0	0
Jospeh Jackson	1		0	0	0	0
Job Langley	1		1	3	0	1
Joseph Doe	1		1	0	0	0
Joseph Johnson	1		0	0	0	0
Thomas Cheslee	1		1	15	10	1
Thomas Cheslee Jun*	1		0	0	0	0
John Crocket	1		0	0	0	1
John Meder	1		0	0	0	0
Paul Cheslee	1		1	0	0	0
Jonathan Brue	1		1	½	0	0
Eliphalet Hill	1		0	5	2	1
Thomas Pike	1		1	2	0	0
Jonathan Leathers	1		0	0	0	0
Ebenezer Leathers	1		0	0	0	0

DURHAM

OXEN	COWS	3 YEAR OLD	2 YEAR OLD	1 YEAR OLD	SWINE
2	3	3	2	2	1
0	3	3	2	3	2
0	0	0	0	0	0
4	0	0	0	0	0
0	0	0	0	0	0
0	0	0	0	0	0
2	2	0	0	0	0
0	1	0	0	0	0
2	0	0	0	0	0
0	1	1	0	0	0
2	1	0	1	0	0
0	0	0	0	0	0
2	2	0	0	0	1
0	1	0	0	0	0
2	1	0	0	0	0
0	1	0	0	0	0
2	2	2	0	1	0
0	1	0	0	0	0
0	0	0	0	0	0
0	0	0	0	0	0

NH 1742 ESTATE TAX

Names	POLS	D/HOUSES	SINGLE HOUSE	PLANTING	PASTURE	HORSES
Joseph Cattline	1		0	0	0	0
Isaac Clark	1		0	0	0	1
Samuel Jackson	1		1	0	1	2
Joshua Davis	1		0	0	0	1
Samuel Meder	1		1	6	0	1
Jeremiah Davis	1		1	5	0	1
John Cheslee	1		1	0	0	0
Thomas Wille	1		1	3	0	1
Joseph Nutter	2	1	0	0	0	0
Joseph Davis 3:^{Tius}	1		0	0	0	0
Thomas Snell	1		1	4	0	0
William Bruce	1		0	0	0	0
Lemuel Cheslee	1	1	0	10	5	1
Samuel Cheslee	1		0	0	0	1
Benjamin Drew	1		0	0	0	0
Shedrack Walton	1		0	0	0	0
John Folliott	1		1	2	0	0
Joshua Burnum	1		0	0	0	0
John Brown	1		0	0	0	0
Lararus Nobel	1		0	0	0	0

DURHAM

OXEN	COWS	3 YEAR OLD	2 YEAR OLD	1 YEAR OLD	SWINE
0	0	0	0	0	0
2	1	0	0	0	1
1	0	0	1	0	0
0	0	0	0	0	0
0	2	0	4	1	0
2	1	1	0	0	0
2	0	0	0	0	0
2	2	0	0	0	0
0	1	0	0	0	0
0	0	0	0	0	0
2	2	2	0	0	3
0	0	0	0	0	0
4	3	2	2	2	1
2	0	0	0	1	0
0	0	0	0	0	0
0	0	0	0	0	0
0	1	1	0	1	0
0	0	0	0	0	0
0	1	8	7	6	7
0	1	0	0	0	0

NH 1742 ESTATE TAX

Names	POLS	D/HOUSES	SINGLE HOUSE	PLANTING	PASTURE	HORSES
Joseph Meder	1	1	0	15	15	1
Moses Meder	1		0	0	0	0
Thomas Gellerson	1		0	0	0	0

OXEN	COWS	3 YEAR OLD	2 YEAR OLD	1 YEAR OLD	SWINE
2	3	0	0	0	0
0	0	0	0	0	0
0	0	0	0	0	0

Durham June 10th 1742

John Williams Sellman

June 9th 1742 John Williams made oath that the within acc't is a true and Exact List of the Poles & Rateable Estates taken by him in that Part of Durham aloted him to take the list of according to the vote of the Gen'l Assembly Last Session according to the best of his Judgement Sworn before

Sam'l Gilman Justice of Peace

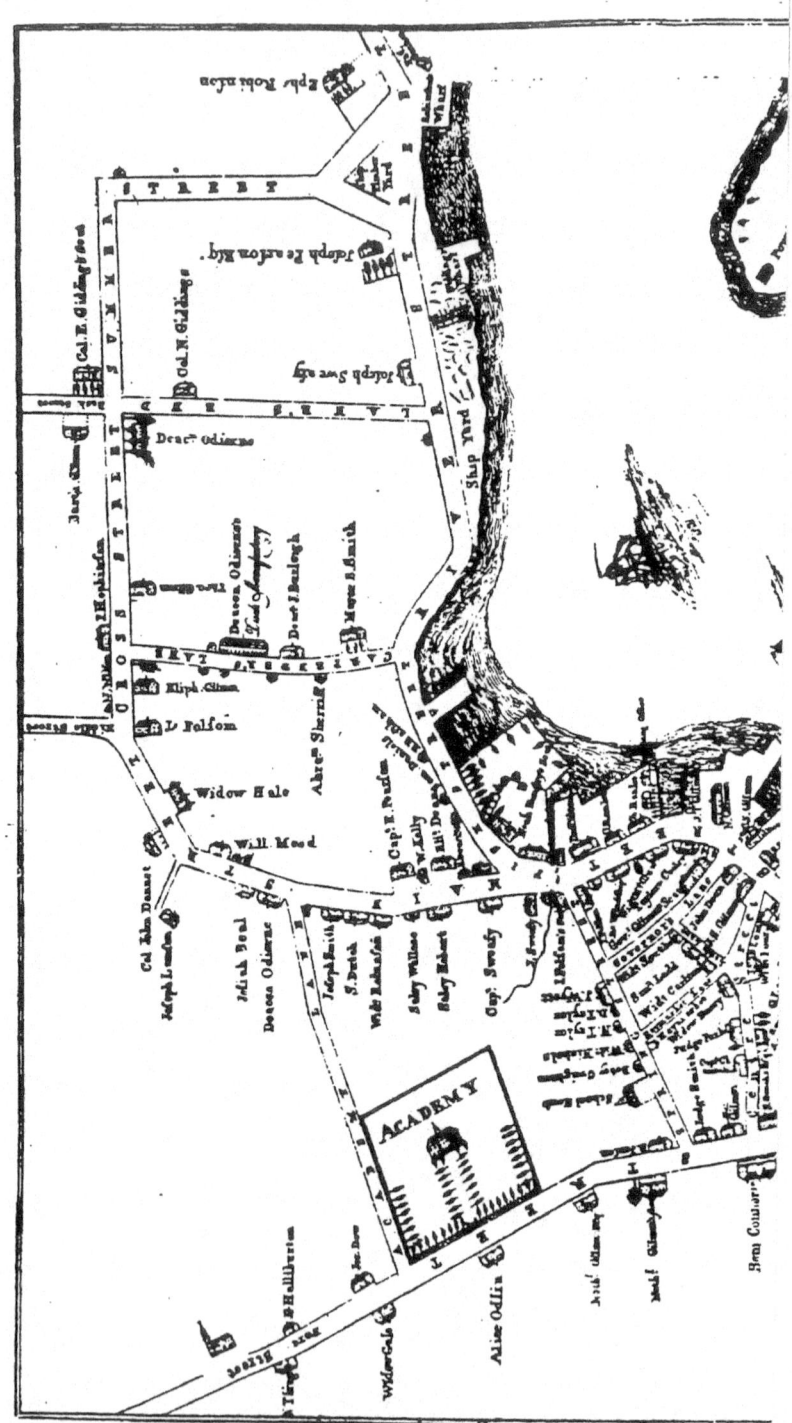

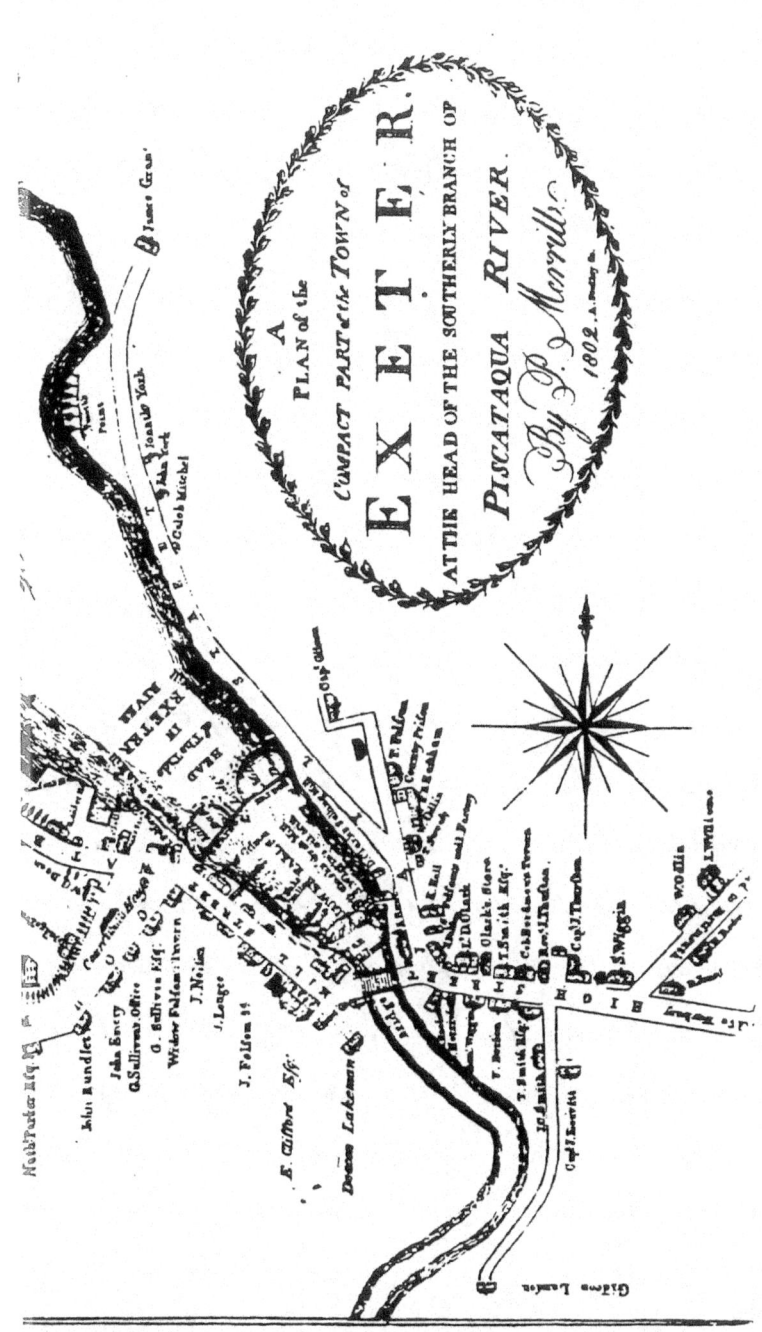

Names	POLS	HOUSING	HORSES	OXEN	COWS	3 YEAR OLD
Town of Exeter (Totals)	63	35	41	36	89	27

Exeter List
Sworn to in the House

June the eighth the five Select men of Exeter that did take those five Invoices Made oath that those several Invoices are a true and Exact accomps of the Rateable Poles and Estate within their Serveral districts according to the vote of the General Assembly Last Sessions according to the best of theire understanding Sworn before Sam^{ll} Gilman Justice of Peace

2 YEAR OLD	1 YEAR OLD	SWINE	PLANTING	PASTURE
35	48	21	390	326

Exeter List
Sworn to in the House

June the eighth the five Select men of Exeter that did take those five Invoices Made oath that those several Invoices are a true and Exact accomps of the Rateable Poles and Estate within their Serveral districts according to the vote of the General Assembly Last Sessions according to the best of theire understanding Sworn before
Sam" Gilman Justice of Peace

Greenland march yͤ 30 1742
heds one hundred and Nienteen
houses Seventy seven
Pastuer six hundred Eighty seven Eakers
Planting two hundred and ninty six eakrs
medo four hundred and forty eakrs
Eighty oxen
Cows 2 hundred fifty fouer
Three years olds eighty nine
two year olds one hundred ninty two
one yeear old one hundred and twenty six
horses Eighty seven
hogs ninteen
mow

        Elenezer Johnson
        James Whidden   Selc'men
        John Brackett

June the 9[th] 1742 the Selectmen of Greenland who Subscribed the above accompt Made Oath that the above is a true and Exact List of the Poles and Rateable Estates in the p[ar]ish of Greenland taken by them according to the act of the Gen" Assembly Made the Last Sessions and According to the best of their Judgment Sworn before Sam" Gilman Justice of Peace

GREENLAND

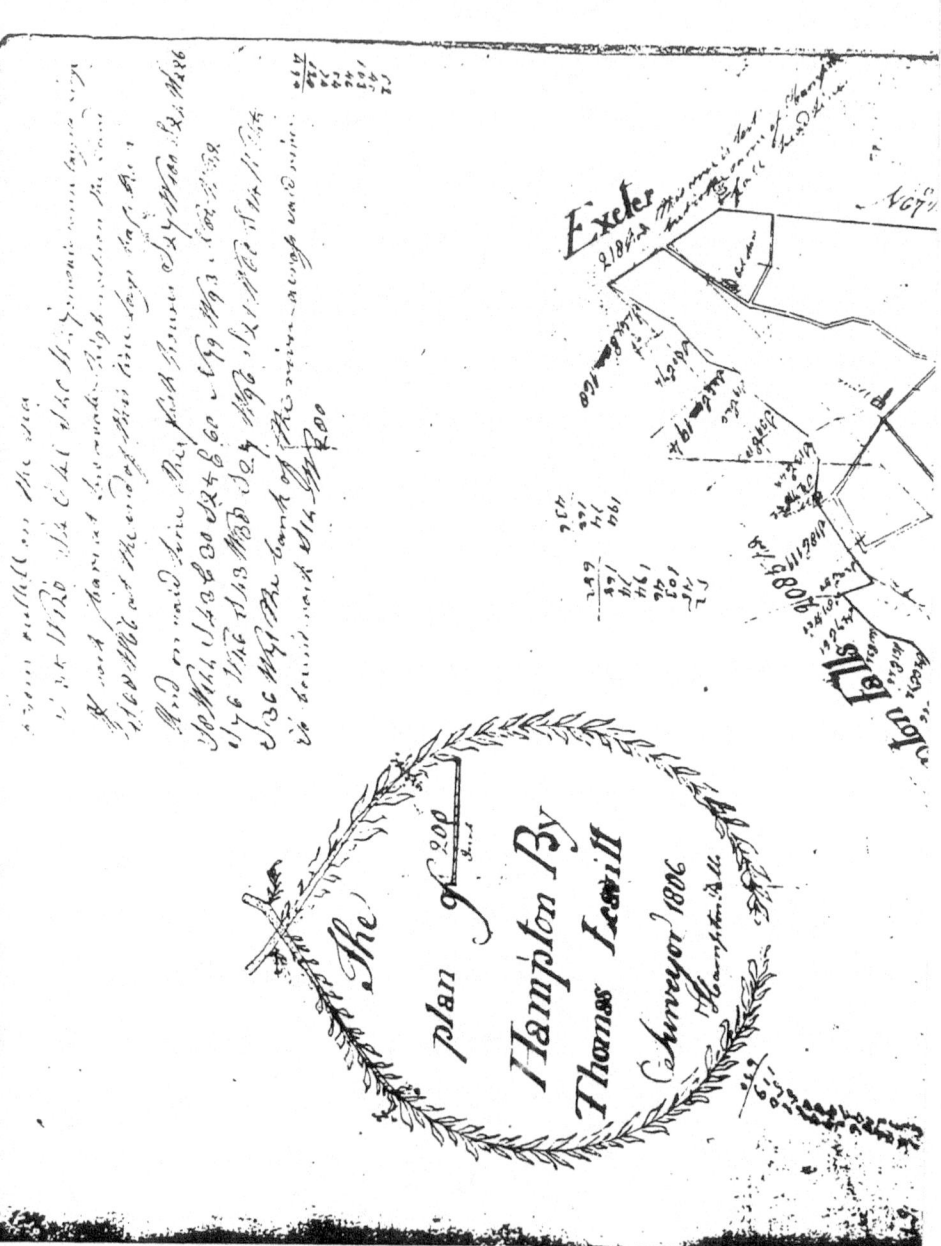

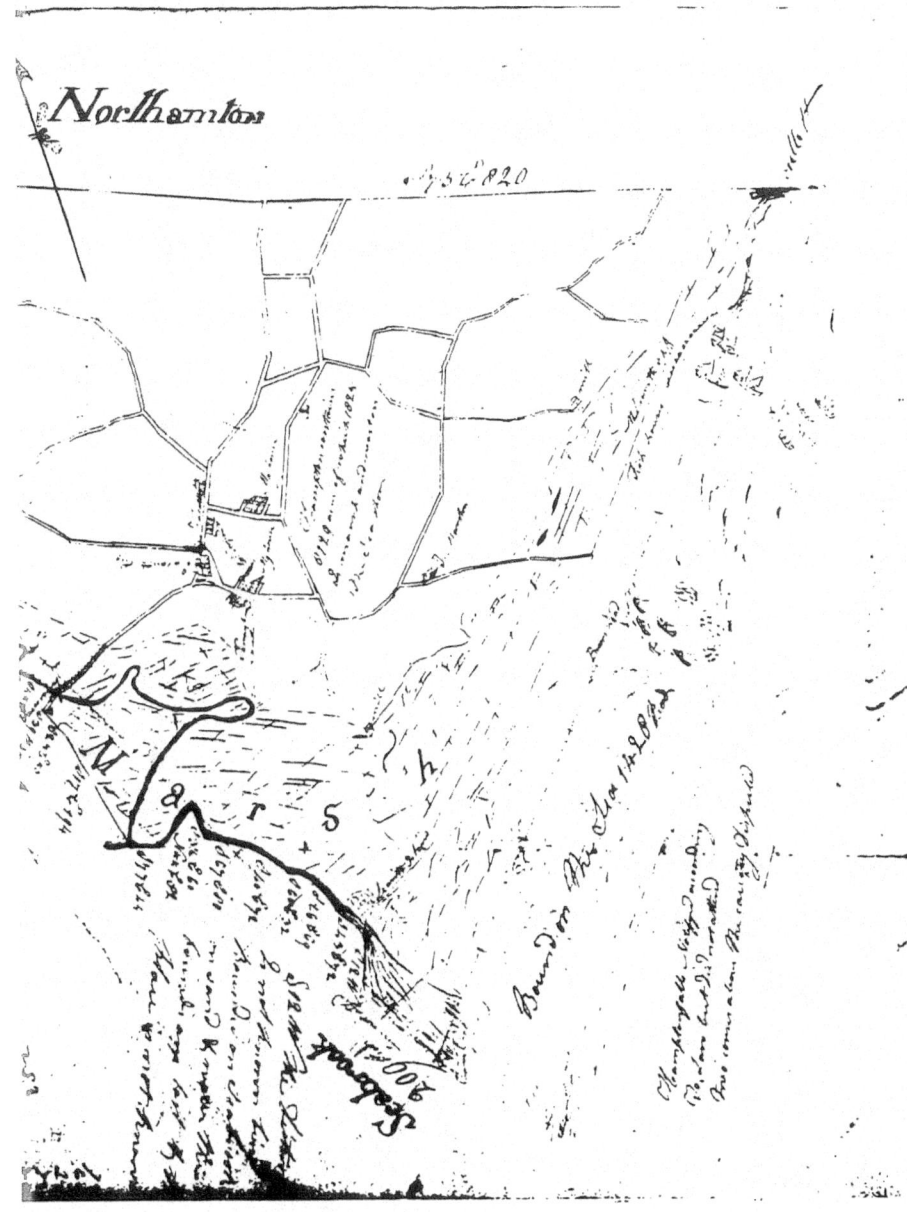

Hampton Invoice for a new proportion in the province 1742

Names	POLS	HOUSES	OXEN	HORSES	COWS	3 YEARS OLD
Jon^a Tucker	3	1	2	1	4	1
Edward Shaw	2	1	0	1	3	0
Ench Samborn	2	1	4	1	3	0
John Newman	1	1	0	1	0	0
Joshua Land	2	1	0	1	3	0
Benj Marston	1	1	1	1	2	0
Phillep Smith	1	1	3	0	3	0
Elisha Smith	2	1	3	2	3	1
Henery Derbon	1	1	2	1	3	1
Jon^a Elkins	2	1	2	2	3	2
Benoni Fuller	1	1	0	1	2	3
Gershim Griffith	1	1	0	1	2	0
Abram Drake Junr	1	1	0	1	2	4
Richard Taylor	2	1	2	1	3	2
Jon^a Thomas	1	1	0	1	3	0
Sam^{ll} Page	2	1	2	2	5	3
Shubal Samborn	1	1	2	1	3	0
Peter Garland	2	1	1	1	3	1

2 YEARS OLD	1 YEAR OLD	SWINE	PLANTING/MOW	PASTURE
3	5	1	025	030
6	5	0	040	025
0	1	0	020	015
0	0	0	000	000
0	1	0	009	015
0	4	0	000	010
3	4	1	035	020
3	4	0	035	020
3	5	0	035	015
3	1	0	015	012
1	2	0	012	008
0	0	0	002	010
0	3	0	010	003
3	4	0	015	015
2	0	0	001	000
5	5	0	040	030
0	4	0	016	015
2	2	0	018	020

NH 1742 ESTATE TAX

Names	POLS	HOUSES	OXEN	HORSES	COWS	3 YEARS OLD
L t John Sherburn	3	1	4	2	4	1
Zac Towle	1	1	0	1	2	1
Abrm Drake	2	1	2	1	2	2
C Jon^a Derbon	6	1	2	1	3	1
Tho Page	1	1	2	0	2	0
Benj James	3	1	0	2	4	0
Solomon Page	1	1	0	1	3	0
Charls Walker	1	0	0	1	2	3
Noah Ward	2	1	2	1	2	1
Thomas Ward	1	1	0	0	2	0
Nat Drake	3	1	2	3	3	1
Nat^l Sargent	1	1	0	1	1	0
John Towle	2	1	0	2	3	0
Thomas Derbon	2	1	4	1	2	1
Reuben Derbon	1	1	0	1	3	3
C John Smith	2	1	2	2	5	1
Benj Smith	1	1	2	1	5	0
Tho Batcheder	2	1	2	0	2	3

2 YEARS OLD	1 YEAR OLD	SWINE	PLANTING/MOW	PASTURE
0	4	0	025	025
5	4	0	005	010
3	4	0	025	025
4	2	0	030	022
0	2	0	016	010
4	4	0	13	010
0	2	0	000	000
0	2	0	000	000
0	4	0	012	006
0	1	0	008	006
1	2	1	025	020
1	2	0	007	004
4	2	0	008	005
2	3	0	020	020
2	2	0	020	010
4	5	1	040	025
1	1	0	002	020
1	3	0	12	0011

NH 1742 ESTATE TAX

Names	POLS	HOUSES	OXEN	HORSES	COWS	3 YEARS OLD
Tho Brown	1	1	0	0	3	0
Tho Brown Jun	1	1	2	1	2	0
Sam^{ll} Hiton	1	1	0	1	0	1
Nathan Philbrick	1	1	0	0	1	0
Sam^{ll} Brown	2	1	2	0	2	1
Zac Brown	1	1	2	1	2	0
Ste Brown	1	0	0	0	2	2
Josh Brown	3	1	2	1	2	0
Nathan Blake	1	1	0	0	2	0
Jn° Batcheldr	1	1	2	1	4	0
Joseph Batcheler	1	1	2	1	3	2
Ste Batchldr Junr	2	1	4	1	3	2
Sam Batcheldr	3	1	2	2	4	1
Sam Batchelder Junr	1	1	0	1	1	0
David Jewel	1	1	0	0	1	0
Job Chapman	1	1	0	1	4	2
Joseph Chapman	1	1	4	1	5	0
David Dow	2	1	2	1	3	0

2 YEARS OLD	1 YEAR OLD	SWINE	PLANTING/MOW	PASTURE
0	0	0	0016	0010
0	2	0	004	002
1	0	0	004	000
0	0	0	000	000
3	0	0	012	015
3	1	0	012	0015
0	0	0	0000	0000
6	2	1	0016	0016
0	0	0	0001	0000
3	1	1	0025	0020
1	2	0	0015	0012
4	4	0	0015	0005
3	3		0016	0012
0	1	0	0000	0005
0	0	0	0000	0000
1	4	1	0015	0012
3	3	1	0030	0020
2	2	0	0020	0016

NH 1742 ESTATE TAX

Names	POLS	HOUSES	OXEN	HORSES	COWS	3 YEARS OLD
Cpt Jabz Dow	2	1	2	0	3	1
Simon Dow	3	1	4	1	2	1
Sam Dow	2	1	2	1	3	4
Jonᵃ Garland	3	1	2	2	4	0
Gedion Shaw	1	0	2	0	2	0
Jonᵃ Moulton	1	1	2	0	1	0
Cpt Jona Marston	3	1	2	1	2	1
Mephi Samborn	2	1	0	1	1	3
Isacc Philbrick	1	1	0	0	0	0
Samᵘ Palmer Junr	2	1	2	1	2	0
Samᵘ Palmer Senr	2	1	2	1	3	0
Chr Palmer	1	1	2	0	3	1
Nehe Hobs	1	1	0	0	0	1
Sam Daulton	1	1	0	0	0	0
Jer Moulton	1	1	2	1	2	0
Joseph Redman	1	1	2	1	5	0
Dr Josiah Moulton	2	1	2	1	2	1
Jnᵒ Lampry	2	1	2	1	4	2

HAMPTON

2 YEARS OLD	1 YEAR OLD	SWINE	PLANTING/MOW	PASTURE
2	2	1	0025	0026
3	2	0	0020	0024
1	2	0	0018	18
3	4	0	0020	0010
0	0	1	0000	0000
1	0	0	0010	016
3	3	0	0035	0030
0	1	0	009	008
0	0	0	000	000
3	1	0	0012	0016
3	3	0	0023	0028
3	2	0	0020	0016
1	0	0	007	005
0	0	0	000	000
0	1	0	0010	0016
0	3	0	0017	0030
3	3	0	0020	0020
1	3	0	0020	0020

NH 1742 ESTATE TAX

Names	POLS	HOUSES	OXEN	HORSES	COWS	3 YEARS OLD
Moris Lampry	1	1	2	1		0
Sam[u] Moulton	2	1	2	1	2	1
Joseph Johnson	1	1	0	1	2	0
Sam[u] Lock	1	1	2	0	1	0
Tho Lane	1	1	0	0	1	0
John Moulton Junr	1	1	2	1	4	0
John Moulton Senr	1	1	2	1	3	1
James Johnson	2	1	2	0	3	0
Dr Joseph Philbrick	2	1	2	0	2	0
Sam[u] Nudd	2	1	4	1	3	1
Nat[h] Lamprey	1	1	2	0	3	0
Amos Knowls	3	1	2	1	6	1
James Johnson Junr	1	1	0	0	1	0
Cp[t] Jabez Smith	1	1	2	1	3	0
Peter Johnson	1	1	2	1	3	1
Jon[a] Page	1	1	0	1	3	1
David Page	1	1	0	1	2	4
Benj Lamprey Jr	1	1	0	1	3	5

HAMPTON

2 YEARS OLD	1 YEAR OLD	SWINE	PLANTING/MOW	PASTURE
1	2	0	0004	0009
1	2	0	00010	0016
0	0	0	0002	0001
0	1	0	002	000
0	0	0	000	000
0	0	0	018	010
3	2	0	015	016
1	2	0	10	9
2	2	0	018	020
3	3	0	030	035
1	3	1	012	014
3	3	0	040	040
0	0	0	000	000
1	2	0	025	020
2	1	0	014	016
3	5	0	016	015
1	3	0	016	015
1	1	0	12	014

NH 1742 ESTATE TAX

Names	POLS	HOUSES	OXEN	HORSES	COWS	3 YEARS OLD
Jon^a Palmer	1	1	2	1	0	0
Joseph Moulton	1	1		1	2	0
Wido Hannah Moulton & her Daughter Eliz	0	1	0	0	3	0
Andrew Mace	1	1	0	0	1	0
Dr Cl Jackson	1	1	2	2	1	1
Wm Stanford	1	1	0	1	1	0
Henry Moulton	1	1	0	1	2	0
Edmond Rand	2	1		2	3	1
Obedi^h Marston	1	1	2		2	0
Wido Toppin Sa	0	1	0	0	2	0
Jer Page	1	1	2	0	3	0
Tho Hains	1	1	2	1	2	0
Jer Fifeld	1	0	0	0	0	0
Jer Marston	2	1	2	1	5	1
Chr Page	2	1	2	1	4	2
Philep Towle	2	1	2	1	3	1
Ed Wilmot	1	1	2	0	2	1

HAMPTON

2 YEARS OLD	1 YEAR OLD	SWINE	PLANTING/MOW	PASTURE
0	0	0	0012	0012
1	1	0	009	010
0	0	0	008	007
0	0	0	000	000
0	0	0	010	000
0	0	0	003	000
0	0	0	005	004
2	2	0	006	0014
1	0	0	002	0020
1	2	0	005	0003
2	1	0	007	0010
2	2	0	008	0009
0	0	0	000	000
3	4	0	036	030
0	4	1	35	030
2	2	0	012	016
1	2	0	012	006

NH 1742 ESTATE TAX

Names	POLS	HOUSES	OXEN	HORSES	COWS	3 YEARS OLD
Ezekiel Moulton	1	1	2	1	3	0
Jacob Marston	1	1	2	0	2	0
Wm Moulton Comp	2	1	2	1	3	0
Nat Mason	1	1	0	0	1	0
James Towle	1	1	2	1	2	1
Joseph Moulton Jun	1	1	2	1	2	1
Benj Hobs	1	1	2	1	4	3
Wm Palmer	1	1	2	1	3	1
Tho Robie	1	1	0	1	3	3
Caleb Marston	2	1	2	1	2	3
Jnº Marston	1	1	1	0	1	1
Joseph Towle Jur	1	1	0	1	3	3
Caleb Marston Jur	2	1	0	1	2	1
Moses Levitt	1	1	0	1	3	0
Samll Marston	2	1	2	1	2	2
Simon Knowls	1	1	2	1	2	1
Marise Hobbs	2	1	2	2	3	3
Jnº Wedgwood	2	1	2	1	3	1

2 YEARS OLD	1 YEAR OLD	SWINE	PLANTING/MOW	PASTURE
3	2	0	008	006
1	1	0	004	011
1	3	0	010	007
0	0	0	001	000
3	5	0	016	020
2	3	0	005	000
3	3	1	016	018
1	0	0	008	012
4	2	0	020	020
2	6	0	20	020
1	1	1	010	015
2	4	0	010	010
3	0	0	008	010
0	2	0	005	005
0	3	0	005	010
1	1	0	007	008
4	0	0	018	020
1	1	1	015	015

NH 1742 ESTATE TAX

Names	POLS	HOUSES	OXEN	HORSES	COWS	3 YEARS OLD
Jnº Hobs	2	1	2	1	3	1
Wm Moulton Of Woods	2	1	2	1	2	0
Jnº Johnson	2	1	2	1	2	3
Jonª Marston Junr	1	1	2	1	3	0
James Godfree	1	1	2	2	4	1
Joseph Taylor	2	1	2	1	4	1
Samˡˡ Levit	1	1	2	1	2	1
Edwᵈ Moulton	1	1	0	0	1	0
Worthton Moulton	1	1	2	0	2	0
Jonª Freez	1	1	0		1	0
Moses Perkins	1	1	2	1	3	2
Henery Fifeld	1	1	0	0	1	0
John Levitt	1	1	0	0	0	1
Benj Johnson	1	1	0	1	1	1
Seth Fogg & Abnr	2	2	2	2	7	2
James Hobs	2	1	2	1	4	1
Reuben Marston	2	1	2	1	4	0
Elisha Page	1	1	2	1	1	2

2 YEARS OLD	1 YEAR OLD	SWINE	PLANTING/MOW	PASTURE
3	3	0	014	012
2	2	0	006	010
1	0	0	008	010
2	2	0	012	016
3	3	0	020	018
2	1	0	015	016
1	5	0	007	010
0	0	0	001	000
0	0	0	005	002
0	1	0	015	010
3	5	1	020	015
2	0	0	020	008
5	2	1	005	004
2	0	1	005	004
0	8	0	30	040
3	3	0	018	018
0	0	0	012	010
1	2	0	10	008

NH 1742 ESTATE TAX

Names	POLS	HOUSES	OXEN	HORSES	COWS	3 YEARS OLD
Sam`ll` Hobs	1	1	0	1	3	0
Francis Page	2	1	2	1	5	0
Danil Fogg	1	1	2	1	2	1
Joseph Page	2	1	0	1	2	0
Jon`a` Knowls	1	1	0	1	2	0
L (t) Ephr Marston	1	1	2	1	4	3
Tho Elkins	2	1	2	1	3	4
Jacob Moulton	1	0	0	0	1	0
Danil Marston	1	1	0	1	4	0
Robert Drake	1	1	2	1	2	1
Joshua Winget Junr	1	1	0	0	1	0
Jona Levitt	3	1	0	1	3	0
Richard Samborn	1	0	0	0	0	0
Caleb Towle	2	1	2	1	4	4
Benj Towle	3	2	4	3	6	2
James Levit	2	1	2	1	3	1
Ben Souter	1	1	0	0	1	0
John Mason	1	0	0	0	0	0

2 YEARS OLD	1 YEAR OLD	SWINE	PLANTING/MOW	PASTURE
1	2	0	008	004
2	5	0	020	020
2	3	0	005	000
0	5	0	012	012
1	2	0	002	002
3	1	0	0020	024
0	0	0	0013	012
0	0	0	000	000
1	1	1	012	016
0	3	0	020	016
0	0	0	005	000
0	0	0	004	008
0	0	0	000	000
2	3	0	025	020
2	4	0	030	030
2	2	0	016	020
0	1	0	000	000
0	0	0	000	000

NH 1742 ESTATE TAX

Names	POLS	HOUSES	OXEN	HORSES	COWS	3 YEARS OLD
John Sleeper	1	0	0	0	0	0
Robert Moulton	1	1	0	1	4	2
Roger Shaw	3	2	2	3	6	0
James Fogg	1	1	1	1	3	0
John Taylor	3	2	2	1	4	1
John Samborn	2	1	2	2	5	4
Jon^a Samborn J^r	1	1	0	0	2	0
John Nay	1	0	2	0	2	0
James Samborn	1	1	2	1	2	0
John Fogg	1	1	1	1	3	0
Enoch Fogg	1	0	0	1	0	0
Reuben Samborn	1	1	0	0	2	0
Stephen Smith	1	1	0	0	1	0
Wm Viber	1	1	0	0	1	0
Jeremi Towle	1	1	0	0	1	1
Jon^a Samborn	2	1	2	0	3	0
Wintrp Samborn	1	0	0	0	0	0
Joshua Towle	3	1	2	0	2	0

2 YEARS OLD	1 YEAR OLD	SWINE	PLANTING/MOW	PASTURE
0	1	0	000	000
3	3	0	012	010
5	5	0	026	026
1	2	1	018	012
2	4	0	025	016
1	4	0	020	025
1	0	0	005	002
0	2	1	010	000
1	0	1	009	008
1	1	0	001	001
0	0	0	002	000
4	4	0	012	010
0	0	0	002	001
0	0	0	000	000
0	1	0	000	008
0	0	1	007	010
2	0	0	000	000
3	1	0	010	005

Names	POLS	HOUSES	OXEN	HORSES	COWS	3 YEARS OLD
Joseph Towle	2	1	2	1	2	1
John Shaw	3	1	2	1	2	4
Thomas Marston	2	1	2	1	5	1
Henery Dearbon Junr	1	1	0	1	2	1
John Godfree	1	1	0	1	2	1
Mr Joshua Wingett	1	1	2	1	3	0
Ebenzr Samborn	3	1	0	1	2	0
James Thomas	1	1	2	1	1	0
Daniel Samborn	1	1	0	1	4	2
Cp Benj Thomas	2	1	2	1	4	3
Simon Derbon	1	1	2	1	3	2
Jeremi Derbon	2	1	2	1	5	2
Timothy Daulton	2	1	0	1	3	3
Samll Smith	1	1	2	0	3	0
Samll Derbon	1	0	2	1	3	1
4 John Derbon	2	1	2	1	6	2
Stephen Samborn	1	1	2	0	1	0
Isaac Marston	1	0	0	1	0	0

2 YEARS OLD	1 YEAR OLD	SWINE	PLANTING/MOW	PASTURE
4	4	0	025	020
2	3	1	06	04
4	6	1	20	14
1	2	0	04	05
3	3	0	10	10
5	4	0	035	20
1	0	0	003	02
2	2	0	000	000
3	4	0	015	007
4	0	1	30	15
2	4	1	25	20
2	4	1	25	20
1	3	0	10	05
2	2	0	10	08
0	1	0	10	07
2	3	0	35	25
0	1	1	12	8
0	2	0	000	000

Names	POLS	HOUSES	OXEN	HORSES	COWS	3 YEARS OLD
Ben Mason	2	1	0	0	1	1

brought to gether	POLS	HOUSES	OXEN	HORSES	COWS	3 YEARS OLD
N:1	61	34	46	41	98	33
N:2	62	38	60	28	91	30
N:3	45	36	48	25	88	22
N:4	50	37	47	33	92	40
N:5	48	28	32	22	75	24
N:6	28	16	22	15	50	23
	294	189	255	164	494	172

2 YEARS OLD	1 YEAR OLD	SWINE	PLANTING/MOW	PASTURE
0	0	0	000	002

2 YEARS OLD	1 YEAR OLD	SWINE	PLANTING/MOW	PASTURE
69	99	4	584	481
60	62	6	495	480
44	59	2	437	439
60	80	6	417	412
38	47	5	329	300
34	44	6	250	172
===
301	391	29	2512	2284
			2284	
			4796	
			89	
			4885	
			35	
			4920	

non Residents for mowing land or marsh

	ACRES
Cpᵗ Ichabod Robie	03
Obediah Johnson	03
Elihu Chase	08
Jonᵃ Dow	03
heirs of Benj Shaw	05
James Moulton & Ben	05
Joseph Batchelder	01
John Batchelder	01
Widow Batchelder Sarah	01
Tho Fuller	06
Ben Hilyard & Jim	03
Wido Emons	04
Coles Marsh	05
Thomas Marston Marsh	06
Elias Philbrick	03
Sam Harris	01
Jonᵃ Derbon Of Stratham	3

HAMPTON

Doomings on Trade Mills Negros in the year 1741
Estates

The above List is a True Coppie of the List of Doomings on Trades Mills & negroes for the year 1741

Ebenezer Samborn Trade	5.00.00
Jeremiah Towle	3.00.00
David Jewel	6.00.00
Gershim Griffith Merch	4.00.00
Nathan Blake	3.00.00
Jon^a Garland	8.00.00
Joshua Lane	5.00.00
Benj Mason	6.00.00
Dr Nath^u Sargent	5.00.00
Nathan Philbrick	5.00.00
Ephraim Marston	1.00.00
Jon^a Thomas	4.00.00
Phillip Towle	6.00.00
Wm Stanford	2.00.00
Dr Cl Jackson	18.00.00
Sam^u Levitt	4.00.00
Henery Moulton	5.00.00

non Residents for mowing land or marsh

	ACRES
Cpᵗ Richard Jennes	04
Francis Lock	05
Eben Philbrick	03
Cpᵗ Joseph Lock	02
David Smith	04
Joseph Philbrick	02
John Garland	02
Sam Fogg	04
Jonᵃ Robenson	02
Acres	89

35 Acres more owned
not given by the
men that owned of   35
makes in the wholl

124 Acres

Doomings on Trade Mills
Negros in the year 1741
Estates

Edward Moulton	1.10.00
James Johnson	2.10.00
Edmond Rand	5.00.00
Noah Ward	3.00.00
William Moulton	3.00.00
Moris Hobbs	1.00.00
Jon^a Levitt	10.00.00
Joshua Wingett Junr	4.00.00
Zacheriah Towle	4.00.00
Caleb Marston Junr	6.00.00
Richard Tayler	1.00.00
Sam^{ll} Batchelder Junr	5
Joseph Johnson	7.00.00
Richard Samborn	4.00.00
Uper Mill On Settle River	20.00.00
Lower Mill On Settle Rivr	15.00.00
Peter Garland Grist Mill	8.00.00
Old Saw Mill	15.00.00

Doomings on Trade Mills Negros in the year 1741
Estates

Jon^a Tuck Grist Mill	8.00.00
Grist Browns Mill	7.00.00
Francis Page Grist Mill	6.00.00
Cp^t Benj Thomas Negro	12.00.00
Dr Sargent Negro	6.00.00
Jeremiah's Marston Negro	10.00.00
Dr Jackson Negro	10.00.00
Abner's Fogg Negro	10.00.00
Enoch's Samborn Negro	10.00.00

we the Subscribers have according to the best of our Judgment and understanding truely taken this within List of Invoice according as we were Directed by the Vote of the General Assembly for a new proportion in the Province In the year 1742 it being the Invoice of the Poles and Estates of the town of Hampton Excluseive of the Parishs at the falls

   Sam^{ll} Palmer
   Jonathan Tuck   Select men
   Ephraim marston   of Hampton
   John Dearbon
   Richard Taylor

Province of
Newhampshire June: 4ᵈʰ: 1742:

The Select men of Hampᵗ: above Named Personally appeared &: made oath yᵗ: according to yᵉ: Best of there Judgment &: understanding thay have Taken truly this within list: of: Invoice as Directed by a vote of the Generall assembly for a new Proportion in the Province aforesᵈ: to be made in yᵉ year: 1742 & that yᵉ within List of Domings is a true copie: of yᵉ: Domings in year 1741:
Sworn before me:
Jabez Smith: Justice of Peace

An Invoice of the Estates and Polls in Hampton Falls: Taken by Select Men: In March Anno Dom 1742 Pursant to an order of the Generall Assembly Passed in in Feby Eod: Anno

Names	POLS	HORSE	OXEN	COWS	3 YEARS OLD	2 YEARS OLD
Samuel Melcher	2	2	0	3	4	0
Benjamin Cram	1	1	2	2	3	0
Jabez Sanborn	2	1	2	2	2	2
Ephraim Sanborn	1	1	0	1	2	0
John Brown	2	1	0	2	0	2
Ben Moulton	2	2	0	4	3	4

1 YEAR OLD	SWINE	MOWING	PASTURE	HOUSE VALUE
2	1	20	15	1@2£
0	0	18	20	1@#1.10
0	0	10	4	1@2£
0	0	0	0	0
1	0	12	6	1@#1
5	1	16	5	1@#1

An Invoice of Estates in Hampton Falls. 1742

Names	POLS	HORSE	OXEN	COWS	3 YEARS OLD	2 YEARS OLD
Jonathan Bachelder	1	1	0	1	1	0
John Bachelder	1	0	0	1	0	0
John Brown	1	0	0	0	0	0
James Moulton	2	2	0	3	3	5
Cap.ᵉ Joseph Tilton	1	1	0	1	1	2
Jonathan Tilton	1	1	0	2	2	2
Jonathan Hilyard	1	0	2	0	0	5
John Cooper	1	0	0	0	0	0
Benj.ⁿ Prescutt	1	1	2	2	0	3
Timothy Morgan	1	1	0	1	0	0
Samuel Prescutt	3	2	2	2	3	4
Elisha Prescutt	2	1	0	3	0	7
Jon.ᵃ Prescutt	1	1	2	3	0	0
Joseph Prescutt	1	1	0	2	0	1
Nathan Tilton	1	1	0	4	0	4
Jon.ᵃ Cram	1	2	2	3	2	4

HAMPTON FALLS

1 YEAR OLD	SWINE	MOWING	PASTURE	HOUSE VALUE
1	0	6	3	1@#1
1	0	0	0	0
0	0	0	0	0
3	0	14	18	1@#1.10
1	0	15	15	1@2£
3	0	15	0	1@2£
0	0	10	15	1@#1.10
0	0	0	0	0
0	0	6	0	1@#1.10
1	0	0	0	1@#0.10
4	0	20	20	1@2£
2	0	20	14	1@2£
2	0	8	20	1@#1.10
0	0	5	0	0
4	0	30	20	1@2£
6	0	25	15	1@2£

An Invoice of Estates in Hampton Falls. 1742

Names	POLS	HORSE	OXEN	COWS	3 YEARS OLD	2 YEARS OLD
Joseph Garland	2	1	2	3	0	1
John Swain	4	1	0	4	2	0
Robert Row	3	1	0	4	3	1
John Prescutt	1	1	0	1	2	0
Reuben Sanborn	2	0	2	4	0	3
Nathan Sanborn	1	1	2	2	1	0
James Prescutt	1	1	2	3	1	0
Widow Abigail Sanborn	0	0	0	2	0	0
Ebenezer Prescutt	1	1	0	3	0	3
Joseph Sanborn	1	1	0	4	4	2
Benjn Sanborn	1	1	2	2	0	3
Thos Levett	2	1	0	3	2	5
Israel Clifford	2	0	0	0	0	1
John Clifford	1	1	0	2	0	0
Joseph Bachelder	1	1	2	2	1	3
Dec^n Nathll Bachelder	2	1	1	3	2	2

1 YEAR OLD	SWINE	MOWING	PASTURE	HOUSE VALUE
5	0	14	12	1@#1.10
5	0	12	5	1@#1
5	0	20	15	1@2£
3	0	12	0	1@#1
3	0	20	20	1@2£
2	0	10	0	1@#1
4	1	15	10	1@2£
0	0	10	0	0
4	0	15	10	1@#1.10
2	0	30	20	1@2£
1	0	20	20	1@2£
2	0	18	12	1@2£
0	0	12	3	1@2£
0	0	0	0	0
8	0	25	25	1@2£
1	0	24	15	1@2£

An Invoice of Estates in Hampton Falls. 1742

Names	POLS	HORSE	OXEN	COWS	3 YEARS OLD	2 YEARS OLD
Deacⁿ Josiah Bachelder	2	1	1	5	3	2
Samuel Lane	2	1	0	3	2	0
Jonathan Nason	2	2	2	3	4	0
Widow Sarah Blake	0	1	0	2	0	0
Joshua Blake	1	1	2	3	1	2
Caleb Swain	1	1	0	1	0	1
Elias Swain	1	0	2	0	0	0
Samuel Tilton	1	1	0	3	2	2
Samuel Blake	2	1	2	3	0	0
Robert Quinby	1	0	0	0	1	0
Capt Jethro Tilton	2	1	2	3	0	0
Capt Nath^{ll} Healy	2	1	2	4	1	3
Abraham Brown	2	1	2	3	2	2
Jacob Green	2	2	2	2	3	2
John Tilton	1	1	2	1	0	0
Capt Ichabod Robey	1	1	0	2	2	1

1 YEAR OLD	SWINE	MOWING	PASTURE	HOUSE VALUE
3	0	24	15	0
3	0	20	20	1@2£
1	0	30	16	1@#1.10
1	0	0	0	0
2	0	30	20	1@2£
4	0	10	8	1@#1
0	0	5	0	0
1	0	12	10	1@#1
4	0	15	7	1@2£
0	0	0	0	1@#0.10
3	1	30	20	1@2£
3	0	25	20	1@2£
4	0	15	5	1@#1
4	0	25	15	1@2£
1	0	0	0	0
1	0	16	12	1@2£

An Invoice of Estates in Hampton Falls. 1742

Names	POLS	HORSE	OXEN	COWS	3 YEARS OLD	2 YEARS OLD
Henry Robey	1	1	0	1	0	2
John Gove	4	1	4	5	1	6
Jonathan Gove	2	1	2	4	3	4
Jonathan Chase	1	1	2	2	2	4
Simon Fogg	1	0	0	1	0	0
Enock Gove	1	0	0	1	1	4
John French	1	0	0	1	0	0
Ebenezer Gove	1	0	2	3	0	0
Ebenezer Knoulton	2	0	0	1	0	0
Ezekiel Carr	1	0	0	1	0	0
Edward Gove	1	1	0	2	1	0
Jeremiah Pearson	1	1	2	1	0	1
Moses Stickney	1	1	0	1	1	2
Daniel Chase	1	0	0	0	0	1
Thomas Brown	1	1	0	3	2	0
Nathan Green	1	1	0	0	0	0

1 YEAR OLD	SWINE	MOWING	PASTURE	HOUSE VALUE
1	0	0	0	0
6	0	30	30	1@2£
6	0	30	25	1@2£
2	0	15	10	1@#1
0	0	1	0	1@#1.10
1	0	10	5	1@2£
0	0	4	0	1@#1.10
1	0	0	0	0
0	0	0	0	1@#0.10
0	0	1	0	1@#1
1	0	8	5	1@2£
2	0	20	6	1@2£
0	0	6	0	1@2£
1	0	0	0	0
4	0	15	10	1@2£
0	0	0	0	0

An Invoice of Estates in Hampton Falls. 1742

Names	POLS	HORSE	OXEN	COWS	3 YEARS OLD	2 YEARS OLD
Benjamin Green	2	0	2	2	3	2
Deacⁿ Jon^a Fiffield	1	1	4	3	2	2
John Philbrick	2	0	0	1	0	0
Thomas Philbrick	1	0	0	0	0	0
Winthrop Dow	1	1	0	2	2	1
John Treadwell	1	0	0	0	0	0
Joseph Worth *	3	1	0	4	3	0
Charles Steward	1	0	0	0	0	0
Jonathan Steward	1	0	0	0	0	0
Joseph Thresher	1	0	0	0	0	0
Jacob Brown	1	1	1	2	2	1
Ralph Butler	1	2	0	3	1	2
Abraham Green	1	1	0	0	0	0
Abraham Dow	1	0	0	1	0	3

1   Houses as 1£ S10-1

2   Houses as 1£=0=0-1

1 YEAR OLD	SWINE	MOWING	PASTURE	HOUSE VALUE
2	0	14	12	1@2£
4	1	30	30	1@2£
2	0	6	0	1@#1
0	0	3	0	0
1	0	6	1	1@#1
0	0	0	0	0
7	0	20	10	$B^1 \& C^2$
0	0	1	0	1@2£
0	0	0	0	0
0	0	0	0	0
2	0	15	15	1@2£
2	0	15	10	1@2£
0	0	1	0	1@2£
3	0	9	9	1@2£

An Invoice of Estates in Hampton Falls. 1742

Names	POLS	HORSE	OXEN	COWS	3 YEARS OLD	2 YEARS OLD
Daniel Perkins	1	0	0	0	0	1
Abner Philbrick	1	1	0	1	4	0
Jonathan Philbrick	1	0	0	2	2	0
Sandress Carr	1	1	0	2	0	0
John Brown	2	1	2	3	3	1
Huldah Davis	0	1	0	1	0	0
Jonathan Hoag	1	0	0	3	2	0
Nathanael Gove	0	0	0	0	2	0
Thomas Cram	4	2	0	2	3	5
John Chase	1	1	0	2	2	2
Jeremiah Brown	1	1	4	1	2	0
Jeremiah Gove	1	1	0	2	0	2
Henry Green	1	0	0	1	0	0
Job Haskall	1	1	0	1	0	0
Amos Cass	1	0	0	0	0	1
Joseph Cass	1	1	0	2	0	0

1 YEAR OLD	SWINE	MOWING	PASTURE	HOUSE VALUE
0	0	1	0	1@#1.10
0	0	15	10	1@2£
3	0	15	10	0
0	0	1	0	1@2£
3	0	28	8	1@2£
0	0	10	3	0
0	0	0	0	0
2	0	0	0	0
4	0	15	10	1@#1
3	0	11	11	1@#1
2	0	14	10	1@#1
2	0	6	4	1@#0.10
0	0	1	2	1@#1.10
0	0	2	0	1@#0.10
0	0	2	3	1@#0.10
2	0	4	4	1@#0.10

An Invoice of Estates in Hampton Falls. 1742

Names	POLS	HORSE	OXEN	COWS	3 YEARS OLD	2 YEARS OLD
John Page	1	1	0	1	3	0
Ephraim Hoyt	1	1	0	2	2	1
William Russell	1	0	0	0	0	0
John Green	1	0	0	1	0	0
Joshua Purington	1	1	2	2	0	0
Daniel Felch	0	1	2	1	1	0
Benjamin Dow	1	1	0	1	1	1
Nath^{ll} Weare Esq*	2	1	2	5	1	4
Benjamin Hilyard	1	0	2	2	0	0
David Swett	1	0	2	3	0	3
Jonathan Swett	1	0	2	2	1	1
Thomas Silea	1	0	0	0	0	0
Amos Levett	1	0	0	0	0	0
Edward Williams	1	0	0	0	0	0
Jabez Smith	1	1	0	1	0	0
Daniel Swet	1	0	0	1	0	0

1 YEAR OLD	SWINE	MOWING	PASTURE	HOUSE VALUE
1	0	5	5	1@#1
0	0	5	5	1@#0.10
0	0	0	0	0
0	0	3	0	1@#1.10
0	0	6	0	1@#1.10
0	0	6	0	1@#0.10
2	0	6	0	1@#1
4	0	40	20	1@2£
3	0	20	20	1@#1.10
0	0	15	20	1@2£
2	0	8	10	1@#1.10
0	0	0	0	0
0	0	0	0	0
0	0	0	0	0
0	0	0	3	1@2£
0	0	0	0	1@2£

An Invoice of Estates in Hampton Falls. 1742

Names	POLS	HORSE	OXEN	COWS	3 YEARS OLD	2 YEARS OLD
Jeremiah Bennett	1	0	0	0	0	0
Matthew Morton	1	2	2	4	0	0
Benjamin Swett	2	0	0	2	0	0
Theo:s Bachelder	2	0	2	2	0	1
John Flood	1	0	0	1	0	0
Joseph Young	1	0	0	0	0	0
John Brown	2	0	0	1	0	0
Timothy Hilyard	1	0	0	2	3	1
Thomas Boid	1	0	0	1	0	0
Enock Barker	1	0	0	0	0	0
Prudence Weare	0	1	2	1	0	1
James Hall	1	0	0	0	0	0
Peter Weare	1	2	2	4	0	2
Mary Shaw	0	0	2	4	0	1
Huldah Kenney	0	0	0	1	0	0
Nathan Hoag	1	1	0	3	0	2

1 YEAR OLD	SWINE	MOWING	PASTURE	HOUSE VALUE
0	0	0	0	0
2	0	10	20	1@2£
1	0	6	4	1@2£
0	0	5	10	1@#1
1	0	0	0	0
0	0	0	0	0
0	0	0	0	1/2 @2£
0	0	30	30	1@2£
0	0	0	0	0
0	0	0	0	0
3	0	15	15	1@2£
0	0	0	0	1@#0.10
5	0	30	10	1@2£
5	0	30	30	1@#1
0	0	0	0	1@#0.10
3	0	10	1	1@#1

An Invoice of Estates in Hampton Falls. 1742

Names	POLS	HORSE	OXEN	COWS	3 YEARS OLD	2 YEARS OLD
Moses Hoag	1	0	0	1	0	0
Ebenezer Sanborn	1	0	0	1	0	0
Ebenezer Sanborn Jun"	1	0	0	0	0	0
Enock Sanborn	1	1	0	1	0	1
Caleb Sanborn	3	0	0	1	0	0
Ebenezer Shaw	2	0	0	1	0	0
Samuel Shaw	1	0	0	0	0	0
Tim Blake Jun"	1	0	0	0	0	0
Philip Pervere	1	0	0	1	0	0
Bradbury Green	1	0	0	1	1	0
John Hardy	2	1	0	1	2	3
Ebenezer Tucker	1	1	0	1	0	0
Isaac Tobey	1	1	0	2	0	0
Joseph Blake	1	1	0	3	0	0
Jedediah Blake	1	0	0	2	0	0
Benj" Swett Jun"	1	2	2	4	0	0

1 YEAR OLD	SWINE	MOWING	PASTURE	HOUSE VALUE
2	0	11	1	0
0	0	0	0	0
0	0	0	0	0
0	0	5	3	1@2£
0	0	1	0	1@2£
0	0	3	0	1@#1
0	0	0	0	1@#0.10
0	0	0	0	0
0	0	0	0	0
0	0	14	18	1@2£
0	0	4	20	1@#1
0	0	2	1	1@#0.10
0	0	0	3	1@#1
0	0	0	0	0
0	0	0	0	1@#0.10
1	0	8	40	1@2£

An Invoice of Estates in Hampton Falls. 1742

Names	POLS	HORSE	OXEN	COWS	3 YEARS OLD	2 YEARS OLD
Thomas Fuller	1	1	2	3	1	2
Cp' Benj Perkins	2	1	0	3	2	2
Joseph Stanyan	1	0	0	0	0	0
Thomas Hunt	1	0	0	1	0	0
Stephen Hoag	1	0	0	0	0	0
Charles Treadwell	1	0	0	1	0	0
Jacob Stanyan	1	1	0	1	0	0
John Flood Jun"	1	1	0	0	0	0
James Stanyon	1	1	2	3	0	2
Jedediah Sleeper	1	0	0	2	0	0
Abner Sanborn	1	1	2	3	1	2
Timothy Blake	1	0	0	0	0	1
Samuel Fiffield	1	0	0	1	0	0
Israel Blake	2	1	0	1	1	3
John Stanyan	1	0	0	1	0	0
Zech Philbrick	1	0	0	1	0	0

1 YEAR OLD	SWINE	MOWING	PASTURE	HOUSE VALUE
1	0	9	10	1@#1
1	0	10	12	1@2£
0	0	0	0	1@#0.10
0	0	0	0	1@#0.10
0	0	0	0	0
0	0	0	0	1@2£
0	0	12	8	1@#1
0	0	0	0	0
3	0	20	10	1@#1
0	0	0	0	1@#1
3	0	30	35	1@2£
0	0	0	0	1@#0.10
0	0	0	0	1@#0.10
0	0	4	3	1@#1
1	0	0	0	1@#0.10
0	0	0	0	1@2£

An Invoice of Estates in Hampton Falls. 1742

Names	POLS	HORSE	OXEN	COWS	3 YEARS OLD	2 YEARS OLD
Walter Williams	1	0	0	0	0	0
Meshech Weare	1	1	4	5	1	0
Nathanael Bussell	1	0	4	0	0	0

The Total of the foregoing Invoices as Follows (viz.)

Heads--	208	Mowing & Planting land	1587 Acres
Horses--	107		
Oxen--	109	Pasture Land	1195 Acres
Cows--	284		
3 Year olds	130		
2 Year olds	165	Houses at 2£	60½
year olds	232	Housee at 1£ $10-	17
Swine	5	Houses at 1£	32
		Housee at 0£ $10-	19

1 YEAR OLD	SWINE	MOWING	PASTURE	HOUSE VALUE
0	0	0	0	0
3	0	55	50	1@2£
0	0	0	0	1@2£

Mowing and Planting Land Belonging to men in other Towns 319 Acres

Pasture Land belonging to men in other towns

58 acres

An account of what Persons were Doomed for their facutries and Trades &c: In Hampton Falls Anno 1742

	£ S D
Joseph Bachelder Doom^d for his Negro man	12:0- 0
Ebenezer Tucker Doom^d for his trade	2 0 0
Daniel Perkins Doom^d for his trade	4 0 0
Jonathan Longfellow Doom^d for his two mills	20 0 0
Benjn Swett Doom^d for his trade	6 0 0
Benjn Swett Junr Doom^d for his trade	4 0 0
Matthew Morton Doom^d for his trade	5 0 0
Daniel Swett Doom^d for his trade	5 0 0
Caleb Sanborn Doom^d for his trade	6 0 0
Ebenezer Shaw Doom^d for his trade	5 0 0
Theophilus Bachelder Doom^d for his trade	3 0 0
Samuel Shaw Doom^d for his trade	1 0 0
Jabez Smith Doom^d for facilty & trade	20 0 0
Capt Jethro Tilton Doom^d for his Negro man	12 0 0
John Bachelder Doom^d for his trade	2 0 0
Nathan Tilton Doom^d for his trade	2 0 0
Capt: Jethro Tilton Doom^d for his trade	3 0 0
Capt: Joseph Tilton Doom^d for his trade	2 0 0

	£	S	D
Samuel Lane Doom.d for his trade	5	0	0
Capt. Ichabod Robie Doom.d for his trade	7	0	0
Samuel Blake Doom.d for his mill	2	0	0
James Prescutt Doom.d for his facilty	20	0	0
James Prescutt Doom.d for his Negro man	0	0	0
Joseph Blake Doom.d for his trade	5	0	0
Caleb Swain Doom.d for his trade	2	0	0
Samuel Prescutt Doom.d for his trade	2	0	0
Edward Gove Doom.d for his trade	4	0	0
John Philbrick Doom.d for his trade	3	0	0
Joseph Thresher Doom.d for his trade	1	0	0
Jonathan Gove Doom.d for his Negro man	12	0	0
Nath.ll Weare Esqr for his mill & Negroman	18	0	0
Daniel Chase Doom.d for his trade	3	0	0
John Treadwell Doom.d for his trade	3	0	0
Jeremiah Bennett Doom.d for his trade	1	0	0
William Russell Doom.d for his trade	6	0	0
Ebenezer Knoulton Doom.d for his trade	2	0	0
Simon Fogg Doom.d for his trade	5	0	0
Sandress Card Doom.d for his trade	4	0	0
Job Haskall Doom.d for his trade	2	0	0
Winthrop Dow Doom.d for his trade	3	0	0
Abraham Green Doom.d for his trade	3	0	0

An account of what Persons were Doomed for their facutries and Trades &c: In Hampton Falls Ammo 1742

	£ S D
Thomas Philbrick Doom^d for his trade	2 0 0
Enock Gove Doom^d for his trade	2 0 0
Charles Steward Doom^d for his trade	5 0 0
Deac^n Joshiah Bachelder Doom^d for his trade	1 0 0
Capt Jethro Tilton & others Doom^d for a mill	10 0 0

Total of the foregoing Doomings 247

Mesheck Weare Jon^a Fyfield, Nathaniel Ely Selectmen June the 8th 1743 the above Select Men made oath - that the above is a True Inventory taken according to the Order of Gen^ll Assembly made at their last sessions of all the Rateable Poles and Estates in the Town of Hampton Falls taken according to the best of their understanding before
    Sam^{ll} Gilman Justice of Peace

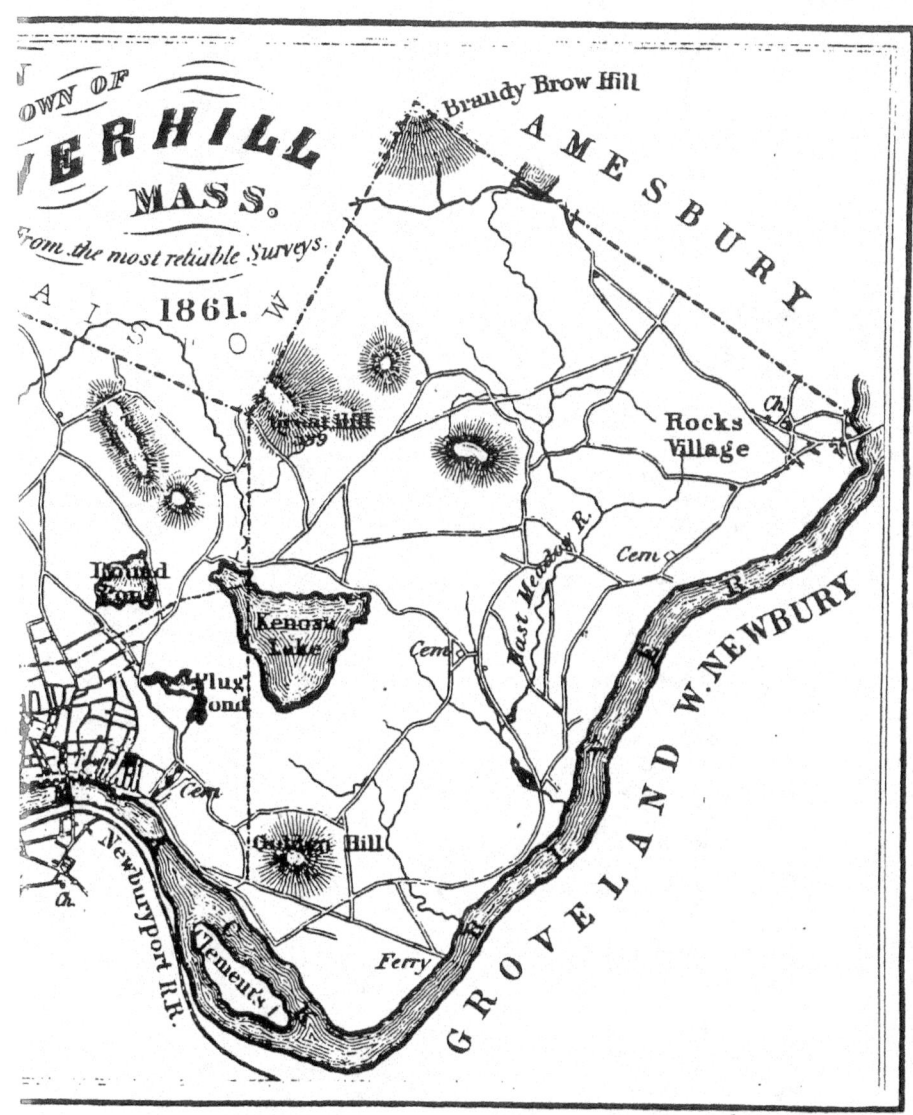

NH 1742 ESTATE TAX

Names	POLS	HOUSING	PLANTING	PASTURE	HORSES	OXEN
Joseph Colbe	1	1	3	0	0	2
Joseph Gile	2	1	4	0	0	2
Stephen Johnson Sei	2	1	10	0	2	2
Daniel Johnson	1	1	1	0	0	0
Moses Gile	1	1	0	0	0	0
humphery Emery	1	1	0	0	0	0
Jonathan hutchans	1	1	1	0	1	0
Jonathan Clemont	1	1	5	2	1	2
Edmund page	1	1	6	0	1	2
Benjamin Richards	1	1	13	2	1	3
Thomas poope	1	0	0	0	0	0
Thomas poope	1	0	0	0	0	0
James heath	1	1	2	0	1	0
Stephen wheeler	1	1	1	0	0	2
John Gooding	1	1	4	0	0	0
Moses Trusel	1	1	0	0	0	0
Lemuel tucker	1	1	2	0	0	0
Thomas hale	1	1	16	2	1	4
Nathanel Knight	3	1	9	0	1	2

COWS	2 YEAR OLD	1 YEAR OLD	SWINE
3	0	0	1
2	0	1	1
2	0	0	0
0	0	0	0
1	0	0	0
1	2	0	0
0	0	0	0
2	0	2	1
3	1	2	1
4	2	3	1
0	0	0	0
0	0	0	0
0	0	0	0
1	0	0	0
1	0	0	0
0	0	0	0
2	0	0	0
4	2	5	0
3	2	1	1

NH 1742 ESTATE TAX

Names	POLS	HOUSING	PLANTING	PASTURE	HORSES	OXEN
Abner herriman	1	1	1	0	1	2
John heath	1	0	0	0	0	0
John heath Junr	1	1	12	2	1	2
John webster	1	1	15	1	1	2
Benjamin heath	1	0	2	0	0	0
Timothy Emerson	1	1	1	0	1	4
James Blye	1	0	7	0	0	0
Benjamin Kimbel	1	1	20	10	1	3
Cornelous Johnson	0	0	2	0	0	0
John Clemont	0	0	6	1	0	0
Benjamin Clemont	0	0	3	0	0	0
Jonathan Emery	2	1	4	0	1	2
Samuel Little	1	1	3	0	1	2
Robert Greenor	1	1	1	0	1	0
Moses Flood	1	0	0	0	0	0
Thomas folensbe	2	1	25	18	1	2
Obediah perry	1	1	0	0	1	0
Samuel Choot	1	0	0	0	0	0
Timothy Noise	2	1	14	0	1	4

COWS	2 YEAR OLD	1 YEAR OLD	SWINE
2	0	0	0
0	0	0	0
4	2	0	0
4	2	2	2
0	0	0	0
2	0	2	1
0	0	0	0
4	0	4	0
0	0	0	0
0	0	0	0
0	0	0	0
1	0	0	0
2	0	0	0
2	0	1	0
0	0	0	0
3	0	2	0
1	0	0	0
0	0	0	0
3	0	1	0

NH 1742 ESTATE TAX

Names	POLS	HOUSING	PLANTING	PASTURE	HORSES	OXEN
Vanus Noise	1	0	0	0	1	0
Jonathan Merrill	1	1	4	0	0	0
Abraham Merrill	1	0	0	0	0	0
Samuel Eatton	2	1	10	2	1	2
Jonathan Stevens	1	1	0	0	0	0
Moses Jackman	1	1	2	0	0	0
Joseph harriman	2	1	10	2	1	2
Joseph arwine	1	1	2	0	1	0
John harraman	1	1	13	3	2	3
Samuel harriman	1	0	0	0	0	0
Leonard harraman	1	1	1	1	1	0
Samuel worthin	1	1	6	0	0	0
Samuel Smith	1	1	8	2	1	2
Josiah heath	1	1	1	2	0	0
James white	1	1	17	6	1	4
Samuel Little	3	1	6	0	1	0
Thomas Stone	1	0	0	0	0	0
Richard heath	1	1	3	0	1	0
Moses Belknap	1	1	2	0	0	2

HAVERHILL

COWS	2 YEAR OLD	1 YEAR OLD	SWINE
1	2	0	0
1	0	0	0
1	0	0	0
4	3	1	0
0	0	0	0
1	0	0	0
5	2	2	2
2	0	0	0
2	1	0	1
0	0	0	0
2	1	0	0
3	0	0	0
3	0	1	1
1	0	0	0
4	4	5	2
3	0	2	0
0	0	0	0
2	0	0	0
3	0	2	0

NH 1742 ESTATE TAX

Names	POLS	HOUSING	PLANTING	PASTURE	HORSES	OXEN
Caleb heath	1	1	2	0	1	2
Benjamin Emerson	2	1	15	0	1	4
Robert Emerson	2	1	15	1	1	6
Samuel Stevens	1	1	0	0	1	0
Jonathan Stevens Junr	1	0	0	0	0	0
Nathaniel Merrill	1	1	2	0	1	2
Georg Little	1	1	14	2	1	2
Jonathan Kimbel	1	1	10	2	1	0
Jeremiah Eatton	1	1	0	4	0	0
Moses Copp	2	1	8	2	1	4
Ebenazer Gile	1	1	2	0	1	0
Otho Stevens	2	1	6	0	1	3
Samuel worthin Jur	1	1	1	0	0	0
James heath	1	1	15	1	1	3
William hand Cock	1	1	2	0	1	0
Mical Johnson	2	0	4	0	1	2
Thomas Craford	1	1	1	0	0	0
John Muzze	1	1	1	0	0	0
John hunkins	1	1	2	0	0	0

COWS	2 YEAR OLD	1 YEAR OLD	SWINE
1	0	0	0
7	2	4	1
4	2	3	1
1	0	0	0
0	0	0	0
1	0	0	0
3	2	2	0
3	4	1	0
1	0	0	0
4	0	1	0
2	0	1	0
3	0	2	0
1	0	0	0
3	0	0	1
2	0	0	0
4	0	0	0
2	0	0	0
1	0	1	0
2	0	3	0

NH 1742 ESTATE TAX

Names	POLS	HOUSING	PLANTING	PASTURE	HORSES	OXEN
Weight Stevens	1	1	2	0	1	0
Sarah Green	0	1	1	0	0	0
Stephen Johnson	1	1	2	0	0	0
Georg Kezzer	1	1	0	0	0	0
John Kezzer	1	1	7	1	1	2
Nahemiah Stevens	1	1	2	0	0	2
Benjamin Stevens	1	0	0	0	0	0
Joseph Stevens Jur	1	0	0	0	0	0
David Copp	1	1	1	0	1	0
Daniel Little	1	1	9	0	1	0
Samuel Stevens	2	1	7	0	1	2
William Stevens	1	1	0	0	0	2
John Stevens	1	1	0	0	1	0
John hog	1	1	7	1	1	2
Peter Eastman	1	1	4	1	1	2
Benjamin philbrook	1	1	1	0	1	2
Timothy Johnson	1	1	12	1	1	2
Jonathan Page	1	1	7	2	1	2
Peter Johnson	1	0	0	0	0	0

COWS	2 YEAR OLD	1 YEAR OLD	SWINE
1	1	0	0
0	0	1	0
1	0	0	0
0	0	0	1
3	0	0	0
1	0	0	0
0	0	0	0
0	0	2	0
2	0	0	0
2	1	3	0
2	0	3	1
1	0	0	0
1	0	0	0
5	2	5	2
4	0	0	1
2	0	3	0
4	1	3	2
5	2	2	3
0	0	0	0

NH 1742 ESTATE TAX

Names	POLS	HOUSING	PLANTING	PASTURE	HORSES	OXEN
John Dow	1	1	4	0	1	2
Daniel poor	1	1	4	1	1	4
Daniel Robords	2	1	2	0	1	2
Joseph Stevens	1	1	15	0	1	2
Jonathan Coborn	3	1	3	5	2	4
Jonathan Eatton	0	0	5	1	0	0
William webster	1	1	3	0	1	2
Thomas Smith	1	0	1	0	0	0
Joseph page	1	1	12	0	1	4
Moses page	1	0	3	0	1	2
Daniel whitteker	1	1	6	0	1	2
Israel webster	1	1	6	0	1	0
Timothy Page	1	1	3	0	1	0
John Currier	1	1	7	0	1	2
Joshua page	1	1	2	0	0	0
John pike	1	1	2	0	0	0
Elipalit page	1	0	1	0	0	0
Philip hoit	1	0	0	0	0	0
Edward Calton	1	1	3	0	0	2

COWS	2 YEAR OLD	1 YEAR OLD	SWINE
2	0	2	2
2	0	2	0
2	0	0	0
1	0	0	0
1	0	2	3
0	0	0	0
2	1	2	1
0	0	0	0
3	1	1	2
1	3	1	0
2	0	2	0
4	3	1	0
1	0	0	0
3	0	1	0
1	3	4	0
1	0	0	0
0	0	0	0
0	0	0	0
1	0	1	3

NH 1742 ESTATE TAX

Names	POLS	HOUSING	PLANTING	PASTURE	HORSES	OXEN
Joseph heath	2	1	8	4	1	2
Gorg Little Senr	1	1	8	3	1	4
William Eastman	1	1	2	0	1	2
Zaciriah Johnson	1	1	2	0	1	0
Stephen Emerson	1	1	12	1	1	2
Nathaniel heath	1	1	10	2	1	2
David heath	1	1	6	0	1	2
John atword	1	1	3	0	1	0
John Davis	3	1	0	0	0	0
William heath	1	0	0	0	0	0
Robert ford	1	1	0	0	1	0
Moses Stevens	1	1	6	2	1	2
Wido Sarah Stevens	0	1	2	0	1	2
Benjamin Stone	1	1	3	0	1	0
Ruben Mase	1	1	3	0	0	0
Ephraim Emerson	1	1	3	0	1	0
Thomas Chaney	1	1	5	2	1	2
Samuel Kimbel	1	1	7	2	1	2
Christopher Bartlet	2	1	8	4	2	4

COWS	2 YEAR OLD	1 YEAR OLD	SWINE
3	0	1	0
4	3	5	1
1	0	0	0
2	0	0	0
3	0	2	0
3	0	1	0
2	0	0	0
2	1	0	0
2	0	0	0
1	0	0	0
2	0	0	0
4	2	1	3
2	2	1	0
1	0	0	0
0	0	0	0
1	0	0	0
4	0	2	0
3	3	2	1
2	0	2	0

NH 1742 ESTATE TAX

Names	POLS	HOUSING	PLANTING	PASTURE	HORSES	OXEN
Jonathan Bartlet	1	0	0	0	1	2
Nathanll Bartlet	1	1	3	1	1	2
Abraham Chase	1	1	5	2	1	0
John Pollord	2	1	1	1	0	0
Samuel heath	1	1	6	0	1	2
Jonathan Robords	1	1	26	30	2	4
Stephen Dow	2	1	18	6	2	2
Jonathan Dow	1	0	0	0	0	0
John Duston	1	1	8	0	1	2
William Ayer	1	1	9	0	1	0
Frances Smylie	1	1	12	3	1	0
John Smylie	1	0	0	0	1	0
Nicolis White	1	1	10	0	2	5
Mr John Brown	0	0	0	2	0	0
James ayer	0	0	0	1	0	0
Nathan^{ll} tucker	1	1	2	0	0	0
Samuel Brown	1	1	0	0	0	0
Daniel Gile	1	1	10	6	2	2
Timothy Dow	1	1	8	3	1	2

COWS	2 YEAR OLD	1 YEAR OLD	SWINE
0	0	0	0
2	0	0	0
2	2	0	1
2	0	0	0
3	0	2	0
6	2	8	0
3	0	3	0
0	0	0	0
1	0	7	3
2	0	1	0
3	0	0	0
0	1	0	0
5	4	4	4
0	0	0	0
0	0	0	0
2	0	0	0
1	0	0	0
3	2	1	1
1	1	3	0

NH 1742 ESTATE TAX

Names	POLS	HOUSING	PLANTING	PASTURE	HORSES	OXEN
Peter Dow	1	1	6	6	1	0
Edmund hale	1	1	6	0	1	2
henry hesaltine	1	1	6	2	1	2
hugh pike	1	1	4	0	1	2
Benjamin petengill	1	1	5	2	1	2
John Kent	1	1	2	0	0	0
Obediah Clemont	0	1	6	0	0	0
Nahemiah heath	1	0	0	0	0	0
Jonathan whitteker	1	1	3	0	1	0
Thomas worthin	1	1	6	0	1	2
Caleb Emery	1	0	0	0	0	0
Nathaniel Smith	1	1	1	0	0	0
Joseph Buck	1	0	0	0	0	0
Lenord Harriman J.	1	0	0	0	0	0
James Noise	1	1	0	0	1	2
Nathaniel Gatchel	1	0	0	0	0	0
Barthomi heath	1	1	3	0	0	0
Joshua Knight	0	0	0	2	0	0
peter patee	1	1	10	0	1	2

COWS	2 YEAR OLD	1 YEAR OLD	SWINE
2	5	0	0
1	1	0	0
1	0	2	0
2	0	0	0
3	0	1	0
0	0	0	0
0	0	0	0
0	0	0	0
1	0	1	0
2	0	2	1
1	2	0	0
0	0	0	0
0	0	0	0
0	0	0	0
2	0	1	2
0	0	0	0
2	0	0	0
0	0	0	0
4	3	2	0

NH 1742 ESTATE TAX

Names	POLS	HOUSING	PLANTING	PASTURE	HORSES	OXEN
David Sanders	1	0	0	0	1	0
Richard pattee	1	0	7	0	0	4
Susanah patte	0	1	2	0	1	0
Thomas paul	1	1	2	0	1	0
John watts	1	1	2	0	1	2
Seth patte	1	1	4	0	1	2
Nathanel	1	1	2	0	0	0
John Currier Jur	1	1	4	0	1	2
Benjamin wheeler	1	1	2	0	1	2
Richard Carlton	1	1	5	0	1	2
Jonathan wheler	3	1	7	0	1	4
william Johnhnson	1	0	3	0	0	2
abraham anis	1	1	4	0	0	2
Caleb Page	1	1	20	10	1	2
Josiah Copp	1	1	4	1	1	2
David Emerson	1	1	4	1	0	2
John Dow Seiner	1	1	5	0	1	0
william whitteker	0	0	4	0	0	0

COWS	2 YEAR OLD	1 YEAR OLD	SWINE
0	0	0	0
1	1	1	0
1	0	0	0
2	0	0	0
2	0	0	2
2	0	0	0
1	0	1	0
1	0	2	0
1	0	1	0
3	0	0	0
3	0	0	0
1	0	1	0
1	0	0	0
6	5	9	3
1	0	0	0
1	0	1	0
2	0	0	0
0	0	0	0

A True invoce of all poles and Ratabel Estates of that part of Haverhill So Called which Is made into a destrect all taken by the May 28 1742 by me Caleb Page Clark

Memorand about ¼ part of the oxen, so Cald should be cald
three year old
Some of the cows should be cald 2year old

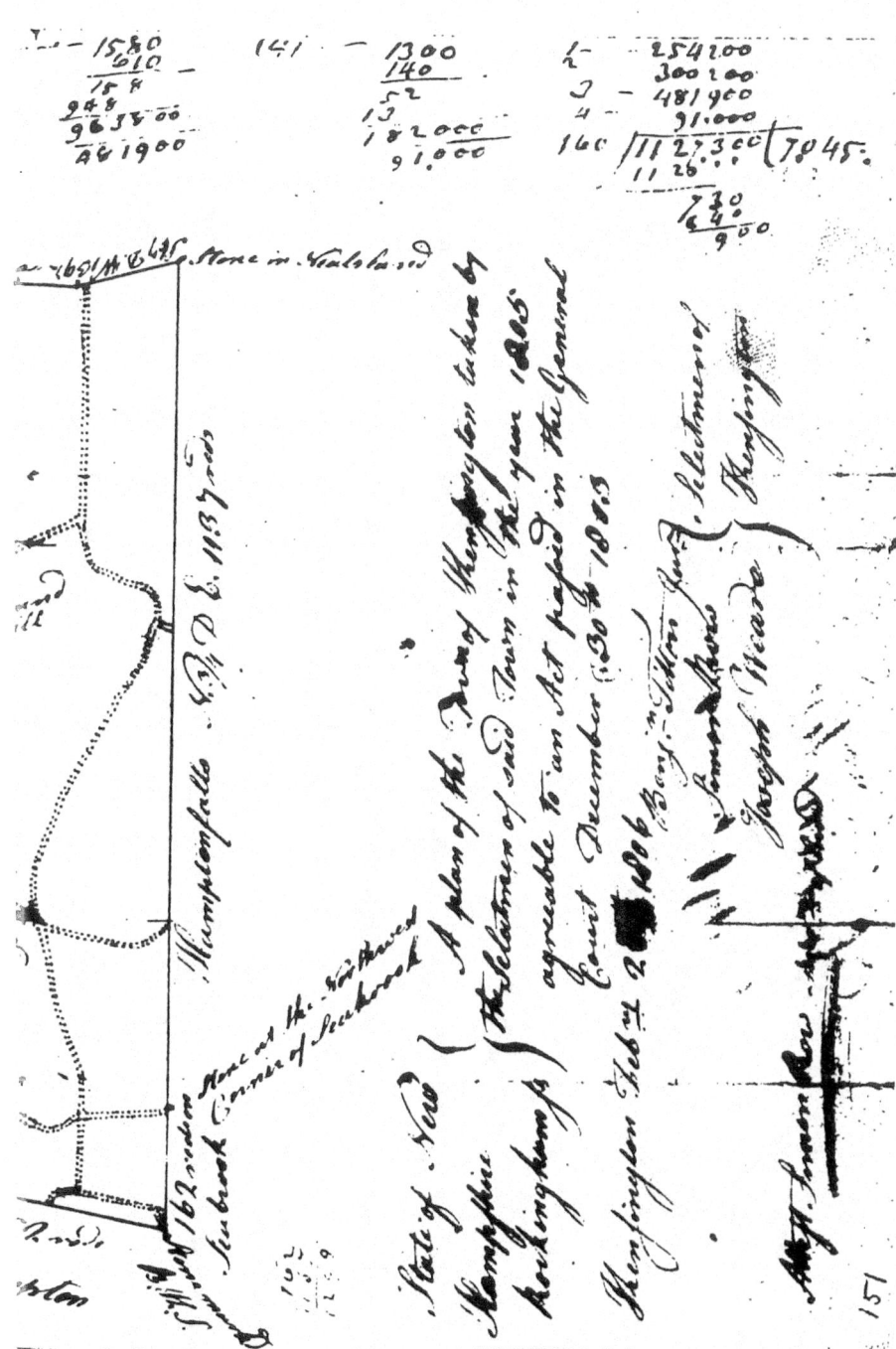

NH 1742 ESTATE TAX

Names	POLS	HOUSING	HORSES	OXEN	COWS	3 YEAR OLD
Philemon Blake	1	1	2	2	2	0
Edward Locke	1	1	1	2	3	0
Edward Tuck	1	1	2	0	3	3
Benjᵃ Row	1	1	0	0	0	0
Jonᵃ Row	1	0	1	2	0	0
Robert Row	1	1	1	0	2	2
Joshua Gilman	1	1	0	0	0	1
Benja Cram	2	1	1	4	1	1
Nathaᵘ Batchlder	1	1	1	2	3	2
John Cram	1	1	1	0	2	2
John Loveret	1	1	1	2	1	0
Samuel Blake	1	1	0	0	1	0
Wade Stickne	1	0	0	0	1	0
Ebenzer Gove	1	1	1	0	1	3
Edward Palmer	1	1	1	2	2	2
John Green	1	1	1	0	2	3
John Green	1	1	1	1	3	0
Benja Page	1	1	1	2	1	2

2 YEAR OLD	1 YEAR OLD	PLANTING & MOWING	PASTURE
2	1	15	12
0	2	7	3
3	6	20	25
0	0	0	0
2	3	3	10
4	5	28	10
3	3	2	12
1	2	15	15
1	4	24	15
0	1	14	10
2	6	6	15
0	0	3	5
0	0	0	0
1	1	7	6
0	2	10	9
3	1	2	4
1	0	19	16
3	2	6	0

NH 1742 ESTATE TAX

Names	POLS	HOUSING	HORSES	OXEN	COWS	3 YEAR OLD
Richard Sanborn	2	1	0	4	3	0
Abraham Priscut	1	1	1	2	1	1
Benj Priscut	1	1	1	2	1	1
James Sanborn	2	1	1	0	2	2
John Sharborn	1	0	1	0	1	0
James Priscut	1	1	1	4	2	0
Jonathan Pulsifer	1	1	0	0	1	0
David Sanborn	1	1	1	2	2	0
Timothy Hucheson	1	1	1	0	1	2
Jonathan Hucheson	1	0	0	2	0	0
Isral James	1	1	1	0	3	1
Caleb Shaw	1	0	1	0	1	0
Abraham Haskils	1	1	0	0	0	0
Jonathan Brown	1	1	1	0	3	2
Ebenezer Dow	1	1	1	0	2	0
Philip Grifen	3	1	1	0	1	2
Jona^n Cass	1	1	1	0	1	0
Gidean Currell	1	1	0	0	1	0

KENSINGTON

2 YEAR OLD	1 YEAR OLD	PLANTING & MOWING	PASTURE
3	*4*	*30*	*20*
0	*0*	*4*	*0*
0	*0*	*4*	*5*
4	*2*	*16*	*20*
0	*0*	*0*	*4*
1	*0*	*12*	*10*
0	*1*	*1*	*0*
0	*0*	*10*	*10*
0	*2*	*10*	*8*
0	*0*	*0*	*0*
3	*0*	*10*	*10*
0	*0*	*0*	*1*
1	*0*	*0*	*0*
2	*2*	*6*	*1*
0	*3*	*5*	*3*
4	*3*	*8*	*7*
0	*4*	*4*	*5*
0	*2*	*0*	*0*

NH 1742 ESTATE TAX

Names	POLS	HOUSING	HORSES	OXEN	COWS	3 YEAR OLD
John Hardie	1	1	1	0	1	0
Ezekiel Dow	1	1	1	2	3	0
Nathan Clough	1	1	1	2	1	0
Obediah Johnson	1	2	1	2	3	4
George Connor	1	1	1	0	1	1
Jereh Green	3	1	1	2	2	2

the asesments amounting to forty £26 pounds

Mowing & Planting Land Belonging to men in other towns 88 acres

Pasture Land Belonging to men in other towns 152 acres

John Bachelder
Richard Samburn   Selectmen
Nathan Clough   Kensington

2 YEAR OLD	1 YEAR OLD	PLANTING & MOWING	PASTURE
2	1	1	3
1	1	10	11
1	4	10	8
5	5	16	20
4	6	6	12
4	5	20	10

June ye 8th 1742 The Selectmen subscribing hereunto made oath that the above is an exact & true List of the Rateable Estates pols in Kensington taken by order of the Gen^{ll} Assembly last session according to their best understanding

Sworn   Sam^{ll} Gilman Just of Peace

NH 1742 ESTATE TAX

Names	POLS	HOUSING	HORSES	OXEN	COWS	3 YEAR OLD
John Tilton	1	1	1	0	4	0
Sharborn Tilton	1	1	0	2	3	2
James Fogg	1	1	1	2	2	1
Chase Hilyard	1	0	0	2	1	0
Moses Sanborn	1	1	0	0	2	0
Benja James	1	1	1	0	2	0
Stephen Hobs	2	1	1	2	4	0
Edward Smith	1	1	1	0	2	0
John Page	1	1	0	2	2	1
Jere^h Batchelder	1	1	1	2	2	0
William Evens	1	1	0	0	2	0
Samuel Page	1	1	2	2	3	0
Simon Batchelder	1	1	1	2	3	0
Benja Brown	1	1	1	2	1	0
Jona Palmer	1	1	0	0	2	0
John Graves	1	1	0	0	1	0
Nehemiah Brown	1	1	0	2	1	0

2 YEAR OLD	1 YEAR OLD	PLANTING & MOWING	PASTURE
3	0	10	10
0	2	10	8
0	2	10	10
1	0	0	0
0	1	0	0
0	1	6	0
0	5	5	18
0	0	2	0
1	2	6	14
2	2	8	4
0	0	1	0
1	3	16	16
1	3	16	16
1	1	9	3
1	0	5	4
0	1	5	2
1	3	4	8

NH 1742 ESTATE TAX

Names	POLS	HOUSING	HORSES	OXEN	COWS	3 YEAR OLD
Anne Brow	1	0	0	0	2	0
Jonathan Dow	1	1	1	0	3	2
Widow Purington	0	1	1	0	2	1
Sam^u Clifford	1	1	1	0	3	2
Theophiles Page	1	1	1	0	4	0
Sam^u Clifford	1	0	1	0	2	3
Philip Dow	2	1	1	0	1	1
Ezekiel Worthyn	1	0	0	0	1	0
John Weare	3	1	2	2	4	1
Abel Ward	1	1	1	0	2	0
John Dow	1	1	1	0	4	2
Joseph Pike	1	1	1	0	3	0
Jere^h Easman	1	2	1	0	3	0
John Batchelder	1	1	1	2	4	0
Josiah Brown	1	1	1	2	2	0
Abraham Sanborn	1	1	1	0	3	5
Joseph Tilton	1	1	1	0	3	2
Jonathan Priscut	2	1	1	2	3	0

KENSINGTON

2 YEAR OLD	1 YEAR OLD	PLANTING & MOWING	PASTURE
2	2	4	4
1	4	12	12
1	3	8	8
3	1	19	16
0	0	10	10
0	3	0	0
2	1	6	6
0	1	0	0
4	3	20	18
0	0	9	7
3	0	10	10
0	0	1	4
3	4	8	7
1	5	25	18
2	2	10	11
3	3	16	20
0	0	10	12
0	7	3	20

NH 1742 ESTATE TAX

Names	POLS	HOUSING	HORSES	OXEN	COWS	3 YEAR OLD
Wadleigh Cram	1	1	0	4	3	0
Thomas Knoulton	1	1	0	0	1	0
Nathaniel Priscut	2	1	0	0	2	0
Joseph Shaw	1	1	1	0	1	2
John Melcher	1	1	1	0	2	0
Nathaniel Priscut	2	1	1	2	2	0
Ebenezer Knoulton	1	1	1	0	1	1
Elihu Chase	1	1	1	2	5	0
John Chapman	1	1	1	0	1	0
Joseph Shaw	1	1	0	0	3	0
Elihu Shaw	1	1	1	0	2	0
Moses Row	1	1	1	0	2	0
John Stanyan	1	1	1	0	2	0
Isaac Fellows	3	1	1	0	1	0
Hezekiah Blake	2	1	1	2	2	3
Moses Blake	1	1	1	0	3	0
Nathaniel Dearborn	1	1	1	0	3	2
Moses Shaw	1	0	1	0	2	0

KENSINGTON

2 YEAR OLD	1 YEAR OLD	PLANTING & MOWING	PASTURE
2	2	16	4
0	0	0	0
2	2	3	17
2	2	10	4
2	2	12	3
1	2	12	7
0	0	1	0
2	5	17	17
0	0	2	0
0	2	3	3
2	1	3	2
2	3	5	3
0	0	5	5
2	0	10	8
0	1	7	4
1	2	4	2
3	3	10	0
2	1	3	0

NH 1742 ESTATE TAX

Names	POLS	HOUSING	HORSES	OXEN	COWS	3 YEAR OLD
Benja Brown	1	0	0	0	0	0
Joseph Row	1	1	1	0	2	1
James Perkins	1	1	2	2	2	0
Reuben Smith	1	1	0	2	1	2
Moses Blake	1	0	1	0	2	0
Shadrach Ward	1	1	1	0	1	0
Abraham Moulton	2	1	1	0	2	3

2 YEAR OLD	1 YEAR OLD	PLANTING & MOWING	PASTURE
0	0	0	0
2	3	10	6
2	3	12	17
1	2	8	5
0	0	3	3
2	0	6	0
4	3	20	15

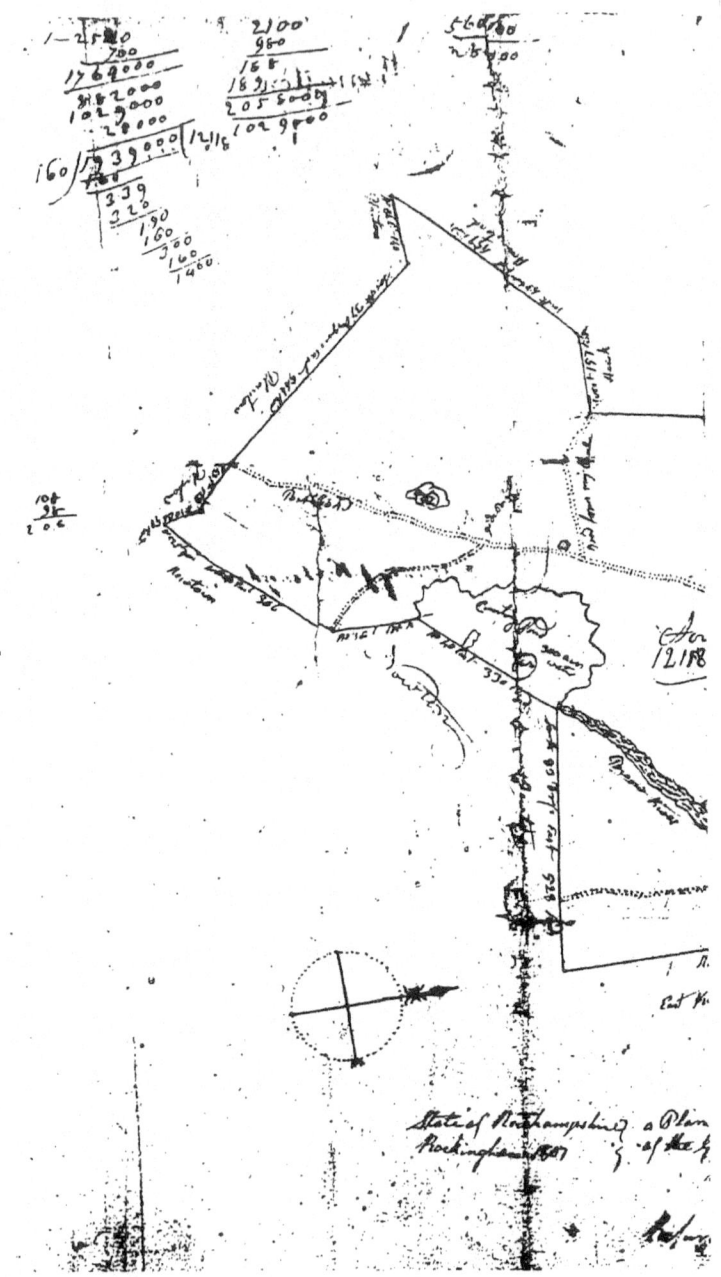

Kingston

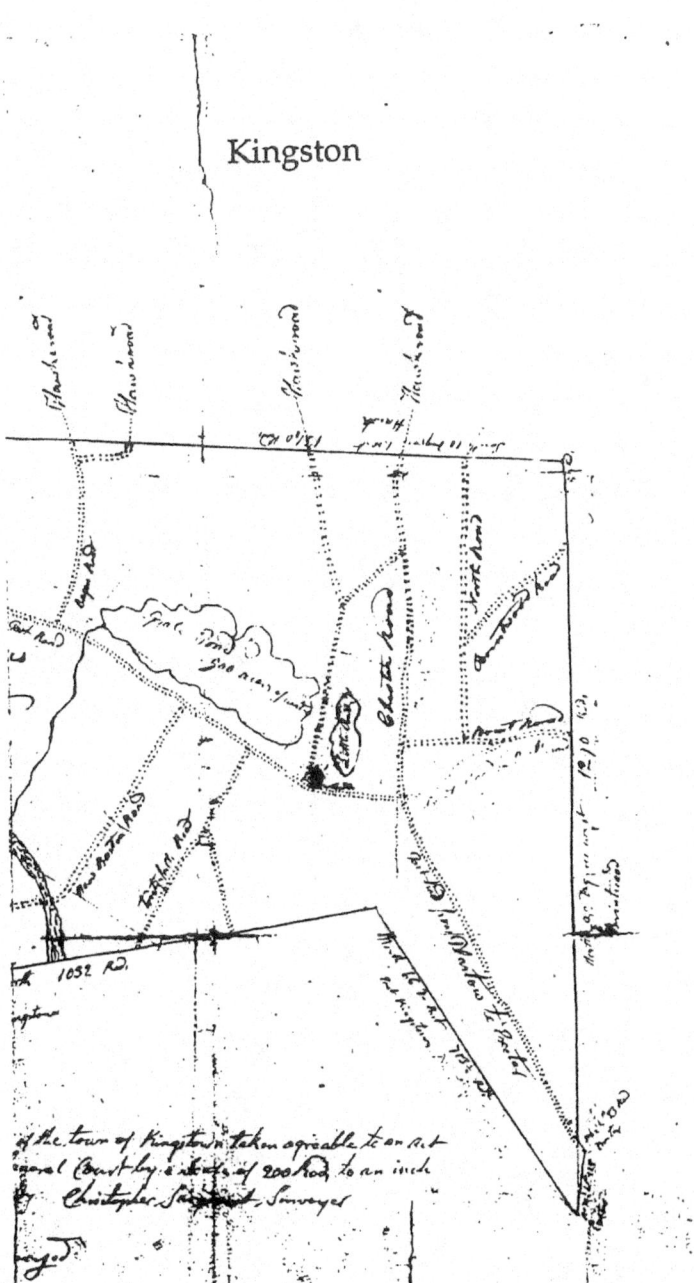

Names	POLS	HOUSES	PLANTING	PASTURE	OXEN	COWS
Eben^r Webster	1	1	8	8	0	1
John Webster	1	1	19	8	4	1
Samuel Locke	1	1	0	0	0	1
Daniel Darling	1	0	0	0	0	1
Nathan Ordway	1	1	4	3	2	3
John Clifford	1	1	7	6	0	2
John Clifford Junr	1	0	0	0	0	0
Obadiah Elkins	1	1	13	5	0	3
Eber^r Sleeper	1	1	13	8	0	3
Joseph Bean	1	1	17	20	0	2
Sam^{ll} Emmons	1	1	8	10	2	3
Eben^r Collins	1	1	16	7	2	4
Nathan Bacheller	1	1	20	20	2	4
Thomas Webster	2	1	1	0	0	1
Ichabod Clough	2	1	13	10	2	2
Abraham Smith	1	1	16	16	2	3
Wiliam Smith	1	1	12	9	2	4
Reuben Muzzey	1	0	3	0	0	0

3 YEARS OLD	2 YEARS OLD	1 YEAR OLD	HORSES	SWINE	MILLS
0	2	2	1	0	
1	0	3	1	0	
0	0	0	0	0	
0	0	0	0	0	
0	0	0	1	0	
0	0	0	1	0	
0	0	0	0	0	
2	0	1	1	0	
0	0	0	1	0	
1	5	3	0	0	
0	1	3	0	0	
0	0	1	1	0	
0	1	2	1	0	
0	0	0	1	0	
0	1	2	1	0	
0	3	1	1	0	
0	1	2	1	1	
0	0	0	0	0	

NH 1742 ESTATE TAX

Names	POLS	HOUSES	PLANTING	PASTURE	OXEN	COWS
Joseph Greeley	1	1	24	26	4	1
Joseph Greeley Junr	1	1	4	1	0	1
Isaac Godfrey	1	1	16	12	2	1
Estate Of Eben^e Fellows	0	1	13	10	2	1
Joshua French	1	1	5	5	0	1
Benj^a Brown	0	0	0	4	0	0
Sam^u French	0	0	1	6	0	0
Jonathan Greeley	1	0	0	0	0	0
Thomas Brown	0	0	0	10	0	0
Jacob Brown	0	0	0	6	0	0
Benj^a Brown		0	0	4	0	0
Eben^e Stevens Esqr	0	0	0	3	0	0
Benj^a Clough	0	0	0	5	0	0
Nehemiah Brown	0	0	0	4	0	0
Abraham Brown	0	0	2	12	0	0
Wiliam Buswell	1	0	0	0	0	0
Sam^u Buswell	1	0	0	0	0	0
Samuel Buswell	1	1	6	2	0	3

KINGSTON

3 YEARS OLD	2 YEARS OLD	1 YEAR OLD	HORSES	SWINE	MILLS
1	3	2	1	0	
0	0	0	0	0	
1	4	2	1	1	
0	1	3	1	0	
2	0	0	0	0	
0	0	0	0	0	
0	0	0	0	0	
1	0	0	1	0	
0	0	0	0	0	
0	0	0	0	0	
0	0	0	0	0	
0	0	0	0	0	
0	0	0	0	0	
0	0	0	0	0	
0	0	0	0	0	
0	0	0	0	0	
0	0	2	0	0	

NH 1742 ESTATE TAX

Names	POLS	HOUSES	PLANTING	PASTURE	OXEN	COWS
Josiah Bacheller	1	1	18	18	2	3
Joshua Prescot	3	1	15	15	0	1
Edward Prescot	1	1	0	0	0	1
Estate Of Rob Stockman	0	1	6	14	0	2
Phinehas Bacheller	1	1	25	25	2	5
Jeremiah Webster	1	1	23	20	2	2
Richard Clifford	1	1	9	5	0	2
Benjamin French	4	1	23	10	2	2
Elisha Blake	1	1	8	8	0	2
Josiah Tilton	1	1	17	13	2	1
Isaac Griffin	1	1	10	10	0	2
John Darling	2	1	8	6	2	0
John Darling Junr	1	0	4	4	2	2
Caleb Clough	1	1	2	3	0	0
Jonathan Greeley	1	1	12	10	2	2
Eben^e Bacheller	1	1	12	10	2	2
Joseph Foster	2	1	2	2	0	1
James Tappan	1	1	10	10	2	3

KINGSTON

3 YEARS OLD	2 YEARS OLD	1 YEAR OLD	HORSES	SWINE	MILLS
1	1	4	1	0	
1	0	1	1	0	
0	0	0	1	0	
0	0	1	1	0	
1	2	4	1	0	
0	0	3	1	0	
1	0	2	1	0	
0	2	2	1	0	
3	3	2	1	0	
1	1	2	1	0	
1	2	2	1	0	
2	0	0	1	0	
0	1	2	0	0	
0	1	1	0	0	
0	1	3	1	0	
0	2	2	1	0	
0	0	1	1	0	
1	2	1	0	0	

NH 1742 ESTATE TAX

Names	POLS	HOUSES	PLANTING	PASTURE	OXEN	COWS
Daniel Clough	1	1	1	8	0	0
Benj^a Morrill	1	1	16	12	2	5
Edward Fifield	1	1	12	8	2	2
Henry Lunt	1	1	8	2	0	0
Simon Noyes	1	0	3	3	0	1
Thomas Newman	1	1	10	10	2	3
Oliver Smith	0	0	16	0	0	0
Joseph Row	0	0	3	4	0	0
Moses Row	0	0	3	3	0	0
Daniel Ladd	0	0	10	0	0	0
Reuben Smith	0	0	10	2	0	0
Joseph Leavits	1	0	3	1	0	0
Patience Stevens	0	0	10	3	0	0
Biley Hardy	0	0	3	1	0	0
Simon Bacheller	0	0	4	0	0	0
Benj^a Sleeper	0	0	20	6	0	0
John Loverain	0	0	3	4	0	0
Moses Leavitt Esqr	0	0	0	3	0	0

KINGSTON

3 YEARS OLD	2 YEARS OLD	1 YEAR OLD	HORSES	SWINE	MILLS
1	0	0	0	0	
0	1	1	1	0	
0	0	2	1	0	
0	0	0	0	0	
0	0	0	0	0	
0	0	1	0	0	
0	0	0	0	0	
0	0	0	0	0	
0	0	0	0	0	
0	0	0	0	0	
0	0	0	0	0	
0	0	0	0	0	
0	0	0	0	0	
0	0	0	0	0	
0	0	0	0	0	
0	0	0	0	0	
0	0	0	0	0	
0	0	0	0	0	

NH 1742 ESTATE TAX

Names	POLS	HOUSES	PLANTING	PASTURE	OXEN	COWS
John Ladd	0	0	0	12	0	0
Wiliam Boynton	2	1	20	20	2	3
Jeremiah Currier	1	1	5	5	0	3
Orlando Bagley	1	1	11	11	0	1
John Currier	1	1	6	6	2	2
Theophilus Clough	1	1	12	14	2	3
Joseph Easman	1	1	12	18	2	5
Thomas Easman	1	1	12	13	2	3
Ralph Blasdell	1	1	8	8	0	2
Jacob Gale	1	1	0	12	0	2
Theophilus Griffin	2	1	10	10	2	3
Wiliam Whicher	1	1	1	2	0	2
Thomas Brown	1	1	3	3	0	2
Jon^a Blasdell	1	1	2	3	0	1
Onesiphorus Page	1	0	4	0	0	1
Daniel Rowell	1	1	5	7	0	3
Peter Thompson	1	0	1	0	0	0
John Griffin	1	0	0	0	0	0

3 YEARS OLD	2 YEARS OLD	1 YEAR OLD	HORSES	SWINE	MILLS
0	0	0	0	0	
2	2	0	1	0	0
0	0	1	1	0	½
0	0	3	0	0	5
0	0	2	0	1	1 ½
2	2	3	1	1	½
0	3	1	0	0	½
0	1	3	1	0	½
0	4	3	1	1	1 ½
0	0	0	1	1	3
0	1	2	0	1	3
0	0	0	0	1	3
2	0	0	0	0	0
0	0	0	1	0	1 ½
0	2	0	0	0	1
0	0	3	1	1	1
0	0	0	0	0	0
0	0	0	0	0	3

Names	POLS	HOUSES	PLANTING	PASTURE	OXEN	COWS
Theo Griffin Jun*	1	0	0	0	0	0
Eliphalet Griffin	1	0	0	0	0	0
Wiliam Boynton Jun*	1	0	0	0	0	0
Moses Blasdel	1	0	0	0	0	0
Benj^a Kendrick	1	0	0	0	0	0
John Carter Jun*	0	0	0	0	0	0
Thomas Carter	0	0	0	0	0	0
Orlando Bagley Esq*	0	0	0	0	0	0
Jacob Bagly	0	0	1	0	0	0
Lt Blasdle	0	0	0	0	0	0
Philip Rowel	0	1	4	12	0	2
Wid Nichols	0	0	0	0	0	0

KINGSTON

3 YEARS OLD	2 YEARS OLD	1 YEAR OLD	HORSES	SWINE	MILLS
0	0	0	0	0	3
0	0	0	0	0	1 ½
0	0	0	0	0	
0	0	0	0	0	0
0	0	0	0	0	0
0	0	0	0	0	¾
0	0	0	0	0	¾
0	0	0	0	0	2 ½
0	0	0	0	0	1 ½
0	0	0	0	0	3
0	0	1	0	0	1
0	0	0	0	0	1

The foregoing is a true Inventory of the Polls Houses Rateable Esatae both Tillage & Pasturing Stock Such as Oxen Cows 3 Year Olds 2 Year Olds Yearling Horses Swine Mills In the East Parish in Kingston Newhampe Taken by order of the General Court in the Month of March 1742

By Us

Phinehas Bachelder
Jeremah Currier   SelectMen for Said Parish
Ebeneer Collins

For the Last Year Was Doomd by Select Men
Assesors In this Parish As Rateable Estate

	£ s d
Wiliam Whicker for his Occupation	2:0 0
Jon^a Blasdle for his Occupation	2:0 0
Josh^a Prescots Saw mill	9:0 0
Grist Mill	12:0 0
Iron Mill at	36:0 0
Saw Mill by it	18:0 0
Another Saw Mill	12:0 0
Jacob Gales Grist Mill	06:0 0
Thomas Webster for his Occupation	04:0 0
Simon Noyes for his Occupation	04:0 0
Jacob Gale for his Tavern	08:0 0
	113-0 0

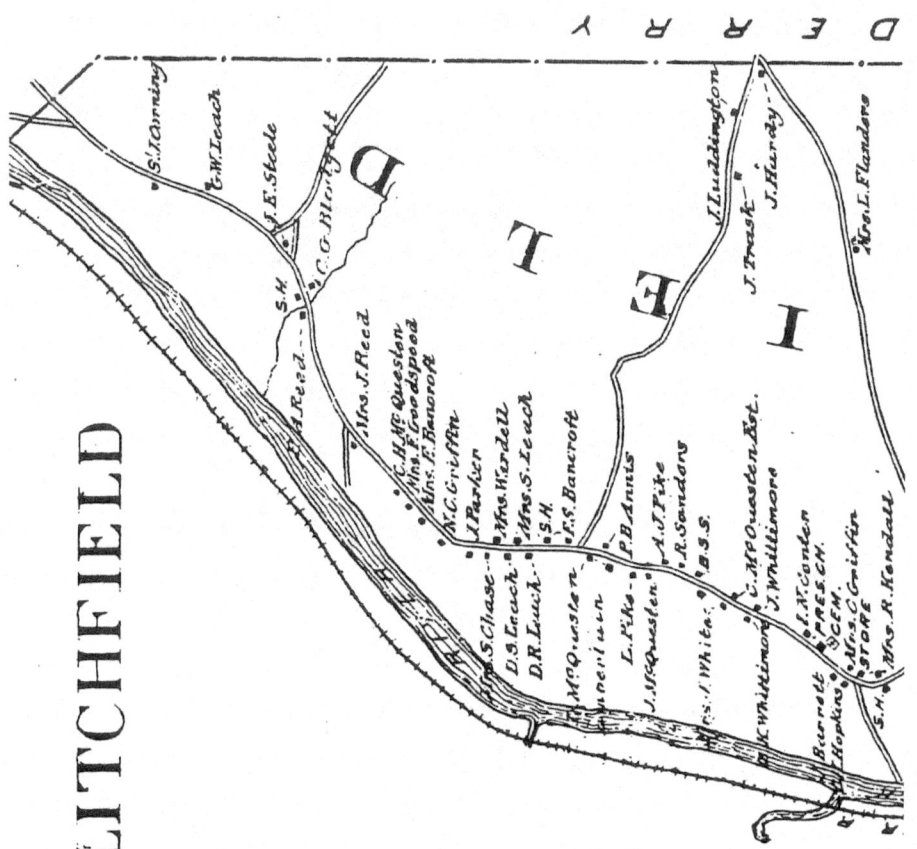

LITCHFIELD

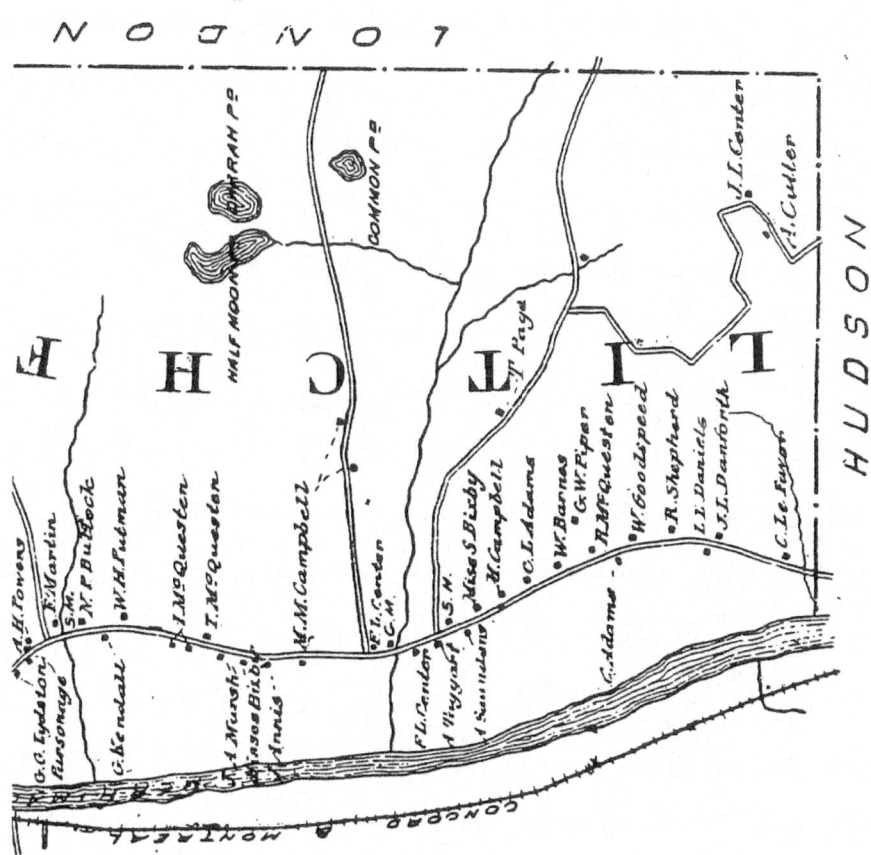

NH 1742 ESTATE TAX

Names	POLS	HOUSE	HORSES	OXEN	COWS	3 YEARS OLD
William Butterfield	1	ℐ1	1	2	4	0
Ebenezer Spaulding	1	ℐ1	0	0	1	0
Robert me Cuen	1	0	0	5	1	0
Steven Spaulding	1	ℐ1	1	3	1	0
Joseph kidder	3	ℐ1	1	0	3	0
Ezekeel hills	1	0	0	2	0	0
henry hills Jun*	1	0	0	2	1	0
Robert M°kean	1	ℐ1	0	2	3	0
Alexander Colwell	1	ℐ1	0	2	2	0
John Carken	1	0	0	0	0	0
Ebenezer Tayler	1	ℐ1	0	0	2	0
William Tayler	1	0	0	0	0	0
John Roberson	1	ℐ1	0	4	0	0
James hills	1	ℐ1	0	2	3	0
Joseph Pollard	1	ℐ1	0	0	1	0
henry hills	1	ℐ1	1	2	2	0
Nathaniel hill	1	1	1	1	2	3
Andrew Cochran	2	ℐ1	1	2	3	0
Samuel more	1	𝒟1	1	2	3	0
William Read	2	0	1	4	5	0
Beniamin Blodget	1	ℐ1	0	2	0	0

LITCHFIELD

2 YEARS OLD	1 YEAR OLD	SWINE	MEADOW	MOWING	PLANTING	PASTERLANDS
0	0	1	0	0	2	2
0	2	1	3	0	1	1
0	4	0	3	0	1	0
0	0	0	4	0	2	0
2	0	0	2	0	4	0
0	2	0	0	0	2	2
0	0	0	0	0	0	0
3	0	1	0	0	7	0
0	0	0	0	0	4	0
0	0	0	0	0	0	0
0	0	0	0	0	3	0
0	0	0	0	0	4	0
0	0	0	0	0	0	0
0	1	0	0	2	6	0
0	0	0	0	0	0	0
0	1	0	2	0	3	1
0	3	0	0	7	7	2
0	0	0	0	1	6	0
0	2	0	0	3	6	2
0	2	1	0	0	0	0
0	0	0	0	0	6	1

NH 1742 ESTATE TAX

Names	POLS	HOUSE	HORSES	OXEN	COWS	3 YEARS OLD
Frances Grimes	1	0	1	0	1	0
Ian Boys	0	ℐ1	1	0	2	0
Paterick Tagart	1	ℐ1	1	0	3	0
Samuel Cochran	1	ℐ1	1	2	3	2
John Blare	0	0	0	2	0	0
Ephraim Powers	1	𝒟1	1	0	5	0
Robert Richardson	2	𝒟1	1	2	2	0
Thomas kar	2	ℐ1	2	0	1	0
Josiah Richardson	1	ℐ1	1	0	2	0
Nathan kindel	1	𝒟1	0	0	3	0
Petter Russell	1	𝒟1	1	0	2	3
James M°night	1	𝒟1	1	0	3	0
Allas kindel	1	𝒟1	1	1	2	0
Robert Read	1	0	0	0	0	0
Christopher kindel	1	0	0	0	0	0
Joseph wilson	1	0	0	0	0	0
Leaonard Cumings	1	ℐ1	1	0	2	2
Beniamin hassell	1	ℐ1	1	0	2	2
Joseph Blanchard or assigns	0	𝒟1	0	0	0	0
James Lindel or assigns	0	ℐ1	0	2	1	0
Jonathan Powers	1	1	0	0	1	0

LITCHFIELD

2 YEARS OLD	1 YEAR OLD	SWINE	MEADOW	MOWING	PLANTING	PASTERLANDS
0	2	0	0	0	0	0
0	0	0	0	0	24	0
0	1	1	0	1	10	0
0	0	0	0	0	5	0
2	0	0	0	0	5	0
0	0	1	0	4	16	2
0	0	0	0	5	8	0
0	0	0	0	0	5	1
0	3	3	0	2	2	2
2	2	0	0	2	6	2
1	0	0	0	10	6	4
0	0	1	0	0	15	1
0	0	1	0	1	8	2
0	1	0	0	0	0	0
0	0	0	0	0	0	0
0	0	2	0	0	0	0
2	0	0	0	4	0	0
2	0	0	0	4	6	0
0	0	0	0	4	15	2
0	0	0	4	0	10	2
0	0	0	0	0	0	0

NH 1742 ESTATE TAX

Names	POLS	HOUSE	HORSES	OXEN	COWS	3 YEARS OLD
Ephraim Butterfield	1	S 1	1	0	1	0
John Bell	1	S 1	1	0	2	2
John hustone	1	S 1	1	0	3	2
Aqula underwood	2	S 1	1	2	2	0
Joshua Converce	1	D 1	1	3	3	0
John Bradgshire	0	D 1	0	0	0	0
William Lund	1	S 1	2	6	5	0
John usher	1	D 1	0	2	4	0
Joseph underwood or assigns	0	S 1	0	2	2	0
Phenehas underwood	1	0	1	2	0	0
Zachariah Sterns	1	0	0	2	4	0
Jonathan Cumings	1	S 1	1	0	3	0
Christepher Temple	1	S 1	0	0	1	0
David whittemore	1	S 1	0	0	3	0
John hervell	1	D 1	1	2	2	0
James Ranken	1	S 1	0	2	1	0
William Bonner Jun"	1	0	0	0	0	0
George nikels	1	0	0	0	0	0
William Bonner	1	S 1	1	0	1	0
John huchardson	1	S 1	0	0	2	0
Alexander parker	1	S 1	1	2	6	0

LITCHFIELD

2 YEARS OLD	1 YEAR OLD	SWINE	MEADOW	MOWING	PLANTING	PASTERLANDS
2	0	0	0	0	0	0
0	2	1	0	1	10	1
0	2	0	2	1	10	1
0	0	0	0	3	5	2
0	3	1	3	5	15	6
0	0	0	0	4	10	0
1	0	0	12	0	17	5
0	2	1	6	0	20	3
0	0	1	0	2	12	4
0	0	0	0	0	12	0
0	0	0	0	0	0	0
2	1	0	0	2	5	1
0	0	0	0	18	12	4
0	0	0	1	2	5	2
2	0	1	0	3	7	2
0	0	0	0	0	2	0
0	0	0	0	0	0	0
0	0	0	0	0	0	0
1	0	1	0	1	3	0
0	0	1	0	1	3	0
2	4	2	0	2	6	2

NH 1742 ESTATE TAX

Names	POLS	HOUSE	HORSES	OXEN	COWS	3 YEARS OLD
James Nahor	1	ᴰ1	1	2	3	0
Robert Nickels	1	0	0	0	0	0
Hugh Nahor	1	0	0	0	0	0
Jonathan howard	1	0	0	0	0	0
David Campbell	1	0	0	0	0	0
Paterick Bonner	1	0	0	0	0	0
Joel Dix or assigns	0	ˢ1	0	0	0	0
Samuel Boid	1	0	0	0	0	0
Henry White	1	0	1	0	2	0
Jonathan Richardson or assigns	0	0	0	0	0	0
John Mᶜkean	1	0	1	0	0	0
Joseph anthony	1	0	0	0	0	0
Jacob Hildreth	1	ˢ1	1	2	2	0

Pursuant to the act of Genᵘ Assembly past at the Last Sessions in new hampshire appointing a Comittee for the Severall new districts to call the first meetings and appointing Clerks to take a true List of the Poles and Estates – on Oath I have taken the above List for Litchfeild upon my Oath and do here Certifie the same to be a true List June 11th 1742

Jacob Hildreth

LITCHFIELD

2 YEARS OLD	1 YEAR OLD	SWINE	MEADOW	MOWING	PLANTING	PASTERLANDS
3	*1*	*3*	*0*	*3*	*9*	*2*
0	*0*	*0*	*0*	*0*	*0*	*0*
0	*0*	*0*		*0*	*0*	*0*
0	*0*	*0*	*0*	*0*	*0*	*0*
0	*0*	*0*	*0*	*0*	*0*	*0*
0	*0*	*0*	*0*	*0*	*0*	*0*
0	*0*	*0*	*0*	*2*	*3*	*0*
0	*0*	*0*	*0*	*0*	*2*	*0*
0	*0*	*0*	*0*	*2*	*4*	*2*
0	*0*	*0*	*2*	*0*	*20*	*0*
0	*0*	*0*	*0*	*0*	*0*	*0*
0	*0*	*0*	*0*	*0*	*0*	*0*
0	*0*	*0*	*6*	*2*	*3*	*2*

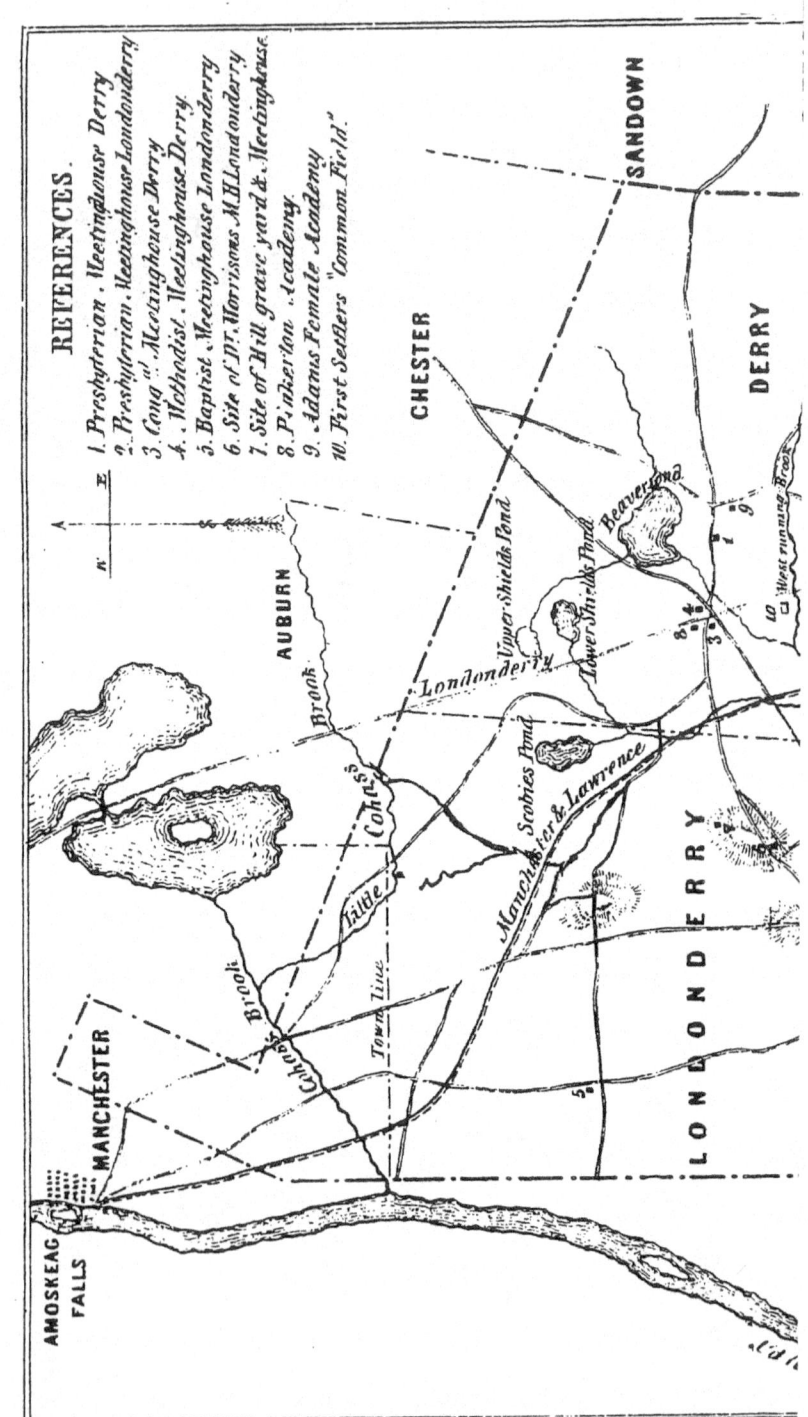

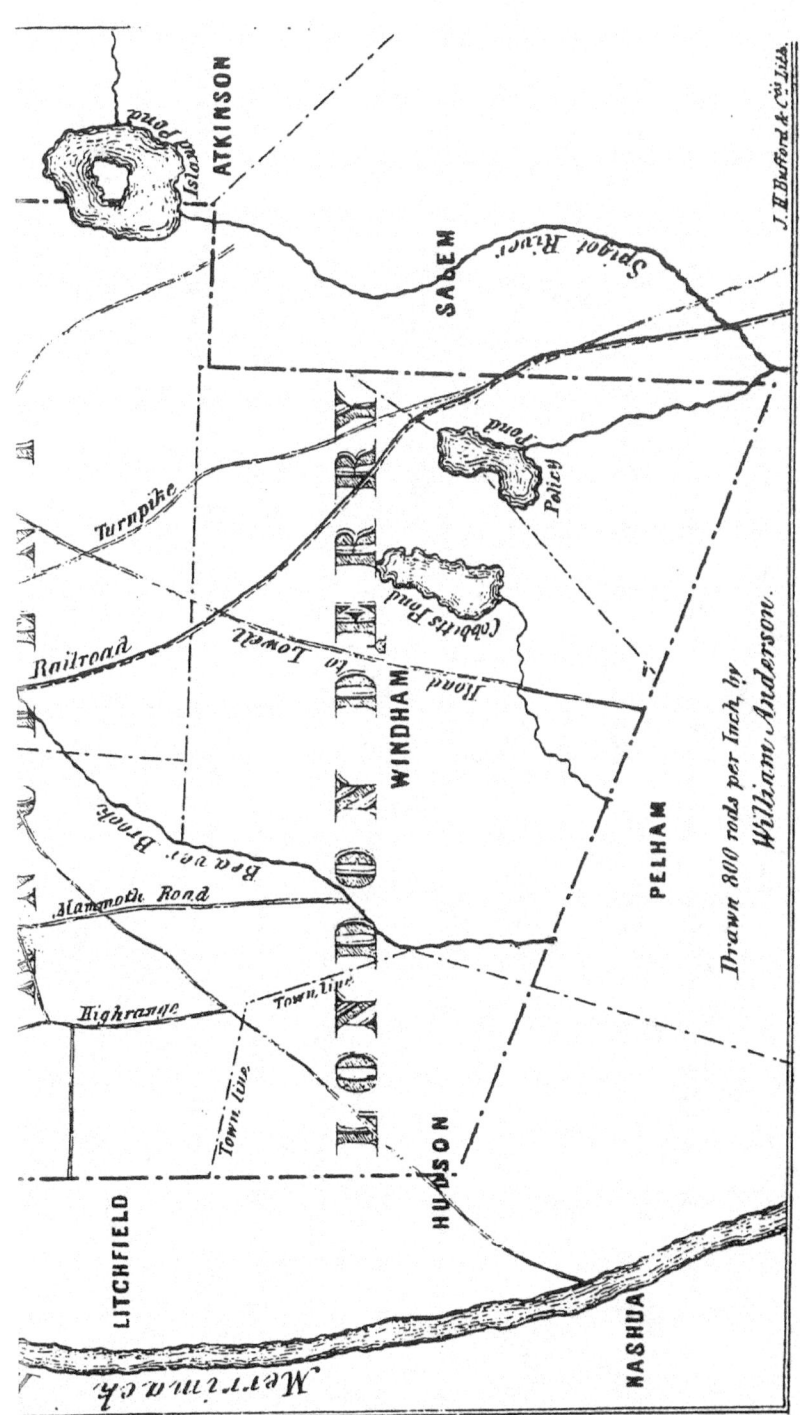

Names	POLS	HOUSES	OXEN	COWS	3 YEARS OLD	2 YEARS OLD
Robᵗ Clark	1	1	0	2	0	0
James Caldwell	1	D-1	2	6	1	0
Willᵐ Adams	2	D-1	2	3	2	0
Deacn John Moore	1	D-1	2	3	0	0
Patrick Douglas	1	D-1	2	5	2	0
John Hunter	1	D-1	2	2	3	1
Widdow Mᶜ Murphy	0	D-1	0	1	1	0
John Brown	1	1	0	1	0	1
Hugh Brown	1	0	0	0	0	1
James Adams Weaver	1	1	0	1	0	0
Widdow Archibald	0	1	0	2	0	1
William Addison	1	1	0	1	1	0
Aleaˣ Robkin	1	1	0	2	0	3
James Gilmore	1	D-1	2	3	0	1
William Gilmore	2	D-1	0	2	0	2
John French	1	0	0	1	0	0
Widdow Moore	1	D-1	2	3	0	2

1 YEAR OLD	SWINE	PLANTING	MOWING	MEADOW	PASTURE	HORSE
1	0	1	3	0	2	1
1	2	9	15	0	10	1
0	1	3	6	½	1	1
0	0	3	3	0	1	1
1	0	4	8	0	0	1
1	0	3	2	1	0	1
2	0	2	1 ½	1	0	0
1	0	2	2	0	2	0
0	0	0	0	0	0	0
0	0	0	½	0	0	0
1	0	1	1	1/6	0	0
0	0	2	2	0	0	0
0	0	3	2 ½	½	0	1
0	0	2	6	0	5	1
1	0	3	3	0	1	1
0	0	0	0	0	0	0
0	0	3	2	0	0	1

NH 1742 ESTATE TAX

Names	POLS	HOUSES	OXEN	COWS	3 YEARS OLD	2 YEARS OLD
Peter Cristy	1	1	0	2	0	2
Robert Gilmore	1	1	0	1	1	0
James Ewing	1	1	0	2	0	0
Arch^{ld} Miller	2	1	0	2	1	0
Sam^{ll} Petterson	1	1	0	1	0	0
William Chambers	1	1	0	2	0	0
Thomas Cristy	1 D-1		2	2	0	1
Robert McUrdy	1 D-1		0	1	0	1
Michail Gordon	1	1	0	2	0	0
William Kellso	1	1	0	2	1	2
Alex^x Kellso	1	1	2	2	0	2
Thomas Horner	1	1	2	4	2	2
William Hogg	1	1	2	4	0	0
William McMaster	2	1	2	7	4	0
Arthur Boyd	1	1	0	1	0	1
Archibald Cunningham	1	1	0	0	1	0
Archibald McEntosh	1	1	0	1	0	0

1 YEAR OLD	SWINE	PLANTING	MOWING	MEADOW	PASTURE	HORSE
0	0	2	2	0	0	0
0	1	1	1	0	0	0
0	0	0	3	0	0	1
0	1	2	6	0	5	1
2	0	1 ½	2	½	0	1
1	0	1	½	½	0	0
1	0	2	3	1	0	0
8	1	2	4	2	0	1
1	0	2	2	0	0	1
0	1	1	3 ½	0	1	1
2	0	2	5	1	0	1
2	1	3	7	2	0	1
2	1	3	3	0	1	1
0	0	2 ½	8	0	0	1
0	0	3 ½	0	0	0	1
2	0	1	1	0	0	1
0	0	1	1	0	0	0

NH 1742 ESTATE TAX

Names	POLS	HOUSES	OXEN	COWS	3 YEARS OLD	2 YEARS OLD
Walter Mc Farland	1	1	0	1	0	0
John Stinson	1	1	0	2	0	0
Nathan Mc Farland	1	1	0	4	0	1
Danl Mc Duffee	3 𝒟-1		2	4	3	2
James Adams Deacn	2 𝒟-1		2	4	3	3
William Willson	1	1	0	1	0	2
Gabriel Bar	1	0	0	0	0	0
Sam^u Bar	1 𝒟-1		2	6	2	2
John Stewart	1	1	0	1	0	0
William Humphry	2 𝒟-1		2	4	0	1
Charles Stewart	1	1	0	2	3	0

1 YEAR OLD	SWINE	PLANTING	MOWING	MEADOW	PASTURE	HORSE
1	0	½	2	0	0	1
1	0	2	1 ½	0	0	1
1	3	1	3	0	0	1
0	0	5	5 ½	0	0	1
0	0	4 ½	8	1 ½	8	2
1	0	1 ½	1 ½	1 ½	1 ½	1
0	0	0	1	0	2	1
2	2	6	4	2	9	1
0	0	1 ½	1 ½	0	0	1
0	1	1	1	2	9	1
0	1	3	3	3	0	1

NH 1742 ESTATE TAX

Names	POLS	HOUSES	HORSE	OXEN	COWS	3 YEARS OLD
Robert Gilmore	1	1	1	0	1	1
Halbart Morrison	1	1	1	0	1	2
Thomas Davison	1	1	1	0	2	2
Joseph Hogg	1	1	0	0	1	0
Rob Cochran	1 D-1	1	1	0	1	2
James Cochran	1	1	0	2	1	1
James Thompson	2 D-1	1	1	2	3	0
Matthew Taylor	2 D-1	1	1	2	4	0
William Nickle	1	1	1	2	3	0
David Craig	0 D-1	1	1	0	2	1
Widdow Stewart	2 D-1	1	1	2	3	0
John Wallace	1	1	0	0	1	0
Thomas Steel	2 D-1	1	1	2	3	1
Sam{u} Allison	2 D-1	1	1	2	3	2
John Morrison	1 D-1	1	1	0	3	2
John Weiz	1 D-1	1	1	1	4	1
David Hopkins	1	1	0	0	1	0

2 YEARS OLD	1 YEAR OLD	SWINE	PLANTING	MEADOW	MOWING	PASTURE
0	0	0	1	0	2	0
0	2	0	2	2	0	0
0	0	1	3	3	0	0
0	0	0	1 ½	0	½	0
2	1	1	3 ½	1	4	0
2	0	1	2	1	4	0
2	0	0	4	1	3	0
0	2	0	4	2	2	0
2	0	2	3	1	1 ½	0
0	0	0	1 ½	3	3	3
1	2	1	3	1	2	0
0	0	0	0	0	0	0
2	0	1	4	1	3	5
1	1	0	3	1	5	7
2	2	0	2 ½	0	4	2
2	2	0	4	2	4	4
0	0	0	2	0	0	½

Names	POLS	HOUSES	HORSE	OXEN	COWS	3 YEARS OLD
Allan Anderson	1	1	1	2	4	1
Sam^{ll} Boyd	2	1	1	0	2	2
Arch^l Mc Urdy	1	1	0	2	2	0
Robert Martin	1	1	1	0	1	0
Sam^{ll} Huston	1 D-1	1	2	2	2	
David Huston	1	0	0	0	0	0
James Rogers	1 D-1	1	2	2	0	
Robert Boies Esqr	1 D-1	1	4	4	0	
Alear Mc Neal	1 D-1	0	0	2	2	
Robert Morrison	1 D-1	1	2	5	0	
Hugh Mountgomery	1 D-1	1	0	3	0	
William Thompson	1	1	1	2	2	0
John Ricky	1 D-1	1	2	2	0	
David Vance	1 D-1	1	0	4	6	
Weaver James Thompson	2	1	1	0	3	0
Sam^{ll} Morrison	1	1	1	0	2	0
Joseph Morrison	1	0	0	2	0	0

2 YEARS OLD	1 YEAR OLD	SWINE	PLANTING	MEADOW	MOWING	PASTURE
1	0	0	4	1	4	5
1	0	1	4	2	2	4
1	0	0	3	2	1/4	0
0	0	0	1/2	1	0	1
1	0	1	8	1 3/4	6	4
2	0	0	0	0	0	0
2	0	0	3	0	4	0
3	4	0	7	0	20	14
2	1	1	3	0	4	2
2	1	0	6	1	6	6
2	1	1	4	0	5	2
2	0	0	2	0	3	3
0	0	0	1 1/2	0	2	2
2	1	1	3	2	9	9
0	0	0	1 1/4	0	3/4	0
2	0	0	3	0	3	0
0	0	0	0	0	0	0

NH 1742 ESTATE TAX

Names	POLS	HOUSES	HORSE	OXEN	COWS	3 YEARS OLD
Nathaniel Martin	1	1	1	0	3	0
William Martin	1	0	0	0	2	0
William Clanding	1	1	1	2	2	1
Samᵘ Kinkead	1	1	0	0	0	1
John Steel	1	1	1	0	2	0
James Reid	1	1	0	2	3	0
John Dicky	1	1	0	0	2	0
James Mᶜ Urdy	1	1	1	2	3	1
Mattʷ Reid	1	1	1	2	4	2
John Hopkins	2𝒟-1		1	2	4	0
James Moore	1	1	1	0	2	0
Thomas Willson	2𝒟-1		1	2	2	0
Daniel Clyd	1	1	1	0	2	0
John Archibald	1𝒟-1		1	2	4	0
Samᵘ Archibald	1	0	0	0	1	0
Hugh Willson	1𝒟-1		1	2	4	0
Widdow Moore	1	1	1	2	6	1

2 YEARS OLD	1 YEAR OLD	SWINE	PLANTING	MEADOW	MOWING	PASTURE
2	0	1	4	0	4	0
0	0	0	0	0	0	0
0	0	0	1	0	0	1
0	0	0	0	0	0	0
0	2	0	1 ½	0	1 ½	0
3	2	0	3	2	3	0
1	0	0	1 ½	0	0	0
0	1	0	3	¼	2	0
0	3	0	2	2	2	0
3	5	1	6	3	2	0
2	0	0	3	1	1	0
0	0	0	4	1 ½	1	0
2	1	0	3	1	1	0
3	2	0	6	3	7	7
2	0	0	0	0	0	0
2	1	0	6	1 ½	5	2
5	3	0	7	2	5	2 ½

NH 1742 ESTATE TAX

Names	POLS	HOUSES	HORSE	OXEN	COWS	3 YEARS OLD
Sam.ᵘˡ Miller	1	1	1	0	2	0
Sam.ᵘˡ Mitchel	2 D-1		1	0	4	0
George Mitchel	1	1	0	0	2	0
James Wilson	1 D-1		1	2	4	2
John Mᶜ Keen	1	1	1	2	3	0
James Mᶜ Keen Esq.ʳ	2 D-1		1	2	3	1
Moses Barnard	1	1	1	2	4	0
Andᵂ Clendening	1 D-1		1	2	3	0
Archibald Clendening	2 D-1		1	0	3	2
John Mitchel	1	1	1	0	3	1
James Nesmith	3 D-1		1	2	5	2
James Clark	1 D-1		1	2	5	2
William Gregg	1	1	1	2	5	1
James Baz	1	1	0	0	1	0
John Mᶜ Conaghay	1	1	1	0	4	0
John Gregg	1 D-1		1	2	4	2
James Miller	1	1	1	0	1	0

LONDONDERRY

2 YEARS OLD	1 YEAR OLD	SWINE	PLANTING	MEADOW	MOWING	PASTURE
0	0	0	2	0	2	0
1	0	0	3	0	5	0
0	0	0	¼	0	½	0
0	2	1	3	3	3	3
2	1	0	2	½	6	3
2	3	1	6	0	6	5
2	0	0	4	½	3	2
0	0	0	2	0	2	0
0	0	0	2	¾	1 ½	½
0	0	0	2	½	1 ½	½
2	0	0	4	2	3	5
2	3	0	4	2	3	5
1	2	0	5	2	9	10
0	0	0	1	0	2	0
0	0	0	1	1	1	0
2	1	0	4	2 ¾	10	8
2	0	0	2 ½	1 ½	2	0

NH 1742 ESTATE TAX

Names	POLS	HOUSES	HORSE	OXEN	COWS	3 YEARS OLD
Allex* Walker	2	1	1	2	2	0
James Anderson	2 𝒟-1		1	2	4	0
And^w Jack	1	1	1	0	3	0
James Morrison	2 𝒟-1		1	2	2	2
David Hunter	1	1	1	2	4	0
Wiliam Robertson	1	1	1	0	2	0
Charles Cox	1 𝒟-1		1	0	1	2
John Durham	1	1	0	0	1	0
John Smith	1	1	1	0	2	0
Nenian Cochran	1 𝒟-1		1	0	2	0
Peter Cochran	1	1	1	2	3	0
William Cochran Jun*	1	1	1	0	2	2
Thomas Jamison	1	1	0	0	0	0
William Aiking	1 𝒟-1		1	2	3	1
James Aiking	1 𝒟-1		0	2	2	1
Nathaniel Aiking	1 𝒟-1		1	0	2	2
John Wallace	2 𝒟-1		1	2	5	0

LONDONDERRY

2 YEARS OLD	1 YEAR OLD	SWINE	PLANTING	MEADOW	MOWING	PASTURE
1	2	1	6	1 ½	2	0
2	2	1	4	2	2	12
2	1	0	1 ½	5	½	1 ½
2	2	3	3	1 ½	2	2
0	4	0	2	3/4	5	0
0	0	0	3	0	3	0
3	6	0	3	0	5	0
0	0	0	½	0	1	0
0	0	1	1	0	1	0
0	0	0	2	0	4	0
0	1	0	2	0	2	0
1	1	1	2	0	1	0
0	0	0	0	0	½	0
1	0	0	2	1	2	2
1	1	0	2	1	4	0
1	1	0	2	1	2	0
2	0	0	9	2	4	5

Names	POLS	HOUSES	HORSE	OXEN	COWS	3 YEARS OLD
John Willson	1	1	1	2	2	0
Alex Mc Collem	1	1	0	2	1	0
Lt Andew Todd	2	1	1	2	5	0
John Bell	2 D-1		0	2	5	0
James Mc Quad	1	1	0	0	1	0
James Smith	2 D-1		1	2	4	0
John Givan	1	1	1	0	0	1
David Morrison	1	1	1	2	3	0
Samll Morrison	3	1	0	2	3	0
Abraham Hoalms	1 D-1		1	2	3	0
John Woodburn	1	1	1	0	2	2
John Craig	2 D-1		1	2	2	0
Widdow Airs	2	1	1	0	3	0
David Bogle	3 D-1		1	2	3	0
John Mc Clarg	1 D-1		1	2	3	0
James Taggard	1	1	1	2	3	0
Christopher Airs	1	1	0	2	2	0

2 YEARS OLD	1 YEAR OLD	SWINE	PLANTING	MEADOW	MOWING	PASTURE
0	2	0	3	1	3	0
0	0	0	3	0	2	0
0	1	1	5	2	5	2
0	0	0	5	1	5	5
0	0	0	0	0	0	0
1	2	0	3	0	4	3
4	0	0	3	0	3	2
0	0	0	2	1	1	0
0	0	0	2	1 ½	1	0
1	0	0	5	1 ½	1 ½	4
2	1	0	5	2	3	0
1	0	0	2	1	2	0
0	0	0	2	0	1	0
0	0	0	2	1	2	0
1	1	0	4	1	2	0
1	0	0	3	0	5	3
0	1	0	3 ½	0	4	0

Names	POLS	HOUSES	HORSE	OXEN	COWS	3 YEARS OLD
James Doak	1	1	1	2	2	0
John Clark	1	1	1	0	2	0
Adam Wier	1 D-1		0	0	2	0
William Hoalms	1	1	1	0	0	2
John Hoalms	1	1	1	0	1	2
Robart Wallaces	1	1	1	0	2	0
John Tagard	1	1	1	2	3	0
Deaⁿ John Craig	1 D-1		1	2	1	0
Arch^d Mc Cormick	1	1	1	2	1	0
Joseph Wallace	2 D-1		1	0	1	2
James Morrow	1	1	1	0	2	3
John Barnet	1 D-1		1	2	3	1
Joseph Bell	1	1	1	2	2	0
George Duncan	1	1	1	2	1	0
Thomas Hogg	1	1	0	0	1	4
John Flands	1	1	1	2	1	0
John Duncan	1	1	1	2	2	0

2 YEARS OLD	1 YEAR OLD	SWINE	PLANTING	MEADOW	MOWING	PASTURE
0	0	0	2	2	1	0
0	0	0	½	0	3	0
0	0	0	3	5	0	0
2	0	0	2	0	2	0
0	0	0	1 ½	0	2	0
0	0	0	1	0	2	0
0	1	0	2 ½	½	4	0
2	1	0	2	0	1	0
1	1	0	2	¾	3	0
2	1	0	2 ½	0	1 ½	0
2	0	0	2	0	4	2
2	2	0	5	2	5	2
1	1	0	2	¾	2	0
0	0	0	3	0	2	4
0	0	0	2	0	4	3
0	0	0	1	0	2	0
1	0	0	3	1	1	0

NH 1742 ESTATE TAX

Names	POLS	HOUSES	HORSE	OXEN	COWS	3 YEARS OLD
William Duncan	1	D-1	1	2	3	0
John Wilson Senr	1	1	1	2	3	0
Joseph Boies	1	D-1	1	2	1	0
James Boies	1	D-1	1	2	2	0
James Nickle	1	1	0	0	2	2
John Douglas	1	1	1	2	1	0
Arch^{ld} Mc Murphy	1	1	1	0	3	0
James Willson	1	1	1	0	3	0
John Pinkerton	1	1	1	0	3	0
Nathaniel Willson	1	1	0	0	2	0
Alex^r Craig	1	1	0	0	1	0
Sam^{ll} Morrison	1	1	1	0	4	0
George Knox	1	D-1	1	0	1	0
John Scoby	1	1	0	0	1	0
John Hale	0	1	1	0	1	0
Scotch John Anderson	0	D-1	0	0	0	0
John Cochran	1	D-1	1	0	3	0

LONDONDERRY

2 YEARS OLD	1 YEAR OLD	SWINE	PLANTING	MEADOW	MOWING	PASTURE
2	0	0	30	0	3	0
2	0	0	3	0	2	0
0	2	0	3	0	1	0
0	0	0	2	0	1 ½	0
0	0	0	1 ½	0	½	0
0	0	0	1	1	2	0
0	0	2	1	1	0	0
0	0	0	3	0	3 ½	0
1	0	0	3	½	0	0
0	0	0	1	0	1	0
0	0	2	1	1	0	0
0	0	0	2 ½	0	2	3
0	0	0	1	0	½	0
0	0	0	1	0	1	0
0	0	0	1 ½	0	¼	0
0	0	0	5	2	7	1
2	1	0	2	0	3	0

NH 1742 ESTATE TAX

Names	POLS	HOUSES	HORSE	OXEN	COWS	3 YEARS OLD
Richard Mc Allester	1	1	0	0	1	0
Hugh Rogers	1	1	1	2	3	0
James Cochran	1	1	0	2	4	0
Joseph Heel	1	1	0	0	2	0
John Alexander	1	1	1	0	2	0
John Cochran	1	1	0	2	1	0
And^w Cochran	1	1	1	0	2	2
Benjamin Willson	1	1	0	0	3	0
Thos Campbell	1	1	0	0	1	0
Robt Montgomery	1	1	1	0	2	0
Randal Alexande^r	1	1	1	0	2	2
John Kaz	1	1	1	0	2	0
Sam^{ll} Mc Keen	1	1	1	0	3	0
And^w Thompson	1	1	1	0	1	0
Thomas Boyd	1	1	0	0	1	0
John Steel	1	1	1	2	0	0
John Davison	1	0	1	4	0	0

LONDONDERRY

2 YEARS OLD	1 YEAR OLD	SWINE	PLANTING	MEADOW	MOWING	PASTURE
0	0	0	0	0	0	0
0	0	0	3	1	1	0
0	2	0	2	0	6	0
0	0	0	1	0	0	0
0	1	0	2 ½	0	3	1
1	2	0	1	0	3	0
0	1	0	3	1	2	0
0	0	0	½	1	0	0
0	0	0	0	0	1	0
0	4	0	3	0	2	0
0	1	0	2	2	1	0
2	1	0	3	½	0	0
1	0	1	4	2	0	0
0	0	1	1 ½	0	1 ½	0
0	0	0	1	½	¼	0
0	2	0	1 ½	3	0	0
0	0	0	0	0	0	0

NH 1742 ESTATE TAX

Names	POLS	HOUSES	HORSE	OXEN	COWS	3 YEARS OLD
William Mᶜ Clanaghan	1 D-1		1	0	2	0
Mrs Scenter	3 D-1		3	2	10	2
Willᵐ Dicky	1	1	1	0	1	0
John Thompson	1	1	0	2	2	0
Samᵘ Thompson	1	1	1	0	1	0
Peter Petterson	1	1	0	0	0	0
James Peterson	1	1	1	0	1	0
David Mᶜ Alester	1	1	1	2	3	1
Willm Mᶜ Alester	1	1	1	2	2	1
William Dicky	2	1	1	0	2	0
Samᵘ Grahams	1	1	1	2	2	0
Hugh Moore	1	1	1	0	1	1
Willᵐ Nutt	1 D-1		1	0	2	0
John Anderson	2 D-1		1	2	1	0
James Anderson	1	1	1	0	2	1
John Mack	1	1	1	0	2	0
Samᵘ Dicky	1	1	1	2	1	1

LONDONDERRY

2 YEARS OLD	1 YEAR OLD	SWINE	PLANTING	MEADOW	MOWING	PASTURE
2	0	0	2	0	1	0
3	3	0	10	5	4	0
0	0	0	1	1	¼	0
0	2	0	3	0	3	0
0	0	0	2	0	1	0
0	0	0	0	0	0	0
0	0	0	1	0	½	0
3	1	0	4	1 ½	1	0
0	0	0	2	1	½	0
0	0	0	1 ½	1	0	1
0	4	0	1 1//2	1 ½	2	1
2	1	0	2	½	1	0
0	2	0	3	0	4	0
0	0	1	2	½	½	0
0	0	1	2	0	1	0
0	0	0	1	½	½	0
0	1	0	2	0	1 ½	½

Names	POLS	HOUSES	HORSE	OXEN	COWS	3 YEARS OLD
James Airs	1	1	1	0	2	2
James Oughtozson	1 𝒟-1		0	0	2	0
Thoᵒ Wallace Junʳ	1	1	1	0	1	2
Thomas Wallace Senʳ	2 𝒟-1		1	2	2	0
James Wallace	1	0	1	0	0	0
Widʷ Arbuckle	0 𝒟-1		1	0	1	1
Charles Mᶜ Cury	1	1	1	0	4	2
James Moore	1	1	1	2	2	0
Samᵘ Gregg	1	1	0	0	4	2
Cpᵗ James Gregg	1	0	0	0	0	0
William Cochran	2 𝒟-1		1	2	2	0
James Cochran	1	0	1	0	1	0
Samᵘ Anderson	1	1	0	0	1	0
Samᵘ Renkin	1 𝒟-1		1	0	4	0
David Dicky	1 𝒟-1		1	0	4	0
William Mᶜ Neal	1	1	0	2	2	0
Danˡ Mᶜ Mullan	1	1	0	0	0	0

2 YEARS OLD	1 YEAR OLD	SWINE	PLANTING	MEADOW	MOWING	PASTURE
0	0	0	2	1	½	0
0	0	0	0	0	0	0
1	0	0	1 ½	0	3	0
2	0	0	2	0	2	0
0	0	0	0	1	1	0
0	0	0	1	0	1	0
0	0	1	3	0	2	0
0	0	0	2	0	2	2
0	0	0	2	0	2	2
0	0	0	2 ¼	0	0	0
1	0	1	1 ½	¾	2	4
0	0	0	0	¼	0	0
2	0	0	1	0	1	0
0	4	0	3	0	8	10
2	2	0	4	0	4	0
1	1	1	2	0	3	2
0	0	0	0	0	¼	0

NH 1742 ESTATE TAX

Names	POLS	HOUSES	HORSE	OXEN	COWS	3 YEARS OLD
Thoˢ Cockoran	1	1	1	0	3	0
John Crumey	2 𝒟-1	1	2	2	0	
Matthew Wrights	1	1	1	0	2	0
George Clark	1	1	1	0	2	0
James Lindsay	1	1	0	0	2	0
John Wallace	1	1	1	0	2	0
James Lessly	2 𝒟-1	1	0	3	0	
William Craig	3	1	1	0	3	2
John Blair	1 𝒟-1	2	0	4	0	
Hugh Ramsey	4 𝒟-1	2	2	6	2	
Thoˢ Willson	1	1	1	0	2	1
William Airs	1	1	1	0	2	0
Samᵘ Murdock	1	1	0	0	1	0
William Murdoch	1	1	1	0	2	0
James Blair	1	1	1	0	2	0
John Cochran	1	1	1	2	2	0
Thos Boies	1	1	0	0	1	0

2 YEARS OLD	1 YEAR OLD	SWINE	PLANTING	MEADOW	MOWING	PASTURE
2	0	0	0	0	5	5
1	0	0	3	¼	5	4
2	0	0	2	0	4	0
0	0	0	2	0	3	0
1	1	0	2	0	3	1
3	0	0	2	0	2	1
0	0	0	3	1	4	0
0	2	0	2	0	2	0
1	0	1	2	1	3	0
0	2	3	4	0	10	10
1	0	0	2	0	4	10
1	0	0	2	0	2	8
0	0	0	0	0	1	0
0	0	0	0	0	2	0
2	0	0	3	0	3	3
0	0	0	2	½	2	0
0	0	0	0	0	0	0

Names	POLS	HOUSES	HORSE	OXEN	COWS	3 YEARS OLD
John Mc Murphy	2D-1	1	2	6	3	

The true Invice of Londonderry taken and Concluded this 7th Day of Aprile 1742 per Thos Boies and Hugh Cromey

2 YEARS OLD	1 YEAR OLD	SWINE	PLANTING	MEADOW	MOWING	PASTURE
2	2	0	9	0	20	30

Province of
newhampshire
    Londonderry June 7ᵗʰ 1742
    this is to testifie to all to whom
    it may conseren that Cᵗ Thomas Boies
    and Hugh Crumey both appeared and
    took ther solom oath that they would
    take and returen a true Invoice of
    all the pols and Esteats in
    Londonderry
        for Robert Hogg Just pe

An acc^t of The transients person in Lo: Derry

Thomas Gilles
James Stewart
Nathaniel Holmes
James Douglass
Thomas Dunfree
John Mc Allester
Neil Hamble
David Mc Killap
John Tuffts
Jonathan Morrison
Hugh Sterling
Benja Smith
George Robinson
Danl Mc Gregore
James Nimock
John Kar
James Dorragh
Arch^{ld} Clendening

Hugh Gregg
James Ferson
John Taggard
Willaim Brimly 41

John Espy
Hugh Bankhead
Hugh Muntgomery
William Cox
Jon^a Cox
Edwd Cox
Joseph Cox
John Stewart
Jo^n Raside
Robert Brimly
William Galt
James Linn
William Betty
Thomas Mc Cleary
Willm Mack
Neal Taggard
David Dinsmore
John Cochran
Josep Cochran

OLD METHUEN

A facsimile of the o...

Map of the Tou...

Scale...

to an...

Drawn and presented to
The Historical Society of Methuen
Mass.,
By A.E. Bodwell Arch't.
Oct. 18th A.D. 1898.

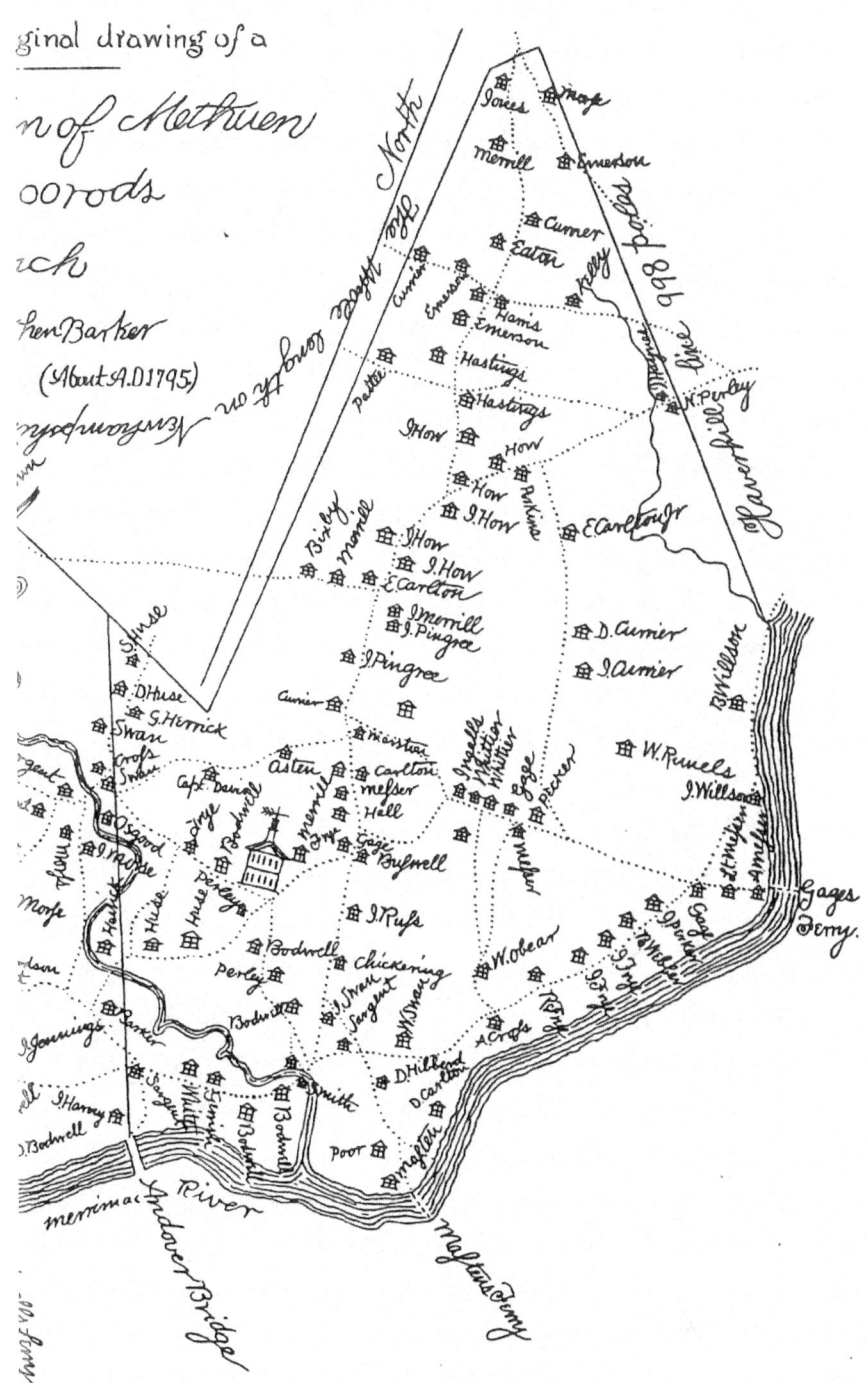

A List of Pools and Estates of the Inhabitants of this district as i was Directed to take an account of May ye 20 1742 John Ober

	POLS	HOUSES	PLOW	MOWING	MEADOW	OXEN
Benoni Rowell	1	1	2	0	1	0
Benini Rowel Jur	1	0	2	1	0	2
Samuel Rowel	1	0	2	1	0	2
Josiah Rowel	1	1	1	0	0	0
John Rowel	1	1	1½	1	0	0
Joseph Davies	1	1	2	0	0	0
John Lowel	1	1	0	0	0	0
David Lowel	1	1	0	0	0	0
Daniel Peasle	2	1	10	2	10	4
John Ober	1	1	6	5	0	4
Richard Kimbel	1	1	3	1	3	2
Richard Kelley	2	2	6	3	6	4
Joseph Peasley	1	1	4	0	6	2
John Lowel	1	1	1	0	0	0
Isarel young	1	2	6	0	15	0
John Page	1	1	2	2	0	0
Samuel Curnor	1	0	0	0	0	2
Ye wido Peseley	0	1	3	2	0	2

COWS	3 YEARS	2 YEARS	HORSES	SWINE	PASTER
1	0	0	1	0	0
0	0	0	1	0	0
1	2	0	1	0	0
1	0	0	0	0	0
0	0	0	0	0	0
0	0	0	0	0	0
1	0	0	0	0	0
0	0	0	0	0	0
3	2	1	1	1	3
3	0	1	1	0	0
2	0	3	1	1	0
3	0	0	1	1	0
2	0	1	1	2	0
2	0	0	0	1	0
4	2	0	0	0	0
5	1	1	0	1	0
2	0	0	0	0	0
1	0	0	0	0	0

NH 1742 ESTATE TAX

A List of Pools and Estates of the Inhabitants of this district as i was Directed to take an account of May ye 20 1742 John Ober

	POLS	HOUSES	PLOW	MOWING	MEADOW	OXEN
John Hall	1	1	0	0	0	2
Jonathan woodberry	1	1	3	0	8	2
Robert Ellenwood	1	1	3	0	3	0
John Cochran	1	1	1	2	0	0
Samuel Armer	1	1	2	4	0	2
Henry Sanders	2	1	9	4	6	2
Oliver Sanders	1	1	3	0	3	2
Timothy Sanders	1	0	0	0	0	0
William Sanders	1	1	4	1	6	2
Samuel Sanders	1	0	0	0	0	0
Abial Keley	1	0	2	0	0	0
John Ober Ju*	1	0	0	0	0	0
Benjamin Corning	1	1	3	2	0	2
Nathanel woodberry	1	1	2	0	1	2
John Giles	1	1	2	0	0	2
Richard Ingerson	1	1	2	0	6	0
Edward Bailey	1	1	1	0	4	0
Ebenezer woodbery	1	1	1	2	0	0

COWS	3 YEARS	2 YEARS	HORSES	SWINE	PASTER
2	0	0	1	1	0
2	2	1	1	0	0
1	0	0	0	0	0
1	0	0	1	0	0
0	0	0	0	0	0
2	1	1	1	0	6
2	2	2	1	0	0
0	0	0	0	0	0
2	3	3	1	0	0
0	0	0	0	0	6
1	0	0	1	0	0
0	0	0	0	0	0
2	0	2	0	0	0
2	1	1	1	0	0
1	0	0	1	0	0
4	2	1	1	0	0
0	0	0	0	0	0
0	2	0	0	0	0

A List of Pools and Estates of the Inhabitants of this district as i was Directed to take an account of May ye 20 1742
John Ober

	POLS	HOUSES	PLOW	MOWING	MEADOW	OXEN
Nathanel Dow	1	1	3	0	4	0
Richard Dow	1	1	4	2	2	2
David Dow	1	1	0	0	0	0
Peter youring	2	1	3	2	2	2
Abial Aston	1	1	4	1	0	2
Isaac Clough	2	1	10	10	0	2
Josiah Clough	1	0	0	0	0	0
Ebenezer Ayers	1	1	10	10	0	8
Daniel Creecey	1	1	3	1	0	0
Jonathan Carles	2	1	9	8	0	2
Samuel Parker	1	1	2	0	7	2
Timothy Swan	1	1	5	8	0	1
Joseph Right	1	1	7	2	0	4
John Bailey	1	1	2	0	2	2
Daniel Gadge	1	1	5	3	0	2
Thomas Gilmore	1	1	5	3	0	2
Simon Bard	1	1	8	0	0	2
Joseph wiman	2	1	0	0	0	0

COWS	3 YEARS	2 YEARS	HORSES	SWINE	PASTER
3	2	0	0	0	0
4	2	0	1	1	0
0	0	0	0	0	0
0	0	0	1	0	0
2	0	0	0	0	0
6	4	3	1	0	0
0	0	0	0	0	0
5	0	2	2	0	0
3	0	1	1	0	0
5	2	2	1	0	0
3	0	2	1	0	0
4	0	4	1	1	0
2	0	3	0	0	0
0	0	2	0	0	0
2	2	0	1	1	0
4	0	0	0	1	0
3	0	0	1	0	0
1	0	0	0	0	0

NH 1742 ESTATE TAX

A List of Pools and Estates of the Inhabitants of this district as i was Directed to take an account of May ye 20 1742

John Ober

	POLS	HOUSES	PLOW	MOWING	MEADOW	OXEN
Ebenezer Ritterdsun	1	1	5	0	0	2
Henry Rittersun	1	1	5	0	0	2
Joseph Wood	1	1	0	0	0	2
Josiah Gadge	1	1	8	3	0	4
Robert Right	1	0	0	0	0	0
John Muglady	1	1	2	0	0	0
Edward wiman	1	1	12	2	6	4
Thomas wiman	1	1	3	1	6	4
William Rittersun	2	1	8	1	6	4
Zachary Colburn	1	1	0	0	6	0
John Forgson	1	1	12	2	6	2
John Colburn	0	0	0	4	0	0
Ephram Colburn	0	0	0	16	0	0
Samuel Butler	0	0	0	4	4	0
John Litellhale	0	0	0	30		0
James varnum	0	0	0	3	0	0
Samuel varnum	0	0	0	3	0	0
John Butler	0	0	0	3		0
John Butler Ju"	0	0	0	4	0	0
Wid Maston	0	0	0	2	0	0
John Cuchson	0	0	0	7	0	0

COWS	3 YEARS	2 YEARS	HORSES	SWINE	PASTER
2	0	0	1	0	0
2	0	0	1	0	0
2	3	0	1	0	0
2	3	0	1	1	0
0	0	0	0	0	0
0	0	0	0	0	0
4	3	1	2	0	0
4	2	2	1	2	1
4	2	0	1	0	0
2	0	0	0	1	0
4	0	0	0	1	0
0	0	0	0	0	0
0	0	0	0	0	0
0	0	0	0	0	0
0	0	0	0	0	0
0	0	0	0	0	0
0	0	0	0	0	0
0	0	0	0	0	0
0	0	0	0	0	0
0	0	0	0	0	0
0	0	0	0	0	0

Names	MOWING	MEDO
wido Proctor	3	0
Samuel Brown	3	0
Epharam Caldwel	0	7
Ebenzer Thorton	0	4
william Colburn	0	2
Joseph Varnum	0	2
Henry Colburn	0	10
Samuel Colburn	0	8
Aron Colburn	0	8
Abraham Colburn	0	8
James Richarson	0	7
Edward Colburn	0	15
Timothy Coalburn	0	8
Robert Coalburn	0	10
Jacob Coalburn	0	15
Azery Coalburn	0	4
Jabes Coalburn	0	4
Ezechal Richerson	0	7
John varnum	0	10
Thomas varnum	0	6
Ebenezer Curles	0	3
Zacharias Coalburn	0	8

Names	PLALT	MOWING	MEADO
Moses Coalburn	0	0	14
Joshua Emery	0	0	10
Timothy Emerson	0	0	6
Jonathan Emerson	0	0	4
Thomas Worster	0	0	6
Edward Calburn	0	0	10
Abiel Rowe	2	3	0
Ebenezer Jones	2	0	2
Nathaniel Mezer	0	0	4
Peter Ayers	0	0	6
Abner Kimbell	0	0	2
Joshua Scott	0	0	10
Thomas Bayle	0	0	5
Ebenezer Buck	0	0	6
Philip Mettchel	0	0	6
James Mettchel	0	0	20
Jonathan Grifen	8	0	6
Thomas Morson	0	0	5

Methuen & Dracut

June 9th 1742 John Ober made oath that the within acc^t is a True & Exact List of all the Poles & Rateable Estates taken by him in that part of Mathuen & Dracutt alotted him to take the List of according to the Vote of the Gen^{ll} Assembly Last Sessions according to the best of his Judgment

Sworn before Sam^{ll}
Gilman Jus: of Peace

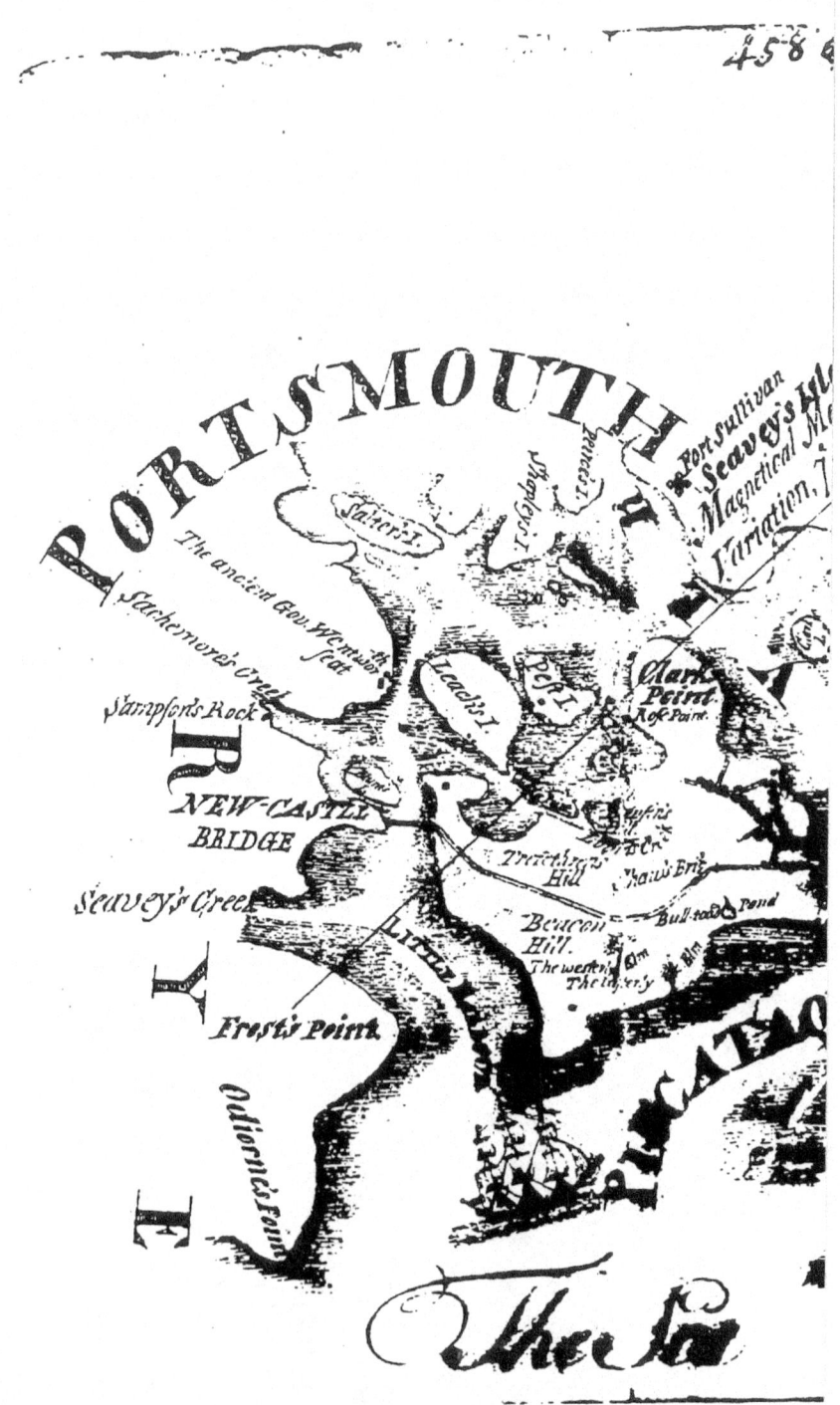

NH 1742 ESTATE TAX

A list of all the Rateable Polls & Estates

Names	POLLS	HOUSES	PLANTING MEADS & MOWING	PASTURE	HORSES	OXEN
Mad^m Walton	0	1	15	20	0	0
Mad Frost ***	0	1	1½	6	0	0
Capt Simpson	2	1	0	2	0	0
Capt Weed	1	1	0	0	0	0
Joⁿ Odiorne ***	1	1	0	0	1	0
Sampson Sheafe ***	1	1	0	0	0	0
John Sherburne *	1	1	20	50	1	4
Batha Odiorne	0	0	0	0	0	0
Jos Newmarch	1	1	1	4	1	0
Thos Bell *** 2	3	1	2	0	1	0
Chris Amazeen	1	1	6	6	0	0
Mad Jackson ***	0	1	2	12	1	0
Nathan White	1	1	0	2	0	0
John Batson	2	1	0	0	0	0
Wm Jones	1	1	4	2	0	0
Edward Martin	1	1	0	0	0	0
Henry Pain	1	1	0	0	0	0
Mary Pedrick	0	1	0	0	0	0
John Stevens	2	1	0	0	0	0
John Oshaw	2	1	4	1	0	1

COWS	3 YEAR	2 YEAR	ONE YEAR	SWINE	VALUE OF & YEARLY INCOME	INCOME OF PROFIT OF TRADE
4			1	0	ℒ.14	
1				0	5	
0				0	5	
1				0	2:10	ℒ-5
1				1	5:10	100
1				0	5:	30
7		2	1	1	20:	
0				0		
1		1		1	4:	20
2				0	6	70:
4		2		1	8:	
5				0	8:	
1				0	3:	
1				1	3:10	
1				0	5:	
0				0	2:	
1				0	1:10	
1	1			0	5:	5
0				0	2:	
3				1	3:	

NH 1742 ESTATE TAX

A list of all the Rateable Polls & Estates

Names	POLLS	HOUSES	PLANTING MEADS & MOWING	PASTURE	HORSES	OXEN
Rueben Mace	1	1	1	0	0	0
Richard Neal	3	1	0	0	0	0
Richard Jorden	3	1	0	0	0	0
Foster Trefethen	1	1	0	0	0	0
Zacª Foss	2	1	0	0	0	0
Wᵐ Frost ***	1	0	0	0	0	0
Benjª Downing	1	1	5	10	1	0
John Salter *	1	1	6	9	1	4
Henry Trefethen	1	1	0	0	0	0
John Martin	1	1	0	0	0	0
Wm Branscomb	1	1	0	0	0	0
Thos Parkes	1	1	0	0	0	0
Benjª Underwood	1	1	0	0	0	0
John Cord	1	1	0	0	0	0
Jon Tuckerman	1	1	0	0	0	0
George Lencord	1	1	0	0	0	0
Nat Sargent	1	1	0	0	0	0
Wm Mordent	1	0	0	0	0	0
Thoms Parker	2	1	0	4	0	0
Elish Luben	1	1	0	0	0	0

NEW CASTLE

COWS	3 YEAR	2 YEAR	ONE YEAR	SWINE	VALUE OF & YEARLY INCOME	INCOME OF PROFIT OF TRADE
0				0		
1				0	2:10	
0				0	1:10	
1				0		2:
1				0	2:10	
0				0	2:	5
3	1	2		0	6:	
3	2			2	4:	
0				0	2:	
0				0	1:	
0				0	2:	10
0				0	1:10	
1				0	2:10	5
0				0	1:10	
0				0	2:10	
0				0	1:10	
1				0	4:	
0				0		
1				0	4:	
0				0	:10	

A list of all the Rateable Polls & Estates

Names	POLLS	HOUSES	PLANTING MEADS & MOWING	PASTURE	HORSES	OXEN
John Pain	1	0	0	0	0	0
Steven Barter	2	1	0	0	0	0
John Trundy	1	1	0	0	0	0
Peter Harvey	1	1	0	0	0	0
Clemt Grandy	2	0	0	0	0	0
Mes Bell	1	0	0	0	0	0
Thomas Winter	1	1	0	0	0	0
Benja Bell	1	1	0	0	0	0
James Stilson	1	1	0	0	0	0
Nath^a White Jr	2	1	0	0	0	0
Tobias Lear	1	1	18	20	1	4
John Yeaton	2	1	2	4	0	0
John Odiorne	1	1	15	13	1	2
Nathan^u Odiorne	1	1	0	0	0	0
John Card Jr	1	1	0	0	0	0
James Trefethen	1	1	0	0	0	0
John Skinner	1	1	0	0	0	0
Sam^u Carder	1	1	0	0	0	0
John Clark	2	1	0	0	0	0
Sam^u Clark	1	1	0	0	0	0

COWS	3 YEAR	2 YEAR	ONE YEAR	SWINE	VALUE OF & YEARLY INCOME	INCOME OF PROFIT OF TRADE
0				0	:10	
0				0	2:	
1				0	2:	
0				0	:10	
0				0		
0				0		
0				1	:10	
0				1	1:10	
0				0	1:10	
0				1	10	
4	1	2		1	10:	
1	1			1	4:	
3		2		0	6:	
0				0	2:	
0				0		
0				0	1:10	
0				0	2:	
0				0	:10	
0				0	1:	
0				0	1:	

NH 1742 ESTATE TAX

A list of all the Rateable Polls & Estates

Names	POLLS	HOUSES	PLANTING MEADS & MOWING	PASTURE	HORSES	OXEN
John Pierce	1	1	0	0	0	0
Richd Yeaton	1	1	0	0	0	0
Henry Langmaid	1	0	0	0	0	0
John Foss	1	0	0	0	0	0
Henry Tredick	1	0	0	0	0	0
Nat Lear	1	0	0	0	0	0
Sam Card	1	1	0	0	0	0
Lewis Tinker	1	1	0	0	0	0
And Mace	1	1	0	0	0	0
Jer^a Jones	1	1	0	0	0	0
Peter Grant	1	1	0	0	0	0
Debo^a Wollis **	2	1	8	30	1	2
Wm Jones J^r	1	1	0	0	0	0
John Leach	1	1	4	10	0	0
Henry Trefethen J^r	1	1	0	0	0	0
Tom Maker	1	0	0	0	0	0
David Mitchel	1	1	0	0	0	0
Wm Larry	1	1	0	0	0	0
Sam Yeaton	1	1	0	0	0	0
Thomas Card	1	1	0	0	0	0

COWS	3 YEAR	2 YEAR	ONE YEAR	SWINE	VALUE OF & YEARLY INCOME	INCOME OF PROFIT OF TRADE
0				0	1:10	
0				0	2:10	
0				0		
0				0		
0				0		
0				0		
0				0	1:	
0				0	1:	
1				0	2:	
1				0	1:	
0				0	1:	
6	1	1		2	8:	
1		1		0	3:	
0				0	4:	
0				0	2:	0
0				0		
1				0	2:	
0				0	1:	
1				0	1:	
0				0	1:	

NH 1742 ESTATE TAX

A list of all the Rateable Polls & Estates

Names	POLLS	HOUSES	PLANTING MEADS & MOWING	PASTURE	HORSES	OXEN
Jos Amazeen	1	0	0	0	0	0
John Martin Jr	1	0	0	0	0	0
Jacob Sheafe	1	0	0	0	0	0
Soloⁿ White	1	0	0	0	1	0
John Crown	1	1	0	0	0	0
Nichols Corny	1	1	0	0	0	0
John Corny	1	0	0	0	0	0
John Trefethen	1	1	0	0	0	0
Robt White	1	1	0	0	0	0
Edward Mastin Jr	1	0	0	0	0	0
Abra^m Trefethen	1	0	0	0	0	0
Rob^{ton} Trefethen	1	0	0	0	0	0
Jonaⁿ Martin	1	0	0	0	0	0
Benj^a Jackson	1	0	0	0	0	0
Foster Trefethen Jr	1	1	1	0	0	0
Jos Clarke	1	0	0	0	0	0
Jacob Clark	1	0	0	0	0	0
Joseph Rice	1	1	0	0	0	0
Henry Foss	1	0	0	0	0	0
James Oshaw	1	0	0	0	0	0

NEW CASTLE

COWS	3 YEAR	2 YEAR	ONE YEAR	SWINE	VALUE OF & YEARLY INCOME	INCOME OF PROFIT OF TRADE
0				0	:10	
0				0		
0				0		
0				0		
0				2	2:	
0				1	2:	
0				0		
0				0	2:	
0				0	2:10	
0				0		
1				0	4:	
0				0		
0				0		
0				0		
1		1		0	3:	
0		1		0		
0				0	1:	
0				0	2:10	
0				0		
0				0	1:	

A list of all the Rateable Polls & Estates

Names	POLLS	HOUSES	PLANTING & MOWING MEADS	PASTURE	HORSES	OXEN
Walden Cenison	1	0	0	0	0	0
Tho⁵ Brown	1	0	0	0	0	0
Benjᵃ Odiorne	1	0	0	0	0	0
Robᵗ Harvy	1	0	0	0	0	0
Samᵘ Rogers	1	1	0	0	0	0
John Randel	1	1	0	0	0	0
Wm Neal	1	0	0	0	0	0
Andrew Pepˣ Frost	1	0	0	0	0	0
Benjᵃ Hale	1	1	0	0	0	0
Stelman Jordan	1	0	0	0	0	0
Robᵗ Carpenter	1	0	0	0	0	0
Edward Card	1	0	0	0	0	0
Sam Lanmaid	1	0	0	0	0	0
John Lasin	1	1	1¼	6	0	0

* 2 year-old steers
** 3 year-old steers
*** Negro/Indian

COWS	3 YEAR	2 YEAR	ONE YEAR	SWINE	VALUE OF & YEARLY INCOME	INCOME OF PROFIT OF TRADE
0				0	:10	
0				0		
0				0		
0				0		
0				0	1:	
0				0	1:19	
0				0		
0				0		
0				0	1:10	
0				0		
0				0		
0				0		
0				0		
0				0	1:5	

A List of all The Rateable Polls & Estates &sr^a for the Parrish of New Castle in the Province of New Hamp^n according to the Direction of an Act of the Prov: afore sd for a New proportioning the Province tax of each Town Made & passed at the Gen^{ll} Assembly begin & held on the 13th Jany taken March y^e 31st 1742

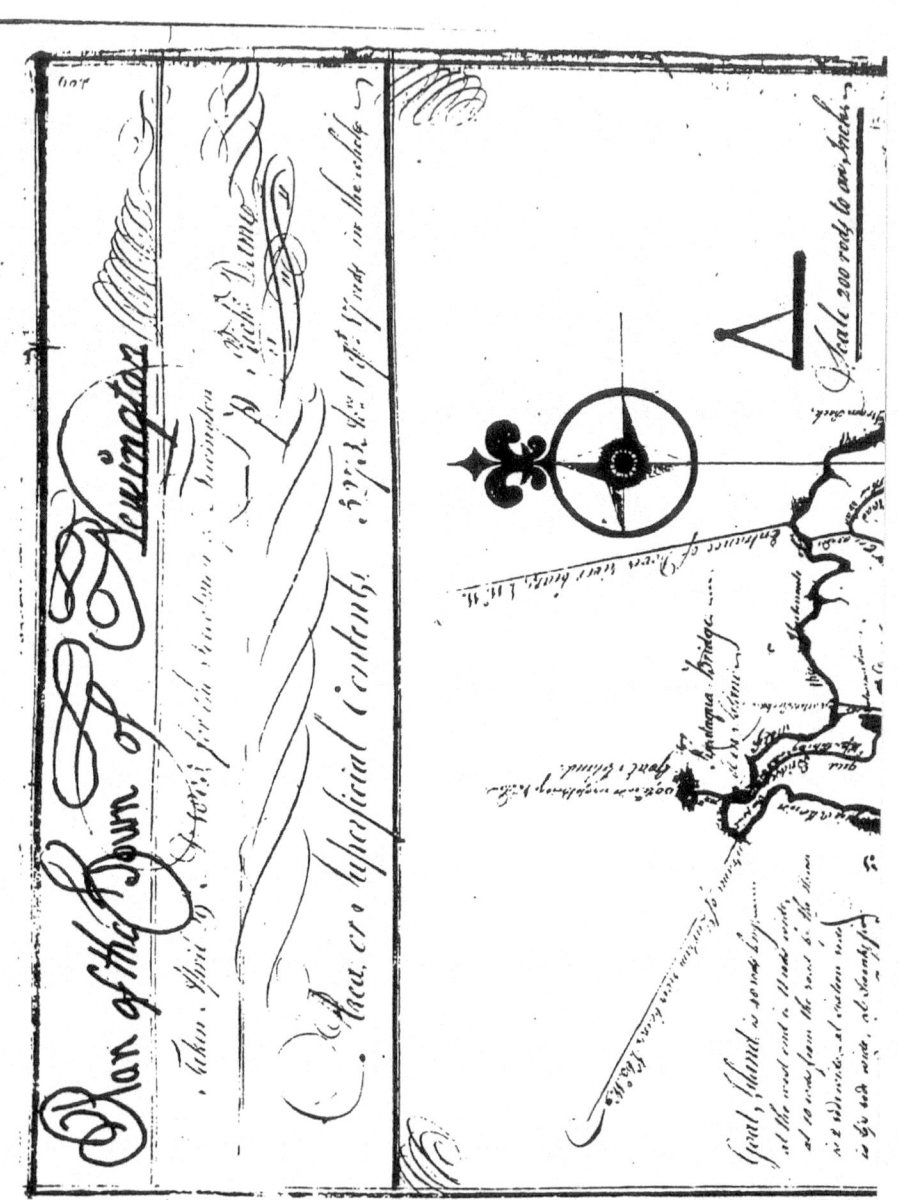

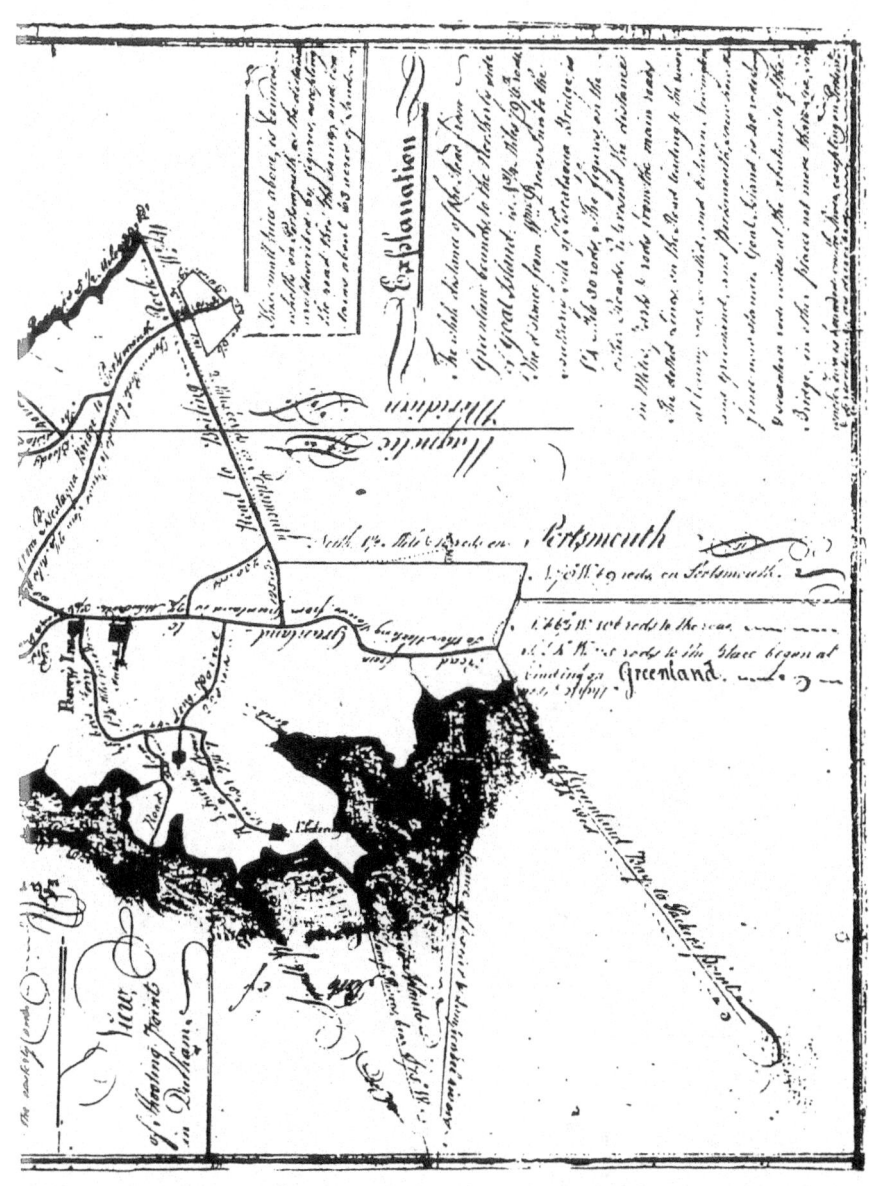

Porvence Newington
of newhampshire
A provence Rate Made Persuent to anact
of General assemble

	£	s	d
Mr John Downing Esqr	00	16	06
Mr John Fabyan Esqr	03	07	06
Mr John Dam	01	01	09
Cap John downing Esqr	13	10	00
Cap Thomas Baldwin	04	13	00
Ens Halabuel Nutter	03	13	11
Mr Elezer Colman	09	03	05
Mr Retcherd downing	04	02	11
Mr Jethro beckford	03	08	00
Mr James Pickren	06	03	03
Mr Thomas Leighten	04	01	09
Mr Joshua Pickren	04	10	00
Mr Thomas Pickren	05	11	09
Mr Seth Ring	08	15	06
Mr Jonathen Downing	02	15	09
Mr James Rollans	01	10	00
Mr Thomos beckford	03	11	09
Mr Joshua downing	01	12	03
Mr Retcherd dam	03	02	06

Mr Samuel rollans	02	11	09
Mr William furbur	01	18	00
Mr Moses dam	01	13	09
Mr John Greek	02	01	00
Mr Alaxend Hodgsdon	01	17	00
Mr Gorg Wallen	02	03	06
Mr John Nutter	04	19	06
Mr John Vinson	03	10	03
Mr Christopher Huntress	03	10	03
Mr James Nutter	01	15	06
Mr Gorg Colbroth	00	19	00
Mr John Hunttres	01	16	06
Mr Samuel Hunttres	02	13	00
Mr Joseph Rollans	01	12	03
Mr Samuel Nutter	03	06	06
Mr Samuel fabyan	02	10	00
Mr Moses furbur	01	12	00
Mr Jathro furur	02	16	00
Mr Nehemiah furbur	02	14	00
Mr John Hoyt	01	15	00
Mr John dam	02	08	09
Mr Phenes Colman	02	04	03
Mr alexander Hodgsdson jur	03	00	00
Mr James Colbroth	01	01	00
Mr Nickles Knight	01	13	00

NH 1742 ESTATE TAX

Mr John Knight	03	11	03
Mr Joseph patterson	03	10	00
Mr Lemuel beckford	02	14	06
Mr John Peckren	01	00	03
Mr Edward Walker	00	18	03
Mr Edward rolans	00	18	00
Mr Jonathan butler	00	18	09
Samuel Rollans jur	00	13	00
John Davis	00	13	00
William Hunttres	00	18	00
James alaxend	00	13	06
John Stevens	01	08	00
Mr Retcherd Plase	01	01	06
Samuel Plase	01	01	06
John Croe	00	17	03
Hattebel Nutter	00	15	00
Mr Edward ars	02	17	00
anton Nutter	00	15	00
Jonathen tecke	02	00	00
John beckford	00	18	00
Jonathen beckford	00	13	00
Wedow Roe	01	11	06
John Watton	00	13	06
Mr bangeman Miller	02	00	00
John Vent	01	02	06

Ebenezer beckford	00	13	06
John downing	00	13	06
Ruben Ham	01	00	06
Josaph rolans Jur	00	16	00
Mathies nutter	00	18	06

a true copy
James Pickren
Lemuel Bickford   Selectmen
John Knight Jur

Newington March ye 25 1742

a true Invoice of all the Estates and polls and Lands and Stocks the Polls 99 Lands 3120 ackers double Houses 26 double Houses one Flore 24 Sengel Houses 13 oxen 64 Horses 77 Cows 227 Three year olds 55 Two years olds 117 year olds 74 Hogs 18 Two negro polls

   James Pickren
    Seleckmen
   Lemuel Bickford
   John Knight Jur

June the 8th 1742 the Selectmen that Signed the above acc^t
Made oath the within Invoice cantains a True & Exact list of the Poles and Estates within their prsh taken by Order of the vote of the Gen^{ll} Asembly Last Sessions according to the best of their understanding Sworn before

   Sam^{ll} Gilman Justice of Peace

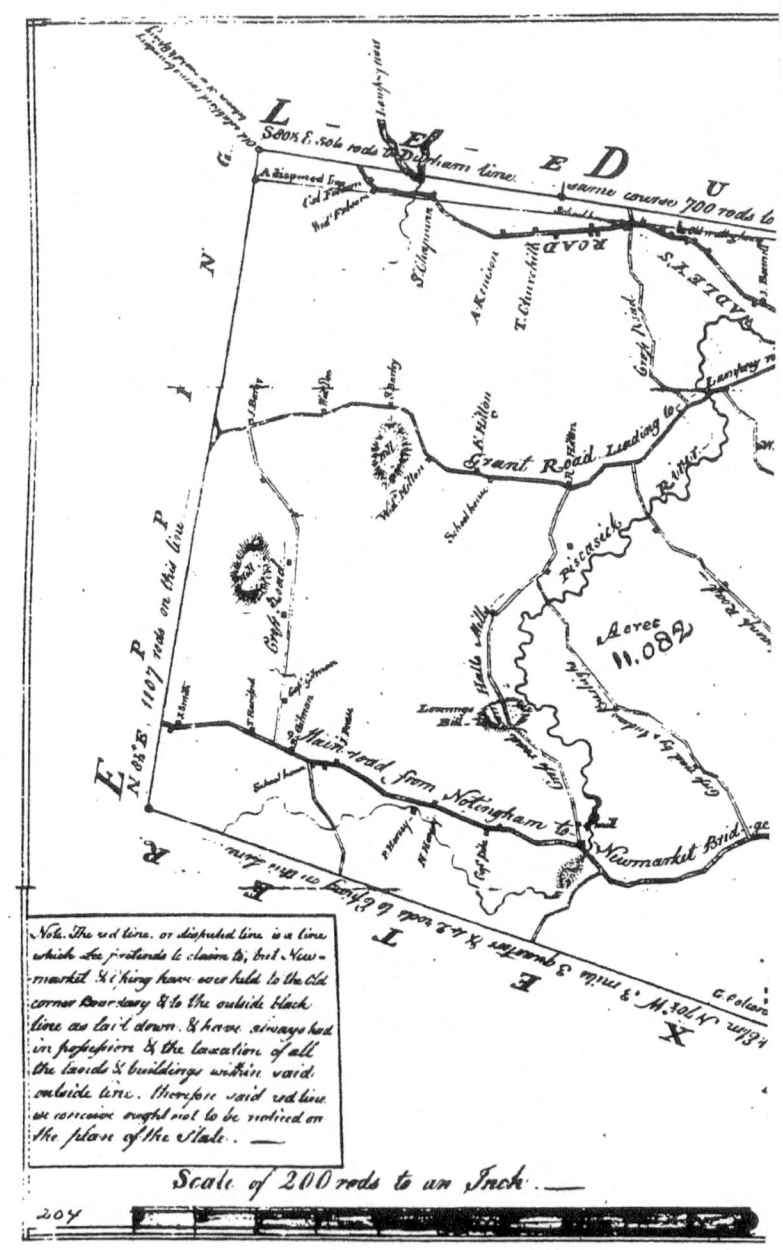

March 1742 A true Invoice of the Polls and Estats both Parsonal And Rateable of the Parsons hereafter Named belongin to the Parish of Newmarket Taken by Rich[d] Mattoon one of the Selectmen of Said Parish

Names	HOUSES	POLS	OXEN	HORSES	COWS	3 YEARS OLD
M[r] Arther Slade	0	1	0	1	0	0
Laf[t] Joseph Hall	1	1	2	1	2	0
Cap[t] Edward Hall	1	1	4	0	4	0
Richard Clark	1	1	2	0	2	0
Winthroup Hilton	1	2	2	0	9	0
Benj[a] Dow	1	2	2	7	7	2
Joseph Smart	1	1	2	0	0	0
Joseph Hilton	1	2	0	0	3	0

2 YEARS OLD	1 YEAR OLD	SWINE	PLANTING	PASTURE
0	0	0	0	0
5	2	1	45	0
3	3	1	50	0
4	3	1	26	0
0	6	0	50	0
2	4	1	35	0
1	0	0	1	0
2	0	0	10	0

NH 1742 ESTATE TAX

Names	HOUSES	POLS	OXEN	HORSES	COWS	3 YEARS OLD
Joseph Metcalf	1	1	0	0	1	0
Mr Thomas Tufts	1	1	0	2	2	0
Hanrey Tufts	0	1	0	0	0	0
Capt Jacob Tilton	1	1	0	0	8	0
Robert Pike	1	1	0	1	2	0
John Wedgwood	1	1	2	2	3	0
William Sargent	1	1	2	1	1	0
Robart Pike Jun*	0	1	2	1	1	0
John Mils	0	1	0	0	0	0
Nathan Preson	1	1	0	0	0	0
Willm Durgan	0	1	0	0	0	0
James Marston	1	1	2	0	3	0
Samll Mighel	1	1	2	0	1	0
John Mighel	0	1	0	0	0	0
Willm Hilton	1	1	0	0	0	0
Widow Mighel	0	0	0	0	2	0
Jonathan Colcord	1	1	2	0	3	0

2 YEARS OLD	1 YEAR OLD	SWINE	PLANTING	PASTURE
1	0	0	1	12
0	0	0	16	0
1	0	0	0	0
7	6	0	65	0
2	0	1	20	0
0	0	1	24	0
0	0	0	10	0
0	0	0	6	0
0	0	0	0	0
0	0	0	0	0
0	0	0	0	0
1	2	1	24	0
0	0	0	6	0
1	0	0	0	0
0	0	0	0	0
1	0	0	6	0
1	0	1	21	0

NH 1742 ESTATE TAX

Names	HOUSES	POLS	OXEN	HORSES	COWS	3 YEARS OLD
Gideon Colcord	0	1	2	0	0	0
Jonathan Colcord Jun	0	1	0	0	0	0
Edward Colcord	0	1	0	1	0	0
Sam*ll* Neal	0	1	0	0	1	0
Walter Neal	1	1	2	0	5	2
Hubartes Neal	0	1	0	0	0	0
Joseph Gilman Jun*	1	1	0	0	2	0
John Fox	1	2	0	0	1	0
John Piner	0	1	0	0	0	0
Isaac Marston Land	0	0	0	0	0	0
Daniel Ames	1	1	0	0	3	0
Simeon Ames	0	1	2	1	0	0
Nathaniel Ames	0	1	2	0	0	0
Jonathan Hoag	1	1	0	1	2	0

2 YEARS OLD	1 YEAR OLD	SWINE	PLANTING	PASTURE
0	*0*	*0*	*0*	*0*
2	*1*	*0*	*0*	*0*
0	*0*	*0*	*0*	*0*
2	*0*	*0*	*0*	*0*
0	*3*	*1*	*21*	*0*
0	*0*	*0*	*0*	*0*
0	*0*	*0*	*2*	*0*
0	*0*	*1*	*7*	*0*
0	*0*	*0*	*0*	*0*
0	*0*	*0*	*12*	*0*
2	*0*	*0*	*22*	*0*
0	*0*	*0*	*0*	*0*
0	*0*	*0*	*6*	*0*
2	*0*	*0*	*28*	*0*

NH 1742 ESTATE TAX

Names	HOUSES	POLS	OXEN	HORSES	COWS	3 YEARS OLD
John Perkins Sr	1	0	0	3	2	1
Rober Perkins	1	2	1	1	0	0
Widow Mary Perkins	0	0	0	4	2	2
John Burley	2	4	1	2	0	2
James Burley	2	4	1	3	0	2
William Burley	1	2	0	0	0	1
Gils Burley	1	2	1	3	0	1
Jacob Burley	1	2	0	2	0	0
William foulsham	1	2	1	2	0	0
Jeremah foulshan	2	4	1	4	4	2
Jermah foulshan Junr	1	2	0	0	0	2
John meed	1	0	0	1	0	0
Joseph burley	2	4	1	6	0	3
John bergin	1	0	1	2	1	0
Jchob Wheten	1	0	1	0	0	0
Hiniman York	1	2	0	2	0	0
Joseph York	1	0	0	0	0	0

2 YEARS OLD	1 YEAR OLD	SWINE	PLANTING	PASTURE
0	1	10	6	
0	0	10	0	
1	0	20	9	
3	1	25	10	
6	1	24	10	
0	0	0	0	
4	1	19	3	
0	0	2	0	
1	0	12	4	
1	1	40	12	
2	0	4	0	
0	0	4	0	
2	1	20	12	
1	0	2	10	
0	0	1	0	
1	0	12	5	
0	0	0	0	

NH 1742 ESTATE TAX

Names	HOUSES	POLS	OXEN	HORSES	COWS	3 YEARS OLD
John York	1	0	0	0	0	0
Sampson Doe	1	0	1	2	1	1
Nathaniel Doe	2	0	1	2	0	0
Samuel Doe	1	2	0	5	2	2
Thomas yung	1	0	0	0	0	0
John yung	1	0	0	0	0	0
Thomas yung Juner	1	0	0	0	0	0
Joseph Judckens	2	2	1	3	2	2
Walter Brint	2	0	1	2	0	0
Nathanel watson	1	0	0	1	0	0
John Craton	1	0	0	0	0	0
Josiah Brley	1	2	1	3	0	2
Ephram folsham	1	0	0	1	2	2
Joseph Smith	2	4	2	7	4	4
hezckah mash	1	0	0	2	1	0
hopstil chzel	1	2	0	2	3	0
Samuel Bracket	1	4	1	4	1	0

2 YEARS OLD	1 YEAR OLD	SWINE	PLANTING	PASTURE
0	0	0	0	
2	0	30	30	
0	1	15	15	
5	1	15	15	
0	0	6	0	
0	0	0	0	
0	0	0	0	
3	1	16	10	
0	1	6	6	
0	0	0	0	
0	0	1	0	
1	1	9	3	
0	0	6	4	
1	2	30	30	
0	0	10	0	
3	1	12	8	
2	0	15	6	

NH 1742 ESTATE TAX

Names	HOUSES	POLS	OXEN	HORSES	COWS	3 YEARS OLD
James Gooden	2	2	1	3	0	0
Beniman york	1	0	1	1	0	0
John Palmer	2	4	1	2	0	1
Nathan Caston	1	2	1	4	0	0
James Palmer	1	0	0	0	0	0
John Benet	1	2	0	1	1	0
Samuel Roling	1	2	1	1	0	0
Robert Roling	1	0	0	0	0	0
James Roling	1	0	1	1	0	2
Thomas Benet	1	2	1	1	0	0
Samuel duley	1	2	0	2	0	0
John barber	1	2	0	2	2	0
Edward fox	2	0	1	1	2	4
Andrew Wedgins	1	1	0	2	0	0
William Taler	1	0	1	1	0	0
Samuel Chatam	1	2	1	0	0	0
John gorman	1	0	0	0	0	0

2 YEARS OLD	1 YEAR OLD	SWINE	PLANTING	PASTURE
1	0	10	3	
0	0	3	0	
2	1	4	0	
0	1	6	0	
0	0	0	0	
2	0	5	6	
1	1	8	3	
0	0	0	0	
0	0	0	0	
0	0	3	0	
0	0	0	0	
0	1	9	1	
1	1	5	3	
0	0	5	0	
0	0	0	0	
0	0	0	0	
0	0	0	0	

NH 1742 ESTATE TAX

Names	HOUSES	POLS	OXEN	HORSES	COWS	3 YEARS OLD
Jonathan fisk	1	0	0	0	0	0
William foulsham	2	4	1	3	0	1
Insen Ephram foulsham	1	4	1	4	2	2
John foulsham	1	2	0	0	0	0
Andrew foulsham	1	0	1	0	0	0
James Hase	1	2	1	0	0	0
John Hase	1	2	1	1	0	0
John Perkins	1	2	2	4	2	1
James keineston	1	0	0	0	0	0
frances durggain	1	2	1	3	0	1
Israel foulsham	2	2	1	1	0	0
John Hoeg	1	0	1	2	0	0
John keineston	1	2	0	1	0	0
Richard Smart	1	0	0	1	0	0
Charls Smart	1	0	0	0	0	0
Benj^a Smart	1	0	1	0	3	2
Robert Smart	1	0	1	2	3	4

NEWMARKET

2 YEARS OLD	1 YEAR OLD	SWINE	PLANTING	PASTURE
0	0	0	0	
2	1	10	3	
0	0	24	10	
0	0	0	0	
0	0	0	0	
1	0	16	4	
0	0	0	0	
4	1	24	10	
0	0	0	0	
3	1	14	7	
0	1	6	0	
4	1	4	0	
0	1	4	0	
0	0	3	0	
0	0	0	0	
0	0	7	9	
2	4	20	15	

A List of the Poles and Eeasteates Teakin By mee the Subcriber one of the Selectmen of newmarket for ye year 1742 Poles---32 houses 30 oxen 32 cows 51 horses 24 3 yr olds 10 2yr 27 yer old 27 swine 8 Mowing and Planting Land 228 acrs Pasture Land 26 acrs

Israel Gilman

June 8th 1742 Robert Smart Made Oath that the Accompt hereunto Annexed is a true & exact List of the Rateabale Polos & Estates within ye prsh of Newmarket that was his District to take according to the Vote of the Genll Assembly Last Sessions according to the best of his understanding. Sworn before
    Samll Gilman Justies of Peace
    This is A true List of the poles and Estates taken by me the Subcriber one of the Selectmen of the Parish of Newmarket for ye yer 1742

heds 80 houses 51 oxen 89 hooses 42: Cows: 121 three year olds: 40 Two years olds: 47 year olds: 62 Swine 31 Land 547 ackrs Pastrars Land 282 Ackrs

                    Robert Smart Sele^{tt} Man

To the Honourable House of Repecsentive in Genearl Ccort Assembeld the with in invoice is Justfy take according to the Best of my skill and Knodedg My in -------- handred me of coming down Sworn Yours humble

        Servent   Richd Mattoon

NOTTINGHAM

ROCKINGHAM CO.

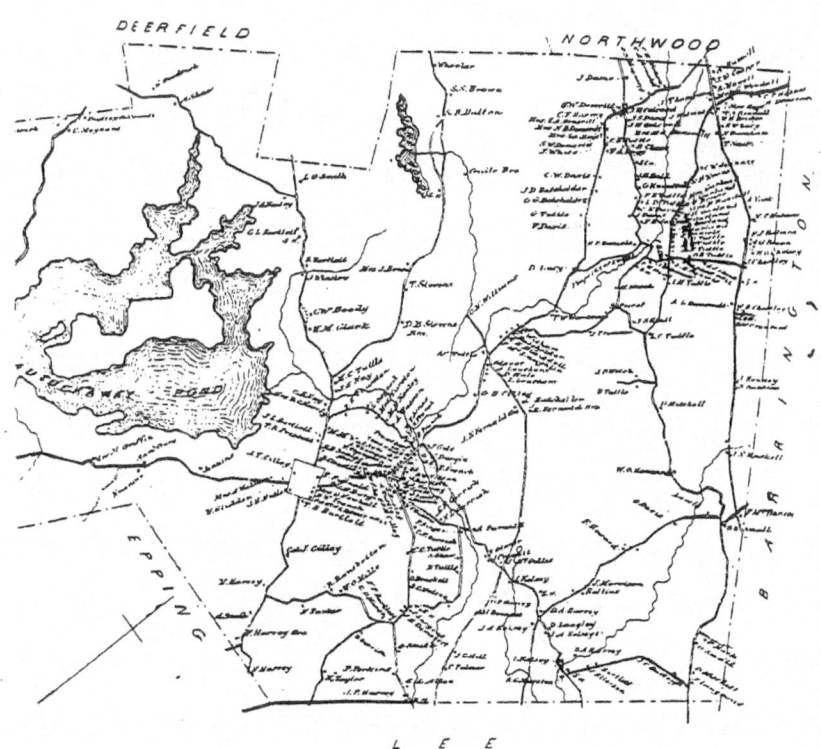

A list of pols & estates of yͤ inhabitance of this district as it was ordered to take and account of May yͤ 20 1740

Pools	067	Henry Baldwin Clerk
Houses	056	Nottingham in yͤ
Oxen	084	New District
Cows	149	
two years old	040	
yearlins	050	
swin	029	
Plow land	183 ackes	
Moing land	246 ackes	
Pastar land	009 ackes	
Horses	36	

Nottingham on
Merrymack

June 9th 1742 Henry Baldwin made oath that the within acct is a True & Exact List of all the Poles & Rateable Estates taken by him in that part of Nottingham on Merrymack aloted him to tak the List of According to the Vote of the Gen[ll] Assembly Last Sessions according to the best of his Judgement

Sworn before
Sam[ll] Gilman Justice of Peace

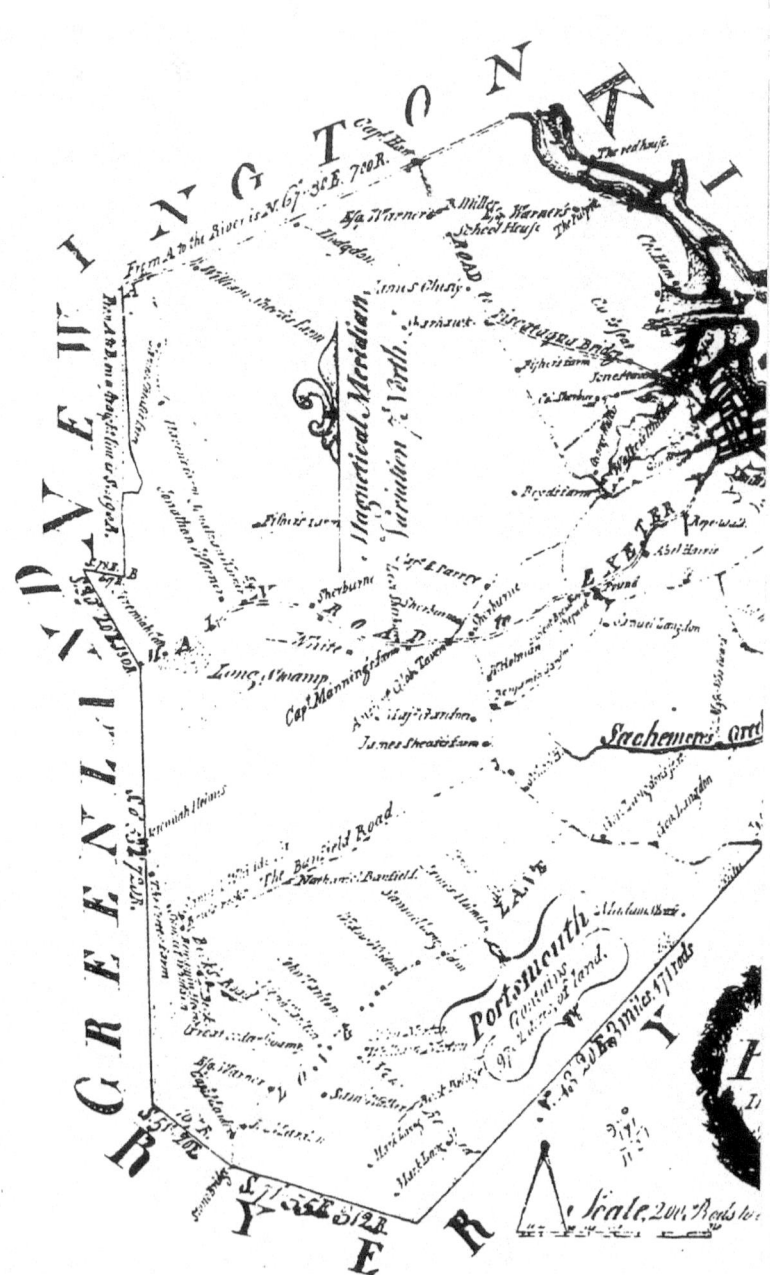

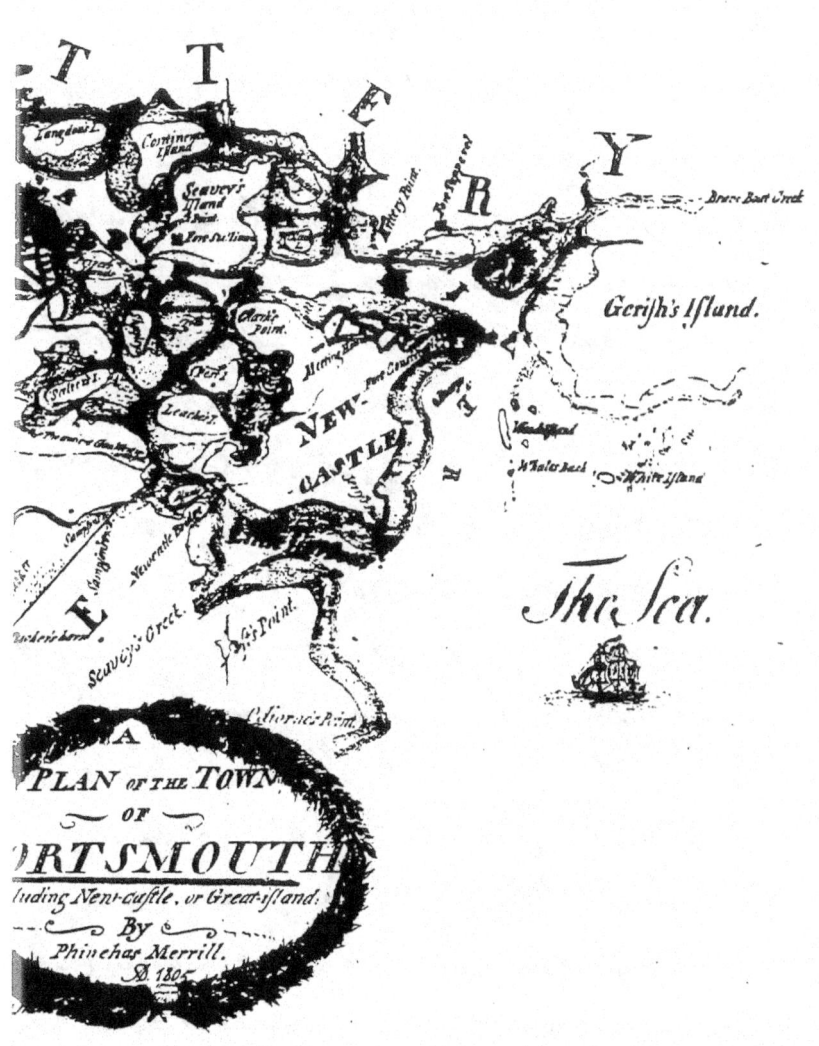

Pursuant to a Vote of ye Genl Court past ye 18th of this inst June requiring ye Select-men or Wardens in every Parish or Precint forthwith to take an exact Invoice of all Polls & Estates within their respective Precincts or Districts in ye following Manner Vizt all rateable Heads from Sixteen years old and upwards Houses Planting meadow mowing & Pasture Land Horses Oxen Cows three years old two year old & yearlings & Swine, of year old & to return their Acct on ye 22 Day of June currt to ye Genel Assembly if then Setting if not ye 2nd Day of ye next Setting of ye Genl Assembly We ye Select=men of ye Town Portsmouth have take as exact an acct as is in our Power agreable to Sd Vote & find that there is 716 Rateable Polls including Negroes three Hundd & eighty two Houses three Hundd Seventy nine acres of Planting Land eigtht Hundd forty two acres of Medw two thousd & fifty two acres of Pasture one

Hund^d fifty swine Horses one Hund^d & thirty three oxen five Hund^d & forty two Cows Seventy one three year olds one Hund^d & fifty five two year olds one Hund^d & thirty five yearlings one Hund^d & ten Swine of a year old

We further Say y^t we have no certain Rule to rate or Doom Person by for thieir Income by Trade or Merchandize & ye Assessors informs us y^t there never was any such Rule in ye Town but y^t they always tax'd ye People by Guess & ye best information they could get of thier Circumstances a ye time of taxing.

The Town of Portsm^o paid to ye Province Tax in ye year 1741 ye Sum of £813.11 when ye whole Prov^l Tax was £57 46-16 which Sum of 813.11 was raised upon ye aboves^d

Polls
Polls & Estates & Trade & Merchandize

June 22ᵈ - 1742

Samᵘ Hart
Hersher burke
John Moffatt
D Peirce
Hen Sherbure Junr

Selectmen of Portsmᵈ

June 22ᵈ 1742 The Selectmen of Portsmouth who Suberibed the above acct made oath that the above is a True and Exact List of the Poles and Rateable Estates in the Town of Portsmº Taken by them according to the act of the Genᵘ Assembly made the Last S
the best of their Judgment Sworn

        Before Samᵘ Gilman Jus of Peace

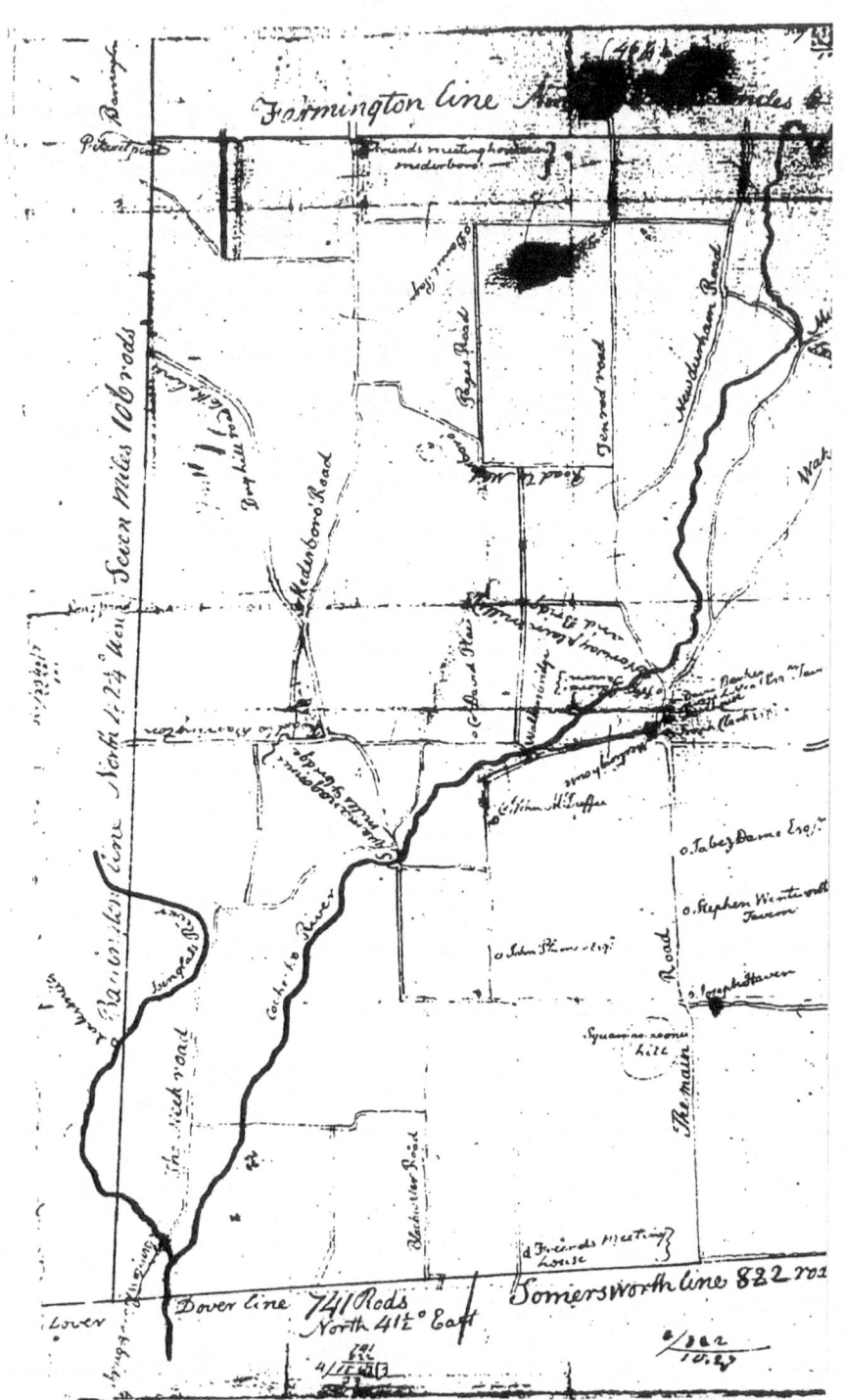

ROCHESTER

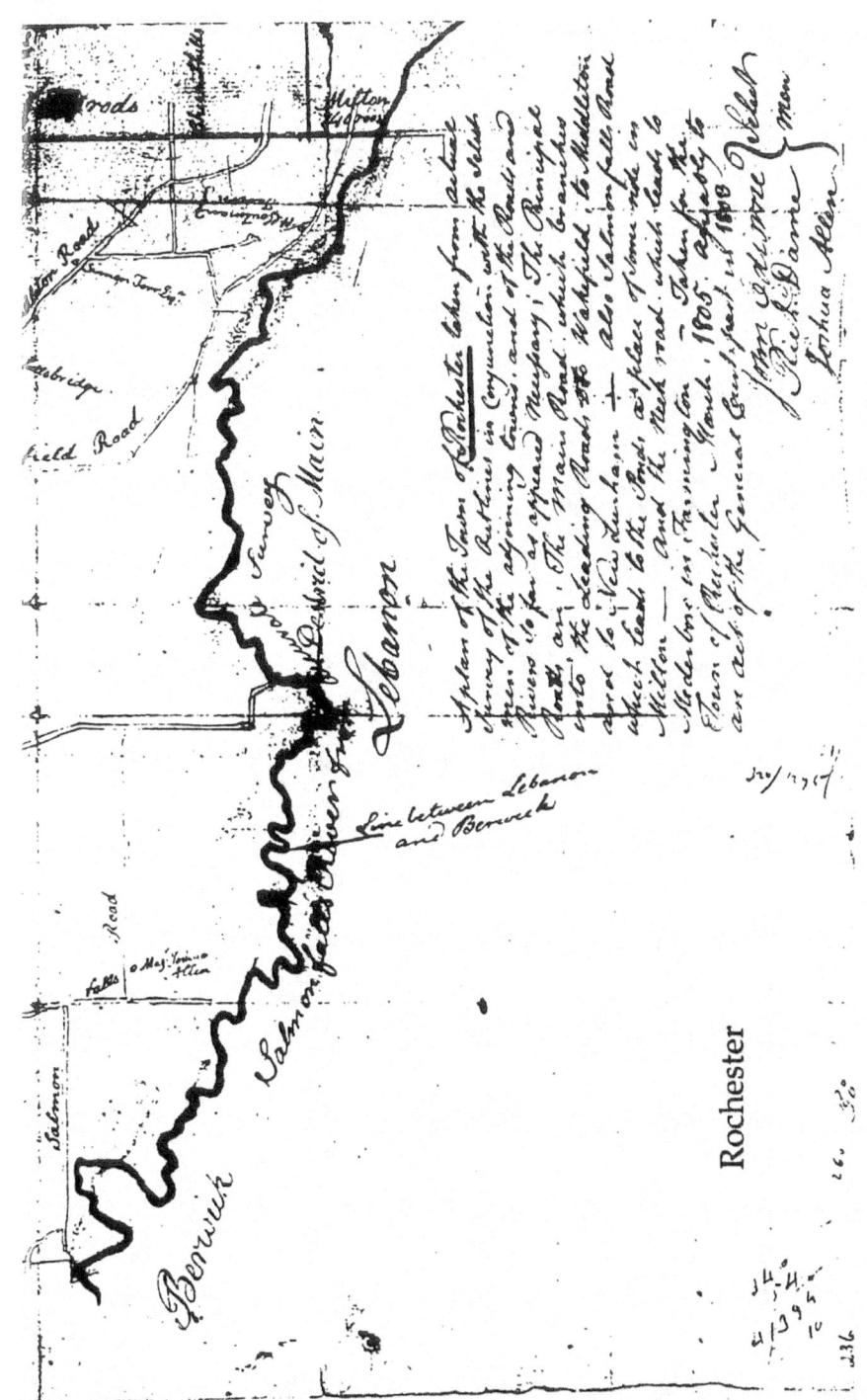

1742 Inventory Of The Town Of Rochester

Names	POLS	OXEN	COWS	3 YEAR OLD	2 YEAR OLD	1 YEAR OLD
Joseph Richards	2	1	2	0	1	1
Jos Heard	1	1	2	4	0	1
Jonathan Copps	1	1	2	0	0	0
Jn° Wentworth	1	1	1	0	0	1
Ichº Horne	1	0	1	0	0	0
Jon Richard Jr	1	1	1	0	0	1
John Allen	1	0	2	0	0	0
Isaac Bussell	1	1	1	0	0	0
Wᵐ Chamberlin	2	2	7	0	0	1
Samˡˡ Richards	1	0	1	0	0	0
Robᵗ Knight	1	0	3	0	1	2
Stepⁿ Berry	2	1	1	0	3	1
Samˡˡ Whitehouse	1	0	1	0	0	0
Eben Plaise	2	0	3	0	1	2
Richᵈ Wentworth	1	0	1	1	2	0
Gershom Downs	1	1	2	0	0	0
Jos Berry	1	0	1	0	0	0

HORSES	SWINE	PLANTING	HOUSING
1	0	8	1
1	0	6	1
1	1	3	0
1	0	4	1
0	0	0	0
1	0	0	0
0	0	6	1
1	0	3	1
2	1	12	1
1	0	2	1
1	1	6	1
1	1	6	1
0	1	2	1
1	0	7	1
1	1	3	1
0	1	3	1
0	0	0	0

NH 1742 ESTATE TAX

Names	POLS	OXEN	COWS	3 YEAR OLD	2 YEAR OLD	1 YEAR OLD
James Bussell	1	0	1	0	1	2
Solⁿ Clark	1	2	1	0	0	0
Phile Dore	1	1	2	0	0	0
Wm Allen	1	0	0	2	3	0
Jⁿ Trickey	1	1	1	0	0	0
Eli^z Tibbets	1	0	1	3	0	0
Jⁿ Ambler	0	0	0	0	0	0
Jos Tibbets	1	2	3	0	1	0
Eph^m Tibbets	1	0	2	0	2	0
Paul Tibbets	1	1	4	0	0	0
Elis^a Tibbets	1	1	2	0	2	0
Aron Tibbets	1	1	2	1	1	0
Sam^{ll} Cousen	1	0	0	0	0	0
Elis^x Hamn	1	1	3	1	1	0
Jⁿ Garland	1	1	2	0	0	0
Benj^a Fost	1	1	1	0	0	0
Wm Ellis	1	0	1	0	1	1
Stepⁿ Harford	1	0	0	0	1	0

HORSES	SWINE	PLANTING	HOUSING
0	0	3	1
1	0	4	1
1	1	3	1
0	0	0	0
1	1	2	1
1	0	5	1
0	0	4	0
1	1	12	1
1	1	6	1
1	1	7	1
0	0	3	1
1	1	7	1
1	0	0	1
0	2	6	1
1	1	2	1
1	0	2	1
0	0	2	0
1	1	2	1

Names	POLS	OXEN	COWS	3 YEAR OLD	2 YEAR OLD	1 YEAR OLD
Elie^r Coloman	1	1	2	2	0	0
Thos Drew	1	1	1	0	1	0
Benj^a Tibbetts	1	0	3	2	2	0
Thos Perkins	2	1	2	0	1	0
Eben Brewster	1	0	1	0	0	0
Sam^{ll} Trambly	1	0	2	0	0	0
Jno Mackafe	2	1	6	0	0	4
Benj^{ai} Hays	1	1	3	0	0	0
Tim^a Roberts	1	2	4	0	2	3
Clem Dearing	1	1	2	0	0	0
Jno Laden	1	1	3	2	3	1
Zebⁿ Dam	2	1	3	0	0	2
Henry Allard	1	0	2	0	0	0
Jno Jennens	1	1	2	0	0	2
James Rogers	2	1	3	0	0	2
Dan^{ll} Mcneele	1	0	1	0	0	0
James Rogers Junr	1	1	0	0	0	0
Sam^{ll} Brown	1	0	0	0	0	0

HORSES	SWINE	PLANTING	HOUSING
1	1	2	1
1	0	2	1
1	2	5	1
1	0	4	1
1	0	3	1
0	0	1	1
1	1	10	1
1	1	5	1
1	2	13	1
1	1	4	1
1	0	5	1
1	1	8	1
1	1	1	0
1	0	4	1
1	1	10	1
0	0	0	0
0	1	4	0
1	1	1	0

NH 1742 ESTATE TAX

Names	POLS	OXEN	COWS	3 YEAR OLD	2 YEAR OLD	1 YEAR OLD
Jon^a Young	1	1	2	0	0	0
So^{ll} Drown	1	0	0	0	0	0
Jno Herd	1	1	0	1	0	0
Wm Thomson	1	0	1	0	0	0
James Plice	1	2	2	0	1	3
Jos Walker	2	0	1	0	0	1
Soll Perkins	1	0	0	0	3	0
Edwd Tibbets	1	1	3	0	0	0
Jno Downing	1	3	0	0	0	0
James Lock	1	0	1	0	0	0
Than Seve	1	1	1	0	0	0
Richd Bickford	1	1	0	0	0	0
Jno Blagdon	1	0	2	0	0	0
Ad^{am} Templeton	1	0	1	0	0	0
Wm Jenings	1	1	3	0	3	2
Mark Jenings	1	1	2	0	0	0
Jos Richards Junr	1	0	1	0	0	0
Jno Peirlo	2	1	1	0	0	0

HORSES	SWINE	PLANTING	HOUSING
1	0	4	1
0	0	0	0
1	1	1	0
1	0	1	0
1	0	2	1
2	0	0	0
0	0	0	0
1	1	4	1
1	0	8	1
1	0	1	0
1	1	3	1
1	0	6	1
0	0	2	0
1	0	0	1
1	0	4	1
1	0	3	1
0	0	2	1
1	0	2	1

NH 1742 ESTATE TAX

Names	POLS	OXEN	COWS	3 YEAR OLD	2 YEAR OLD	1 YEAR OLD
Jos Hodgsdon	1	1	0	0	0	0
Jnº Hammock	2	0	2	0	0	0
Jnº Hammock Junr	1	0	1	2	0	0
Jnº Bickford	1	1	3	0	0	0
Samll Merry	1	0	1	0	0	0
Samll Merry Junr	1	0	1	2	0	0
Hen Sevey	1	0	0	0	0	0

Saml Roberts
Wm Chamberlin   Selectmen
John Downing

HORSES	SWINE	PLANTING	HOUSING
0	1	1	2
1	1	7	0
1	0	0	0
1	0	5	0
1	0	1	0
1	0	3	0
0	0	0	0

June 9th 1742 Tim't Robert J Wm Chamberlin John Dowing J Made oath that the within act is a True & Exact List of all the Poles & Rateable Estates taken by Select of town of Rochester alloted them to Take ye list of according to the note of the Genll Assembly Last Sessions According to the Best of their Judgement

Sworn before Samll Gilman Jus: of Peace

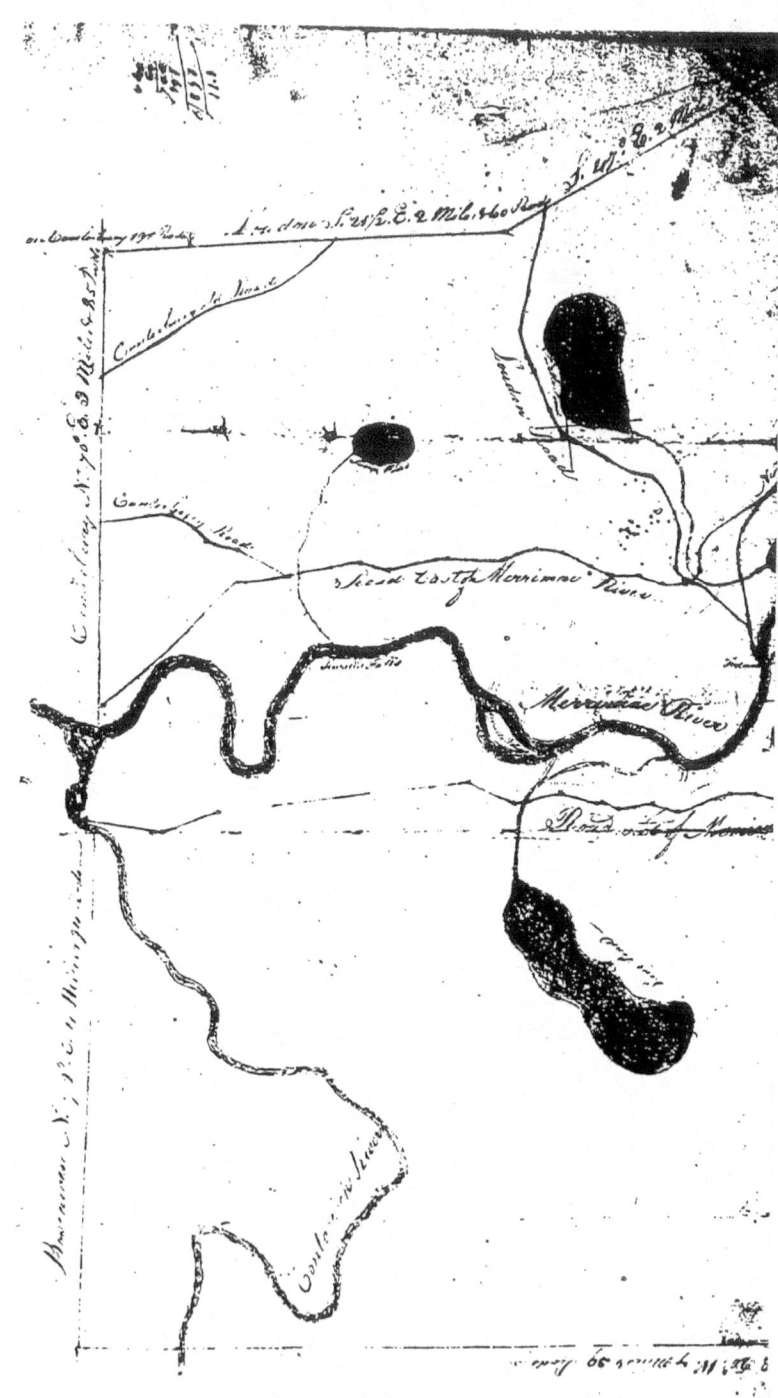

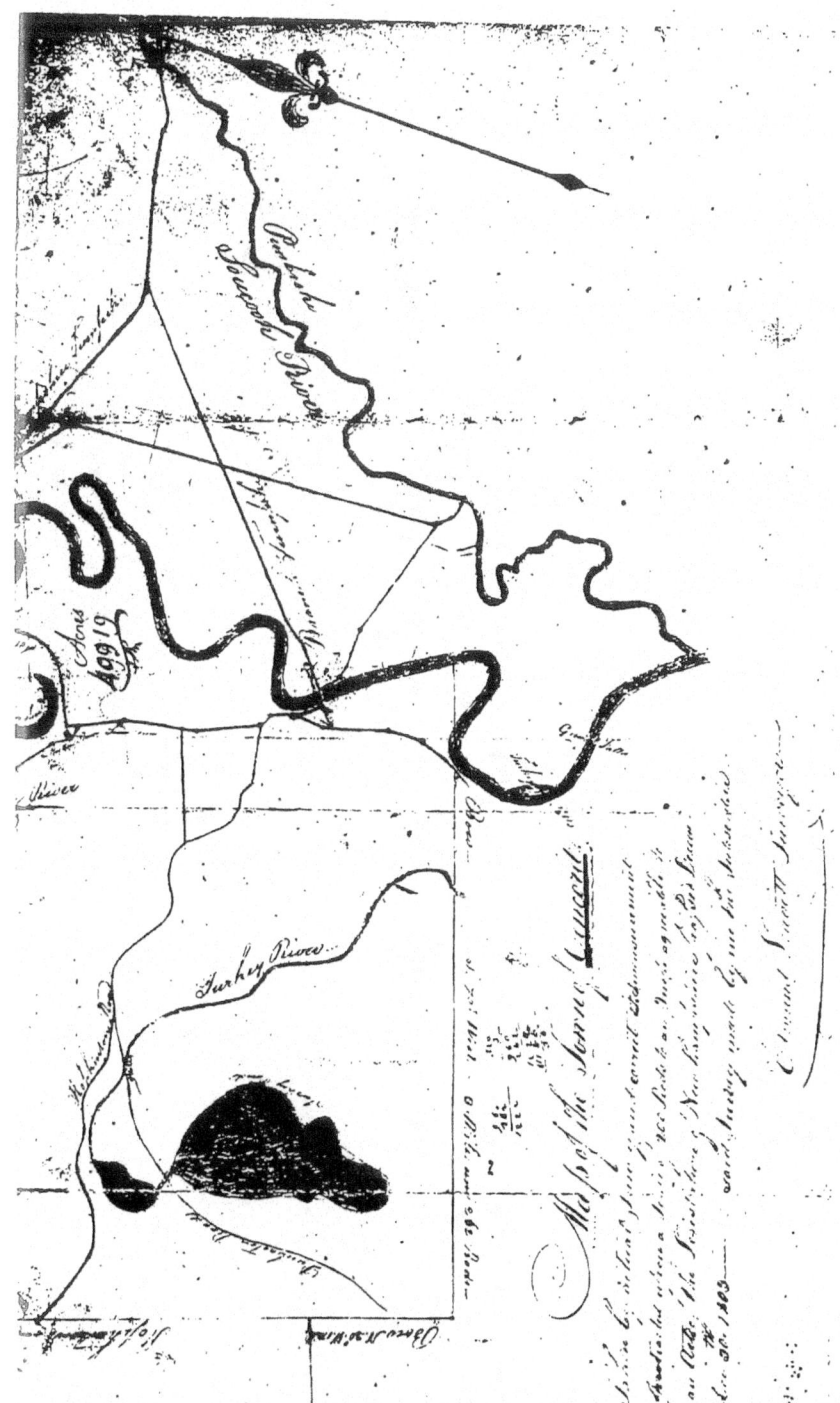

NH 1742 ESTATE TAX

Names	HEADS	HOUSEING	ACRES OF PLOW LAND	ACRES OF MOWING	ACRES OF PASTURING	HORSES
Benjamin Abbott	1	0	3	4	2	1
Edward Abbott	1	1	10	10	3	1
George Abbott	1	1	5	6	0	1
James Abbott	1	1	5	5	0	1
Nathll Abbott	1	1	7	5	0	1
Isaac Abbott	1	0	0	0	0	0
Samuel Burbank	2	1	4	4	0	1
Widow Barker	0	1	4	3	0	0
Abraham Bradlee *	2	1	8	9	0	1
Jeremiah Bradlee	1	1	1	6	0	0
Timothy Bradlee	1	1	2	1	0	1
Jonathan Bradlee	1	1	5	4	0	1
Daniel Chase	1	1	5	5	0	1
John Chandler	1	1	8	12	0	1
Lot Colbe	1	1	5	4	0	0
Ezra Carter	1	0	0	0	0	0
Abraham Colbe	1	1	0	3	0	1
Samson Colbee	1	0	0	0	0	0
David Chandler	1	1	2	0	0	1
Jeremiah Dresser	1	1	4	4	0	0

OXEN	COWS	3 YEAR OLD	2 YEAR OLD	YEARLINGS	SWINE
2	1	0	0	1	0
2	3	0	1	1	2
2	2	1	1	1	0
2	1	1	4	1	0
2	2	0	4	2	0
0	0	0	0	0	0
2	2	0	0	0	2
2	2	0	3	0	2
2	2	2	2	1	1
2	1	0	2	1	0
2	2	0	0	0	1
2	2	0	2	0	1
2	2	0	0	0	0
2	4	0	2	0	3
0	1	3	1	2	0
0	0	0	0	0	0
2	1	0	0	3	0
2	0	0	0	0	0
2	1	0	0	0	0
2	1	0	1	1	1

NH 1742 ESTATE TAX

Names	HEADS	HOUSEING	ACRES OF PLOW LAND	ACRES OF MOWING	ACRES OF PASTURING	HORSES
Cap.t Ebenezer Eastman *	2	1	20	24	3	4
Joseph Eastman	2	1	3	3	2	0
Ebenezer Eastman Jun.r	1	1	2	3	0	0
Philip Eastman	1	1	3	0	0	0
Obediah Eastman	1	0	3	0	0	1
Zebediah Farnum	1	0	2	1	0	1
Barachias Farnum ***	1	1	1	4	0	1
David Foster *	1	1	3	2	0	1
Ephraim Farnum	1	1	5	3	0	1
James Farnnum	1	1	3	2	1	0
Stephen Farington	1	1	8	5	0	1
Obediah Foster	1	0	0	0	0	0
Joseph Farnum	1	0	1	1	0	1
Benjamin Foster	1	0	0	0	0	1
Samuel Gray	1	0	0	0	0	0
Joseph Hall	1	1	2	5	2	0
Ebenezer Hall	1	0	0	0	0	0
George Hall	1	0	0	0	0	0
Richard Hazeltine	1	1	6	5	0	1
Abner Hoit	1	1	2	1	0	0

OXEN	COWS	3 YEAR OLD	2 YEAR OLD	YEARLINGS	SWINE
4	6	0	2	2	2
2	3	0	0	0	1
2	3	0	1	1	0
0	2	1	0	0	0
2	0	0	0	0	0
0	1	0	1	0	1
2	3	0	1	0	1
2	2	0	0	0	0
4	2	1	1	4	0
2	2	1	0	0	0
2	1	0	1	0	1
0	0	0	0	1	0
2	1	0	0	0	0
0	1	0	0	2	0
0	0	0	0	0	0
2	2	0	0	0	0
0	2	2	0	0	0
0	0	0	0	0	0
2	2	2	2	0	0
0	2	0	1	2	0

NH 1742 ESTATE TAX

Names	HEADS	HOUSEING	ACRES OF PLOW LAND	ACRES OF MOWING	ACRES OF PASTURING	HORSES
Jacob Hoit	1	0	0	0	0	0
Stephen Hoit	1	0	0	0	0	0
David Kimball	1	1	5	2	0	1
Philip Kimball	1	0	2	2	0	0
Abraham Kimball	1	1	4	2	0	0
Stephen Lurvee	1	0	0	0	0	0
William Lyon	1	1	0	0	0	0
John Merrill	2	1	8	6	0	1
James Osgood	1	1	5	3	0	0
Samll Putnee	2	1	3	8	0	1
William Putnee	1	0	0	0	0	0
Seborn Peters	1	1	0	1	0	0
James Peters	1	0	0	0	0	1
Obediah Peters	1	0	0	0	0	0
Benjamin Rolfe	1	1	20	14	2	1
Nathll Rolfe	1	0	11	9	2	1
Samll Rolfe	1	0	0	0	0	1
Ezra Rolfe	1	0	0	0	0	0
John Russ	1	1	3	5	0	0
Aaron Stevens	1	1	8	9	2	1

OXEN	COWS	3 YEAR OLD	2 YEAR OLD	YEARLINGS	SWINE
2	0	0	0	0	0
0	0	0	0	0	0
2	2	0	1	0	0
0	2	0	0	0	0
2	1	0	0	1	0
0	0	0	0	0	0
0	0	0	0	0	0
0	3	0	1	0	4
2	2	1	0	1	0
0	3	1	1	0	3
0	0	0	0	0	0
0	1	0	0	0	0
0	1	0	0	0	0
0	0	0	0	0	0
4	2	2	4	2	0
4	3	1	4	2	0
0	0	0	0	0	0
0	0	0	0	0	0
0	0	0	0	0	0
2	1	2	1	1	0

NH 1742 ESTATE TAX

Names	HEADS	HOUSEING	ACRES OF PLOW LAND	ACRES OF MOWING	ACRES OF PASTURING	HORSES
Nathan Stevens	1	1	3	1	0	1
Jeremiah Stickney	2	1	12	10	1	1
Jacob Shute	1	1	3	1	0	1
Ezekiel Steel	1	0	0	0	0	1
Judah Trumble	1	0	0	0	0	0
Ebenezer Virgin	1	1	5	5	0	1
John Urann	1	0	0	0	0	0
John Webster	1	1	4	8	0	0
Isaac Walker Jun*	1	1	0	1	0	0
Timothy Walker Jun*	1	1	4	2	0	0
Edward West	1	1	0	1	0	0
Nathanll West	1	1	1	1	0	0
William Walker	1	0	0	0	0	0

* 1 negro
*** 1 sawmill, 1 gristmill, 1 negro

OXEN	COWS	3 YEAR OLD	2 YEAR OLD	YEARLINGS	SWINE
2	1	0	0	0	0
3	3	1	3	1	0
0	1	0	0	0	0
0	1	0	0	0	0
0	1	0	0	0	0
2	3	2	3	2	4
0	0	0	0	0	0
0	1	0	0	1	0
0	0	1	0	0	0
0	1	1	1	2	1
0	0	0	0	0	0
1	0	0	0	0	0
0	1	0	0	0	0

Rumford May y̅e̅ 19th 1742

The aforegoing List and Inventory of the Rateable Polls and Estates in the District of Rumford was taken and given in upon Oath agreable to an Act of the General Assembly of the Province of New Hampshire saving the Polls & Estates of the aforesaid Edward West, Sampson Colbe and Jacob Hoit they being gone out of said district and did not return till after the Time was expired for taking of said List and Inventory, the List & Inventory of the Polls & Estates of the said Edward West, Sampson Colbe and Jacob Hoit was taken according to the best Information that could be had thereof

Per
Benjamin Rolfe
Clerk of Rumford

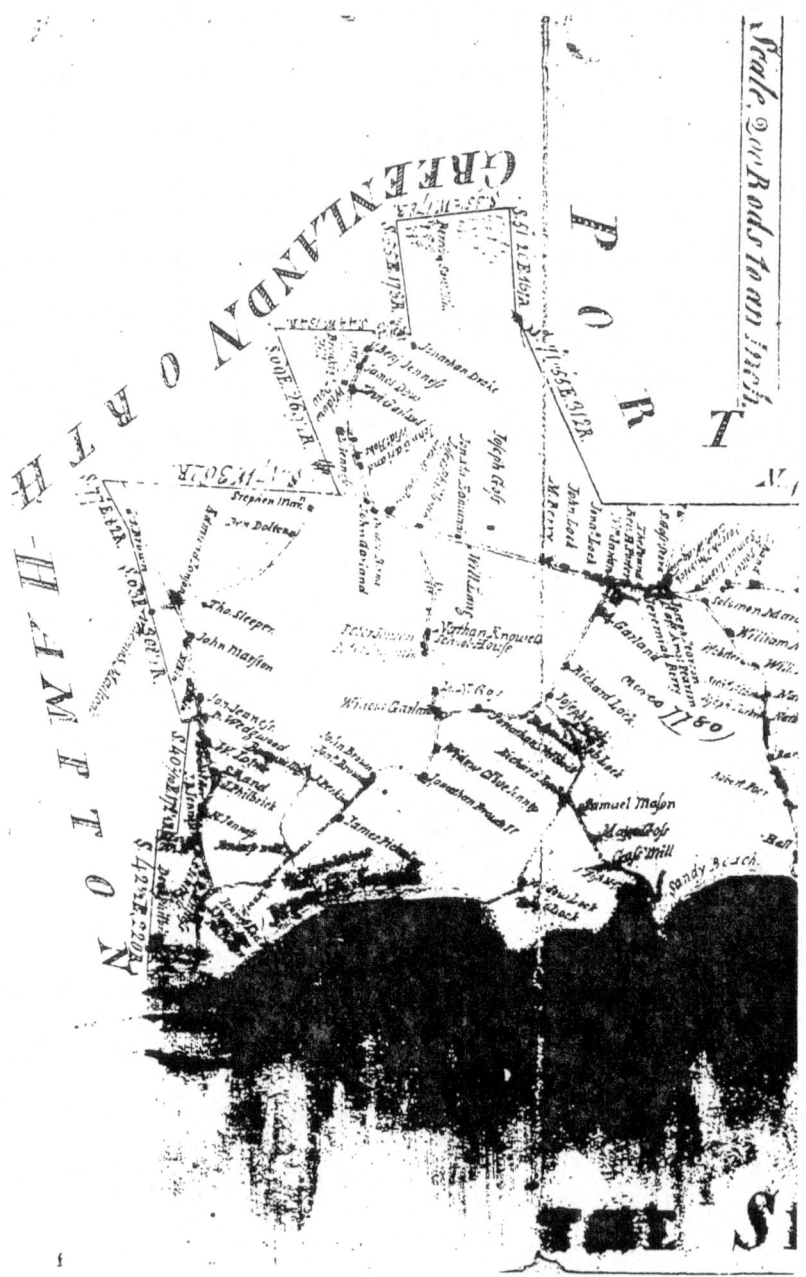

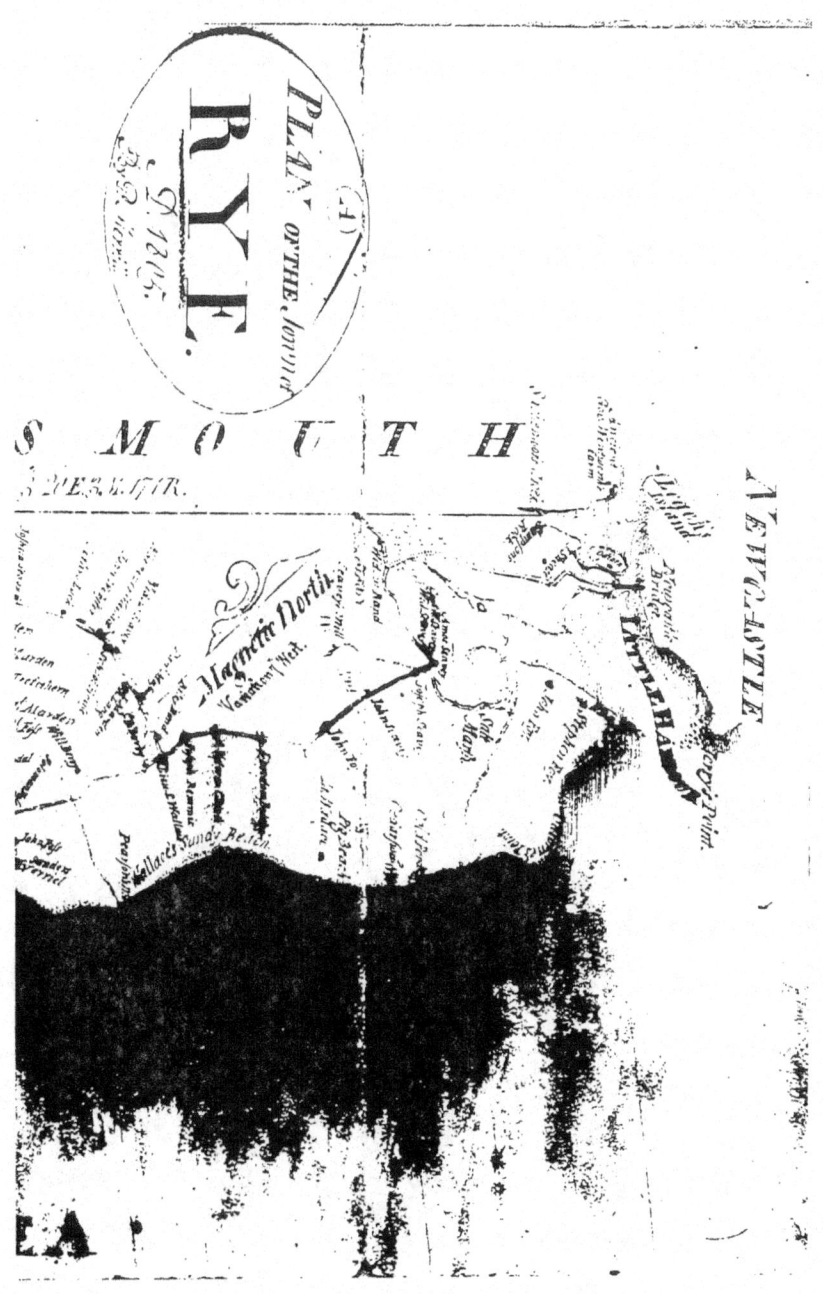

Names	POLS	HOUSING	PLANTING	HORSES	OXEN	COWS
John Knowls	2	1	20	1	0	1
John Knowls Juner	1	0	0	0	0	1
Jams Knowls	1	0	0	0	0	0
Job Innes	1	0	3	1	2	1
Joshua Innes	1	1	12	1	2	3
John Innes	1	1	12	1	2	1
Joseph Connear	1	0	0	0	0	0
Daneal Molten	1	1	15	1	0	2
James Lock	1	1	6	1	2	0
D William Lock	1	1	10	1	0	1
Eliazen Lock	1	0	6	0	0	2
Elisha Lock	1	0	0	0	0	0
William Lock Juner	1	1	1	1	0	1
John Lock	1	1	20	1	2	4
Richard Lock	1	0	0	0	0	0
Jams Porkens	2	1	20	1	2	1

Capp Jeny Saw Mill James Perkins
and gris mill at 14--0-0   Richard Rand Select men
William Seavey Gris Mill   att 6-0-0

3 YEAR OLD	2 YEAR OLD	1 YEAR OLD	SWINE
3	1	1	0
0	2	0	0
0	0	0	0
0	0	0	0
0	0	1	0
1	0	0	0
0	0	0	0
3	1	2	0
0	1	0	0
2	0	0	0
2	0	1	0
0	0	0	0
3	1	0	0
4	2	0	0
0	0	0	0
2	0	4	1

NH 1742 ESTATE TAX

Names	POLS	HOUSING	PLANTING	HORSES	OXEN	COWS
D Richard Innes	1	1	0	1	2	4
William Seavy	1	1	60	1	4	5
James Seavy	1	1	20	1	2	2
William Seavy Juner	1	1	0	0	0	0
Beniman Seavy	1	1	10	1	0	2
Beniman Seavy June*	1	1	5	0	0	2
William Seavy Tasher	1	1	0	0	0	2
Thomas Wotsen	1	0	0	0	0	0
Philip Pain	1	1	5	1	0	1
John Pain	1	0	0	0	0	0
Samuel Woles	1	1	20	1	2	3
Joseph Seavy	1	1	5	1	2	2
Joseph Seavy June*	1	0	0	0	0	0
Hinary Seavy	1	0	0	0	0	0
William Rand	1	0	5	0	2	2
Thomas Rand	1	1	5	0	0	2
Joshua Rand	1	1	5	1	2	2

3 YEAR OLD	2 YEAR OLD	1 YEAR OLD	SWINE
5	3	6	1
4	3	0	1
1	0	0	0
0	0	0	0
2	2	0	0
2	1	1	0
2	0	0	0
0	0	0	0
0	1	0	0
0	0	1	0
2	0	0	0
0	0	0	0
0	0	0	0
0	0	0	0
1	1	1	0
2	0	2	0
1	0	2	0

NH 1742 ESTATE TAX

Names	POLS	HOUSING	PLANTING	HORSES	OXEN	COWS
Samuel Bracket	2	1	50	1	2	4
Nathanel Beary	1	1	5	1	0	2
Ralond Sanders	1	0	0	0	0	1
John Sanders	1	0	0	0	0	1
Joshua fors	1	1	15	1	1	2
Nathanel fors	1	0	0	0	0	0
Nehemiah Beary	1	1	5	1	0	0
William Marden	1	1	2	0	0	1
Samuel Beary	1	1	5	1	0	2
Jothom Beary	1	0	0	0	0	2
Samuel Marden	1	1	1	1	0	1
William tucker	1	1	1	0	0	1
Zakriar Beary	1	0	1	0	1	0
Ebenezer Marden	1	1	1	0	0	1
John Jones	1	0	0	0	0	0
Jams Marden	2	1	15	1	2	2
Stepen Marden	1	1	4	1	0	2
D Nathanel Rand	1	1	1	0	0	1

RYE

3 YEAR OLD	2 YEAR OLD	1 YEAR OLD	SWINE
2	4	4	0
0	0	0	0
0	0	0	0
0	0	0	0
0	0	0	0
0	0	0	0
2	2	2	0
0	2	0	0
0	2	0	0
2	0	0	0
0	0	0	0
0	0	0	0
0	0	0	0
0	0	2	0
0	0	1	0
4	0	0	0
2	0	2	0
2	0	0	0

NH 1742 ESTATE TAX

Names	POLS	HOUSING	PLANTING	HORSES	OXEN	COWS
John Rand	1	0	0	0	0	0
Joshua Rand	1	0	2	1	0	2
William Beary	1	1	6	0	1	2
Solomon Doust	1	1	8	1	2	1
William Marden	1	1	0	0	0	1
Jonathan Marden	1	0	0	0	0	1
Samuel Doust	1	1	6	1	2	2
Wolas fors	1	0	0	0	0	0
Siman Knowls	1	1	2	1	0	1
Jathro Gors	1	1	2	0	0	1
Hinkson fors	1	1	20	1	2	4
Josiah Webster	1	1	17	1	0	1
William Chamberlin	1	1	1	0	0	1
William Pain	1	1	1	0	0	0
William Langmaid	1	0	0	0	0	0
Richard Rand	1	1	2	0	0	1
Hazikkiah Innes	1	1	10	0	0	3
Wido Innes	0	1	10	1	2	4

3 YEAR OLD	2 YEAR OLD	1 YEAR OLD	SWINE
0	0	0	0
2	0	2	0
0	0	0	0
0	1	0	0
0	0	0	0
0	0	0	0
0	2	0	0
0	0	0	0
2	0	2	0
0	0	2	0
0	2	0	0
3	3	2	0
0	0	0	0
0	0	0	0
0	0	0	0
1	0	2	0
1	1	0	0
2	3	0	0

NH 1742 ESTATE TAX

Names	POLS	HOUSING	PLANTING	HORSES	OXEN	COWS
Joseph Philbrook	1	1	0	0	0	0
Joses Philbrook	1	0	30	2	2	6
Richard Innes Ju^r	1	0	5	0	0	0
Richard Innes Taske	1	0	0	0	0	0
Stephen Palmer	1	1	0	0	0	1
Wido Molten	0	1	0	0	0	2
Cristepr Palmer	1	1	4	0	0	1
William Palmer	1	0	0	0	0	2
Hinary Elkens	1	1	10	0	0	3
Jonathan tool	1	1	10	0	0	2
Iseak Libi	1	1	30	1	2	1
Jacob Libi	1	1	30	0	0	2
John Libi	1	0	0	0	0	0
Samuel Libi	1	0	0	1	0	0
David Smith	1	1	15	1	0	2
John Lane	1	1	9	1	0	2
Frances Lock	2	1	15	1	2	3
Jams Fuler	1	0	0	0	0	2

3 YEAR OLD	2 YEAR OLD	1 YEAR OLD	SWINE
6	0	0	0
5	0	2	1
2	0	0	0
0	0	0	0
0	0	0	0
3	0	2	0
0	0	0	0
0	0	2	0
2	2	1	0
2	2	0	0
2	2	1	0
0	2	0	0
0	0	0	0
0	2	0	0
0	3	0	0
0	0	2	0
0	3	1	1
0	0	0	0

NH 1742 ESTATE TAX

Names	POLS	HOUSING	PLANTING	HORSES	OXEN	COWS
Joseph Fuler	1	1	9	0	0	1
John Fuler	1	0	6	0	2	0
Jarmier Fuler	1	0	4	0	0	0
Joseph Masten	1	1	15	1	0	1
Joseph Brown	2	1	10	0	2	2
Samuel Brown	1	0	0	1	0	0
Ephafram homs	1	1	3	1	2	1
Wido Dow	0	1	0	0	0	2
Cap Joseph Lock	1	1	30	2	2	4
Joseph Lock juner	1	1	4	1	2	2
Frances Innes	1	1	5	1	2	1
Esral Dolby	1	1	4	1	0	1
John Dolbe	1	1	4	0	0	1
Jonathan Dolbe	1	0	0	0	0	0
Samue Seavey	1	1	12	1	2	3
Osam Doust	1	1	3	1	0	1
Samuel Weals	1	1	0	0	0	0
Samuel Seavy Jun^{er}	1	1	0	0	0	0

3 YEAR OLD	2 YEAR OLD	1 YEAR OLD	SWINE
0	0	1	0
0	0	0	0
0	0	0	0
1	2	2	0
2	2	1	0
0	0	0	0
0	0	0	0
0	2	1	0
5	3	1	0
1	0	0	0
0	2	1	0
0	0	4	0
0	0	1	0
0	0	0	0
0	2	0	0
2	2	0	0
0	0	0	0
0	0	0	0

NH 1742 ESTATE TAX

Names	POLS	HOUSING	PLANTING	HORSES	OXEN	COWS
Jonathan Gors	1	1	0	0	2	0
Ebenezer Beary	1	1	10	1	2	2
Jonathan Lock	1	1	8	1	2	2
Thomas Gors	1	0	0	1	0	1
Ebenezer Philbrook	2	1	10	1	2	3
Jams Philbrook	1	1	0	0	0	2
John Garland	1	1	12	0	2	4
John Garland Juner	1	0	0	1	0	0
Widow Knowls	2	1	10	1	2	2

RYE

3 YEAR OLD	2 YEAR OLD	1 YEAR OLD	SWINE
0	0	0	0
0	2	1	0
0	2	0	0
2	0	1	0
1	0	1	0
0	0	0	0
0	3	1	0
0	2	0	0
0	1	1	0

June the 8th 1742 the Selectmen that signd the above account made oath that the above is a true & Exact List of at the rateable Poles and estates within the dist of Rye of their understanding Swown before
   Sam^{ll} Gilman Justice of Peace

Taken by order of the Genl Assembly Last Sessions According to the best of their understanding
Sworn before   Sam^{ll} Gilman Justice of Peace

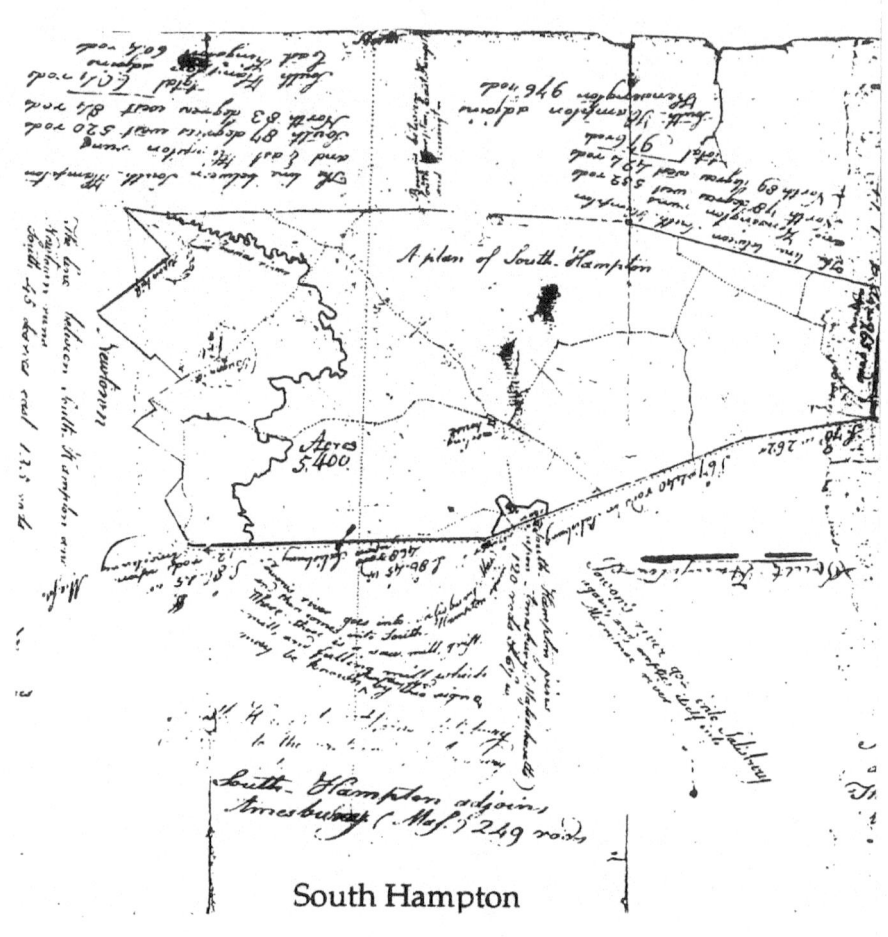

South Hampton

SOUTH HAMPTON

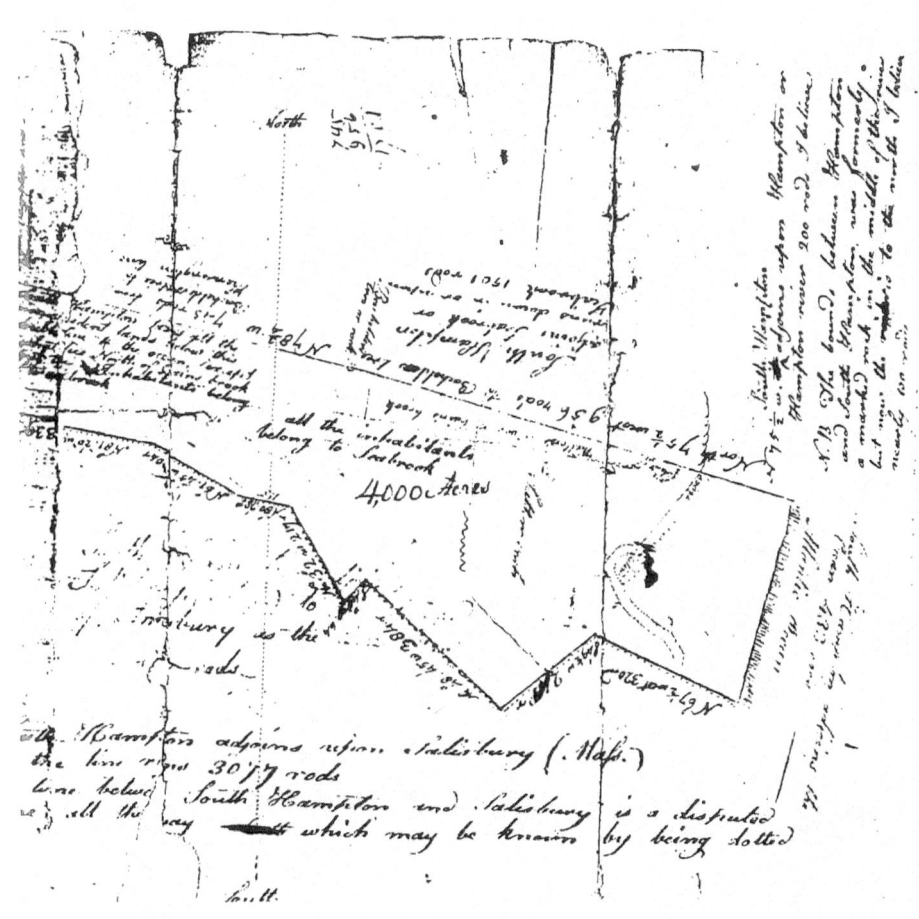

NH 1742 ESTATE TAX

The invoice of yͤ part of yͤ Destrict Called Amesbury	HEADS	HOUSEING	PLANTING	MOWING	PASTURE	HORSES
Jonathan Currier	3	1	2	0	5	0
Richard Currier	1	1	3	3	5	1
Jonathan Kimball	1	1	2	2	2	1
Benjamin Kimball	1	1	1	0	1	1
Caleb Hobbs	1	0	0	0	0	0
Roger Easman	1	1	3	1	3	1
Jacob Morss	2	1	3	0	4	1
Caleb Hobbs Jun	1	1	0	0	0	0
Jonathan Watson	1	1	1	0	1	1
James George	1	1	1½	0	3	1
Jno Elliot	2	1	1	0	2	1
Jonathan Farran	2	1	3½	0	6	1
Samll Goodwin	1	1	1	1	1	1
Phillip Challis	1	1	1	2	4	0
David Goodwin	1	1	1	1	2	1
Mick͠ Hoyt	1	1	1	2½	4	1
Aaron Currier	1	1	1½	½	5	1
David Colby	1	1	1½	0	1	0
Zeccheus Colby	1	1	1½	0	1	0
Jacob Colby	1	1	0	0	0	0
Roglers Colby	1	0	0	0	0	0

SOUTH HAMPTON

OXEN	COWS	3 YEAR OLD	2 YEAR OLD	YEARLING	SWINE
2	4	2	0	2	2
2	2	0	2	1	1
2	3	0	3	2	1
0	2	2	0	1	1
0	2	0	0	0	0
2	2	0	0	1	1
0	1	0	1	0	0
0	0	0	0	0	0
2	2	0	0	0	0
2	2	0	0	0	1
2	1	0	1	0	1
4	3	0	1	1	1
0	2	0	1	0	1
0	0	0	0	0	0
0	1	0	0	0	0
2	2	0	2	2	0
0	1	0	3	2	1
0	2	2	0	1	1
0	1	0	1	0	1
0	2	0	0	0	0
0	0	0	1	0	0

NH 1742 ESTATE TAX

The invoice of ý part of ý Destrict Called Amesbury	HEADS	HOUSEING	PLANTING	MOWING	PASTURE	HORSES
David Elliot	1	1	1	1½	0	0
Thomas Carter	1	1	0	0	0	0
Abraham Morrill	1	1	1½	2	3	0
Robart Martin	1	1	1½	1½	1½	0
George Martin	1	0	0	0	0	0
Ezra Tucker	1	1	2	1½	0	1
David Bagly	1	1	1	3	0	1
Andrew Whicher	1	1	1	1	0	0
Daniel Sargent	1	1	1	0	2	0
Gideon Bartlet	1	1	0	0	1	0
Willm Rowel	1	1	2	3	1	1
Cuttin Feaver	1	1	2	2	5	1
Willm Shargent	1	0	0	0	0	0
Joseph Bartlet	1	1	4	6	10	3

SOUTH HAMPTON

OXEN	COWS	3 YEAR OLD	2 YEAR OLD	YEARLING	SWINE
2	2	0	1	2	0
0	0	0	0	0	0
2	2	0	0	3	0
0	1	0	0	0	1
0	0	0	0	0	0
0	2	0	0	0	0
2	2	0	0	1	1
0	1	2	1	1	0
0	1	0	0	0	1
0	2	0	4	0	0
0	3	2	0	2	1
0	2	0	2	0	1
0	0	0	0	0	0
2	5	2	4	5	1

NH 1742 ESTATE TAX

The invoice of y' part of y' Destrict Called Amesbury	HEADS	HOUSEING	PLANTING	MOWING	PASTURE	HORSES
John Straw	1	1	3	5	0	1
John Peaslee	1	1	4	7	16	1
John Peaslee Jun	1	1	5	8	4	1
Samll Plummer	2	1	2	3	2	1
Peter Morss	1	1	4	4	0	1
William Sayer	1	1	1	0	1	0
Samll Jacman	1	1	0	0	0	0
John Webster	1	1	0	3	0	1
Nathan Hunt	1	0	0	0	0	0
Edmond Sayer	1	1	1	0	0	0
Benjamin Hadley	1	1	1	0	0	2
Richard Goodwin	1	0	0	0	0	0
Nathan Goodwin	1	0	0	0	0	0
Josph Hadley	2	1	3	0	3	1
Thomas Williams	1	1	1	3	0	1
Jeremiah Calton	1	1	3	10	8	1
Thomas Stevens	1	1	2	0	2	1
Aaron Stevens	1	1	2½	0	0	0
Thomas Jonson	1	1	2	4	0	1

OXEN	COWS	3 YEAR OLD	2 YEAR OLD	YEARLING	SWINE
2	2	0	0	1	0
2	2	2	1	3	0
2	3	0	1	3	0
2	1	0	0	0	0
4	3	0	0	1	0
2	2	0	0	1	0
0	1	0	0	0	0
2	2	0	2	5	0
0	0	0	0	0	0
2	0	0	0	0	0
0	1	0	2	0	0
0	1	0	0	0	0
0	1	0	0	0	0
2	2	0	1	2	0
0	2	0	0	2	0
4	3	0	0	0	0
0	1	0	0	0	0
0	1	2	0	0	0
2	1	0	1	2	1

NH 1742 ESTATE TAX

Names	HEADS	HOUSEING	PLANTING	MOWING	PASTURE	HORSES
Richd Fitts	1	1	3	3	5	1
Abner Morril	1	1	4	4	3	1
Ezek Morril	1	1	5	7	13	1
Orlando Weed	1	0	0	0	0	0
Jno Morril	1	1	0	0	0	0
Paul Morril	1	1	3	4	0	1
Sam^{ll} Currier	1	1	4	3	15	1
Hen Currier	1	1	3	6	15	1
Rubⁿ Currier	1	1	2	4	10	1
Danl French	1	1	3	4	10	1
Eben French	1	1	3	5	20	1
Josep French	1	1	3	5	20	1
Sam French J^u	1	1	3	2	10	1
Hen French	1	1	1	4	10	1
Eph^r Carter	2	1	4	2	20	1
Josh^a Clough	1	1	1	3	1	0
Jo^s Flandrs	1	1	2	2	4	0
Jno Flanders	2	1	4	1	5	0
Tho Rowell	1	1	2	5	10	1
Elijah Rowel	1	1	2	1	0	1

SOUTH HAMPTON

OXEN	COWS	3 YEAR OLD	2 YEAR OLD	YEARLING	SWINE
2	3	0	0	2	0
0	3	0	0	4	0
0	3	0	0	0	0
0	1	0	0	0	0
0	0	0	0	0	0
2	2	0	0	1	0
0	3	0	0	4	1
2	4	0	0	5	1
0	3	2	0	1	0
2	3	0	0	1	1
2	0	1	2	3	1
0	3	2	3	1	1
2	3	0	0	2	0
2	2	0	1	1	1
2	2	0	1	1	0
0	1	0	0	1	0
0	1	0	0	0	0
2	2	0	1	3	1
0	2	0	1	2	0
0	0	0	0	1	0

NH 1742 ESTATE TAX

Names	HEADS	HOUSEING	PLANTING	MOWING	PASTURE	HORSES
Tho Merrill	2	1	5	10	25	1
Josph Merrill	1	½ 1	0	0	0	0
James Merril	1	½ 1	0	0	0	0
Danl Carter	1	1	2	0	3	0
Joseph Towel	1	1	0	1	0	1
Joseph Gould	1	1	1	0	4	1
Joseph Jones	1	1	2	0	6	1
David Weed	1	0	0	0	0	0
Tho Morril	1	0	0	0	0	0
Joseph Morrill	1	1	2	1	5	1
Ruben Dimond	3	1	1	1	10	1
Sam Barnard Jun	1	1	3	1	4	1
Sam Straw	2	1	3	2	6	1
Nath^{nel} Morril	1	1	4	4	10	1
Nath^{nel} Merril	1	1	1	2	6	0
John Bartlet	1	1	2	2	6	1
Jerem^{ah} Flandrs	1	1	3	4	20	1
Sam Morril	1	1	3½	2	8	0
Lawre^{nce} Straw	1	1	2	4	3	1
Widow Weed	0	1	1	1	5	0

SOUTH HAMPTON

OXEN	COWS	3 YEAR OLD	2 YEAR OLD	YEARLING	SWINE
0	4	0	2	0	0
2	2	0	0	1	1
0	2	0	0	1	0
2	2	0	0	0	1
2	3	0	2	3	1
0	1	2	0	0	0
0	2	0	0	0	0
0	1	0	0	0	0
0	0	0	0	0	1
0	1	0	1	0	0
2	3	0	3	3	1
0	2	0	2	2	0
2	2	0	0	1	2
0	1	0	1	0	1
0	2	0	2	1	1
2	2	0	0	1	0
0	3	0	2	4	1
2	2	0	1	3	1
2	2	0	0	1	1
0	2	0	0	0	0

NH 1742 ESTATE TAX

Names	HEADS	HOUSEING	PLANTING	MOWING	PASTURE	HORSES
Ezekl Hoyt	1	1	2	0	2	0
Jonath Flandrs	1	1	0	0	0	0
Richd Collins	1	1	0	3	3	0
William Collins	1	0	0	0	0	0
Jacob Fowler	1	1	4	3	20	1
Abner Fowler	1	0	0	0	0	0
Ephr Brown	1	1	4	6	20	1
Stph Flandrs	1	0	0	0	0	0

SOUTH HAMPTON

OXEN	COWS	3 YEAR OLD	2 YEAR OLD	YEARLING	SWINE
0	2	0	0	1	0
0	1	0	0	0	0
0	2	0	2	0	0
0	0	0	0	0	0
0	3	0	1	2	0
0	0	0	1	0	0
0	4	0	0	6	1
0	0	0	0	0	1

NH 1742 ESTATE TAX

Names	HEADS	HOUSEING	PLANTING	MEADOW	PASTURE	HORSES
Asa Flanders	1	1	2	2	10	1
Sam^u Flanders	1	1	2	2	10	0
Daniel Page	1	1	2	1	0	1
Abra^m Brown	2	1	3	6	16	2
Amos Page	1	1	1	5	1	1
Caleb Clough	2	1	3	3	9	1
John Dow	1	1	3	3	1	1
Benj^a Brown	4	1	0	7	1	2
Sam^u French	2	1	0	6	20	1
Nathl Maxfield	1	1	4	6	8	1
Philip Flanders	0	0	0	2	13	0
Philp Flanders Ju	0	0	4	1	7	0
Jonathan Jewel	1	0	0	0	0	0
Abrd^l Bronell	0	0	0	5	12	0
Nathan Dow	1	0	0	0	0	0
Ben^j Currier	0	0	0	0	10	0
Solmon Shephard	0	0	3	0	20	0
Sam^u Barnard	1	0	0	0	15	0
Joseph Chandler	2	1	0	0	5	0
Nathan Gould	2	1	2½	0	15	0

SOUTH HAMPTON

OXEN	COWS	3 YEAR OLD	2 YEAR OLD	YEARLING	SWINE
0	1	0	0	0	0
0	1	2	1	0	0
0	3	0	0	2	0
2	4	0	2	6	1
0	1	0	0	0	0
0	1	0	3	0	0
0	2	0	0	0	0
2	3	0	1	6	0
0	3	2	2	3	0
0	2	3	0	0	0
0	0	0	0	0	0
0	0	0	0	0	0
0	0	0	0	0	0
0	0	0	0	0	0
0	1	0	0	0	0
0	0	0	0	0	0
0	0	0	0	0	0
0	0	0	0	0	0
0	0	0	2	1	1
0	2	0	2	0	1

NH 1742 ESTATE TAX

Names	HEADS	HOUSEING	PLANTING	MEADOW	PASTURE	HORSES
Jacob Currier	0	0	1	2	10	0
Jn° Bartleway	0	0	0	0	4	0
David Ring	1	0	0	4	0	0
Israel Currier	0	0	2	0	5	0
John True	1	1	4	6	10	1
Joseph Tucker	1	1	0	0	0	0
Widow French	0	1	3	4	8	1
Jonath Hoyt	1	1	1	0	0	0
Joseph Maxfield	0	0	2	4	3	0
Jn° Easman	0	0	0	0	9	0
Ben^j Morril	0	0	0	2	0	0
Jn° Page	1	1	5	0	10	1
Seth Bartlet	0	0	0	0	10	0
Jn° Evens	0	0	2	4	10	0
Sam Brown	0	0	0	0	15	0
Widow Griffon	1	1	2	2	8	1
Ben^t Baker	1	1	3	5	8	1
Timothy Townsend	0	0	0	0	20	0
William Straw	0	0	0	0	6	0
William Morrill	0	0	0	0	6	0

SOUTH HAMPTON

OXEN	COWS	3 YEAR OLD	2 YEAR OLD	YEARLING	SWINE
0	0	0	0	0	0
0	0	0	0	0	0
0	0	0	0	0	0
0	0	0	0	0	0
1	2	0	0	1	0
0	0	0	0	0	0
2	2	0	0	4	0
0	1	0	0	0	0
0	0	0	0	0	0
0	0	0	0	0	0
0	0	0	0	0	0
0	1	4	5	2	0
0	0	0	0	0	0
0	0	0	0	0	0
0	0	0	0	0	0
0	2	0	1	0	0
1	1	0	1	1	0
0	0	0	0	0	0
0	0	0	0	0	0
0	0	0	0	0	0

Names	HEADS	HOUSEING	PLANTING	MEADOW	PASTURE	HORSES
Zeccheas Clough	0	0	0	0	7	0
Jonat[hn] Jones	0	0	1½	0	6	0
John Currier	0	0	1½	2	0	0
John Easman	0	0	0	2	4	0

OXEN	COWS	3 YEAR OLD	2 YEAR OLD	YEARLING	SWINE
0	0	0	0	0	0
2	1	1	1	1	0
0	0	0	0	0	0
0	0	0	0	0	0

NH 1742 ESTATE TAX

Names	HEADS	HOUSEING	PLANTING	MOWING	PASTURE	HORSES
Jonathan Calton	1	1	4	4	3	1
John Shargent	1	0	0	0	0	0
Moses Calton	1	1	3	3	0	1
Nathan Peaslee	1	1	0	6	3	0
George Hadley	1	1	0	2	0	1
Samuel Hadley	1	1	2	0	3	0
John Hadley	1	0	0	0	0	0
James Ordeway	1	0	0	0	0	0
Jacob Peaslee	1	0	0	0	0	0
Moses Peaslee	1	0	3	3	5	0
James Peaslee	1	0	3	3	0	1
Joseph Peaslee	1	1	4	6	5	1
David Peaslee	1	0	0	0	0	0
John Challis	1	1	3	0	0	1
John Martain Ju	1	0	0	0	0	0
Francis Chass	1	1	3	3	0	1
Samuel Peaslee	0	1	3	6	6	0
John Martain	1	1	3	3	1	1
Joshua Moody	0	0	2½	0	0	0
Samuel Davies	2	1	4	6	0	1

SOUTH HAMPTON

OXEN	COWS	3 YEAR OLD	2 YEAR OLD	YEARLING	SWINE
4	3	0	0	0	0
0	0	0	0	0	0
4	2	2	0	0	0
4	1	0	0	2	0
0	1	0	0	2	0
0	2	4	0	0	0
0	0	0	0	0	0
0	0	0	0	0	0
0	1	0	0	0	0
0	1	0	1	2	0
2	0	0	0	0	0
0	2	0	2	1	1
0	0	0	0	0	0
2	1	0	0	0	0
0	1	0	0	0	0
4	2	0	4	0	0
0	0	0	0	0	0
1	3	0	0	1	0
0	0	0	0	0	0
2	1	0	2	0	2

NH 1742 ESTATE TAX

Names	HEADS	HOUSEING	PLANTING	MOWING	PASTURE	HORSES
Thomas Davies	2	1	0	0	0	1
Moses Sanders	1	1	3	3	0	0
David Straw	1	0	0	0	0	0
Shargent Hath	1	1	2	0	3	0
Enock Brown	1	1	0	0	0	0
Philip Shargent	1	1	2	2	1	0
David Shargent	1	1	1	3	8	1
Peter Colby	1	1	1	2	0	0
Samuel Hadley	1	1	0	3	5	1
Daniel Kelley	1	1	1	1½	8	1
Benjam Woodbridge	0	0	1	1	0	0
Henry Bagly	1	1	2	3	2	1
Josiah Bartlet	0	0	0	2	4	0
Charles Chass	0	0	0	0	4	0
Daniel Gould	1	1	2	0	3	1
Timothy Whitcher	1	1	1	0	0	0
Nathaniel Ash	1	1	2	3	3	0
Thomas Towel	1	1	1½	3	3	1
Henry Flood	1	0	0	0	0	0
William Shargent Ju	1	0	0	0	0	0

SOUTH HAMPTON

OXEN	COWS	3 YEAR OLD	2 YEAR OLD	YEARLING	SWINE
2	1	0	0	4	1
1	1	0	0	0	0
0	0	0	2	0	0
0	0	0	0	0	0
0	0	0	0	0	0
0	2	0	2	1	0
0	3	0	0	1	1
0	0	0	2	0	1
0	1	2	0	0	0
2	2	0	0	0	0
0	0	0	0	0	0
2	1	0	1	2	1
0	0	0	0	0	0
0	0	0	0	0	0
0	2	2	0	0	0
0	1	0	0	0	0
2	1	0	1	2	1
2	1	0	0	0	0
0	0	0	0	0	0
0	0	0	0	0	0

NH 1742 ESTATE TAX

The invoice of yᵉ part of Salisbury Called byfield	HEADS	HOUSEING	PLANTING	MOWING	PASTURE	HORSES
Jnᵒ Collins	1	1	3	0	10	1
Joseph Page	1	1	5	0	8	0
Samᵘ Smith	1	1	1	0	0	1
Jnᵒ Eaton	2	1	3	0	6	0
Samᵘ Fowler	1	1	3	0	5	0
Bejaᵐ Selley	1	1	2	0	0	1
Ephraim Eatton	1	1	4	1	10	1
Jabez Eatton	1	1	4	1	10	1
Samᵘ Walton	1	1	2	0	0	1
Jonathan Walton	1	0	0	0	0	0
Jermʰ Wheler	1	0	0	0	0	0
John Eatton Ju	1	1	0	0	0	0
David Fowler	1	0	0	0	0	0
Samᵘ Selley	1	0	0	0	0	0
John Worthen	1	1	4	0	0	0
Elihu Dow	1	1	2	0	6	0
Elifess Dow	1	0	0	0	0	0
Judah Dow	1	1	3	0	8	0
Bildad Dow	1	1	0	0	1	0
Noah Dow	1	1	1½	0	11	0

SOUTH HAMPTON

OXEN	COWS	3 YEAR OLD	2 YEAR OLD	YEARLING	SWINE
0	2	3	5	4	0
2	2	1	1	0	1
0	2	0	2	2	0
0	1	1	0	4	0
0	1	0	0	2	0
0	0	4	0	0	0
0	2	0	3	0	0
0	3	2	2	1	0
0	1	0	0	0	0
0	0	0	0	0	0
0	1	0	0	0	0
0	1	0	0	0	0
0	1	0	0	0	0
0	1	0	0	0	0
0	2	0	0	0	0
0	2	0	0	0	0
0	0	0	0	0	0
0	0	0	0	0	0
0	0	0	0	0	0
0	1	0	0	0	0

NH 1742 ESTATE TAX

The invoice of ỹ part of Salisbury Called byfield	HEADS	HOUSEING	PLANTING	MOWING	PASTURE	HORSES
David Norten	1	1	1½	0	0	0
Joseph Norten	1	0	0	0	0	0
Trustrom Collins	1	1	4	0	2	1
Bejaᵐ Collins	1	1	3	0	4	0
Samᵘ Collins	1	0	0	0	0	0
Thomas Selley	1	1	2	0	2	1
Benjamin Hoyt	1	1	2	2	0	0
Richd Smith	1	0	0	0	0	0
Jacob Smith	1	0	0	0	0	0
Joseph Todd	1	1	1	0	0	1
James Jacman	2	1	3	4	20	1
Israel Shepherd	2	0	2	0	0	0
Sanders Car	0	0	2	0	4	0
Widow Smith	0	1	8	0	20	1

SOUTH HAMPTON

OXEN	COWS	3 YEAR OLD	2 YEAR OLD	YEARLING	SWINE
0	1	0	0	0	0
0	0	0	0	0	0
0	2	0	1	0	0
0	1	0	1	0	0
0	0	0	0	0	0
0	0	0	0	0	0
0	2	0	0	0	0
0	0	0	0	0	0
0	0	0	0	0	0
0	0	0	0	0	0
2	3	1	1	2	0
0	2	0	0	0	0
0	0	0	0	0	0
4	3	1	2	3	1

NH 1742 ESTATE TAX

a List of the Salt Meadow

Name	acres	Name	acres
John Collins	12	Joseph Page Ju	2
Trustrom Collins	4	Sam Smith	3
Benjamin Collins	3	Widow Smnith	20
John Dow	2	Benjamin Sylli	2
Noah Dow	2	Abraham Brown	15
Bildad Dow	2	Ephraim Brown	2
Samll	6	Benjamin Brown	4
Jabez Eaton	4	William Busel	15
Ephriaim Eaton	5	Ephraim Brown	2
Samll French	2	Samuel Brown	10
Widow French	3	Thomas Clough	4
Nathaniel Maxfield	3	Aaron Clough	5
Paul Morrill	4	Sanders Carr	5
Jn° Page	3	Jeremiah Dow	5
Samuel Dow	2	Samuel Eaton	3
John Easman	2	John Eavens ju	2
Benjamin Easman ju	2	Benjamin Easman	2
Henry Eaten	4	Eliphelet French	2
Timothy French	6	Thomas Flanders	2
Phillip Flanders	2	Andrew Greele	20
Phillip Greele	1	Daniel Gill	6
John Gill	6	Benjamin Hoyt	2
Jeremiah Fog	1	Benjamim Morrill	2
Jacob Morrill	4	John Morrill	5

Reuben Morrill	4
Abraham Morrill	2
Moses Merrill	3
Stephen Merrill	3
William Osgood	2
David Osgood	2
John Pike	2
Onecipheris Page	5
John Peurinton	3
Jonathan Stevens	1
William Smith	14
Elias Smith	6
Capt Jeremiah Stevens	2
James Tucker	3
John True Decn	8
William True	3
James Thorn	2
Abner Samborn	6
Benjamin Green	3
Thomas Brown	3
Jonathan Brown	3
Samuel Melcher	4
Cap^{tn} Banfield	4
Cap^{tn} Orneld Widow	6

First New District South Hamton

June the 8th 1742 Reuben Diamond made oath that these two sheets of Papper containe a True and exact accompt of the Rateable Poles & Estates that lies within the district that he was appointed to take by the Comittee that was appointed by an act of the Last Gen[u] assembly of the Province of new hampshire Sworn before Sam[u] Gilman Justice of Peace

Reuben Diamond

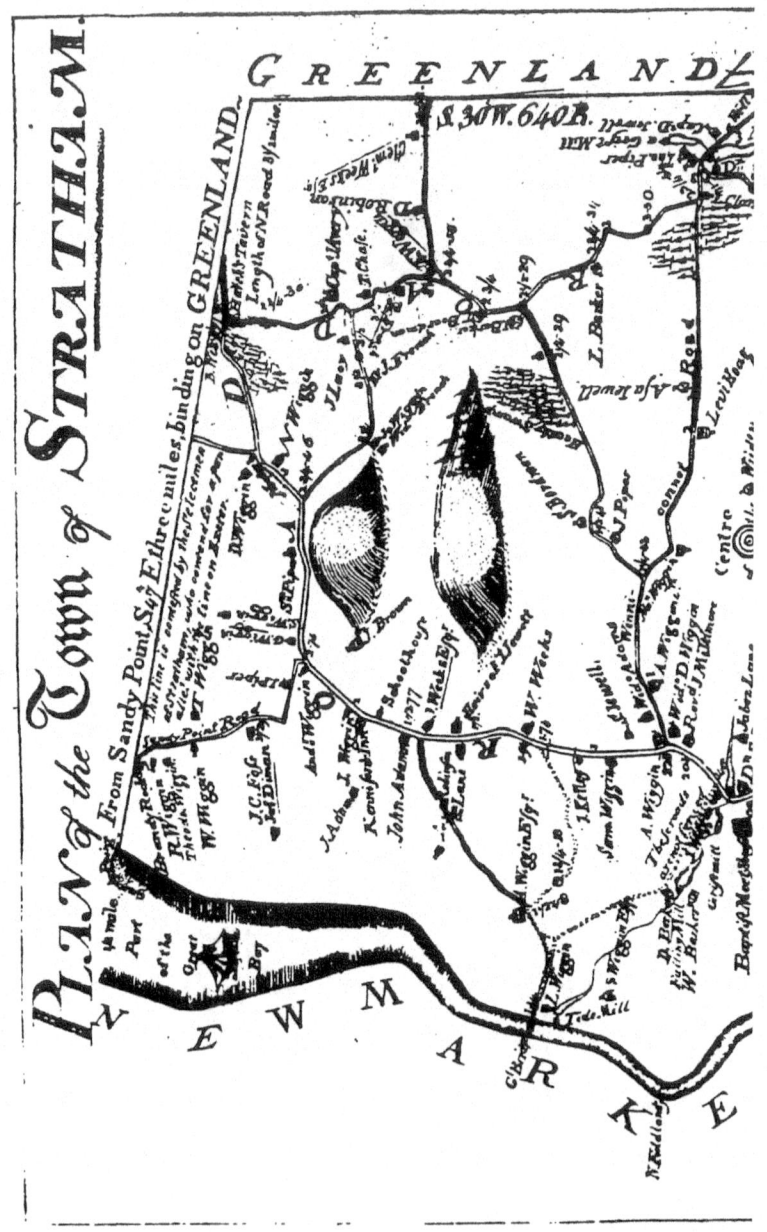

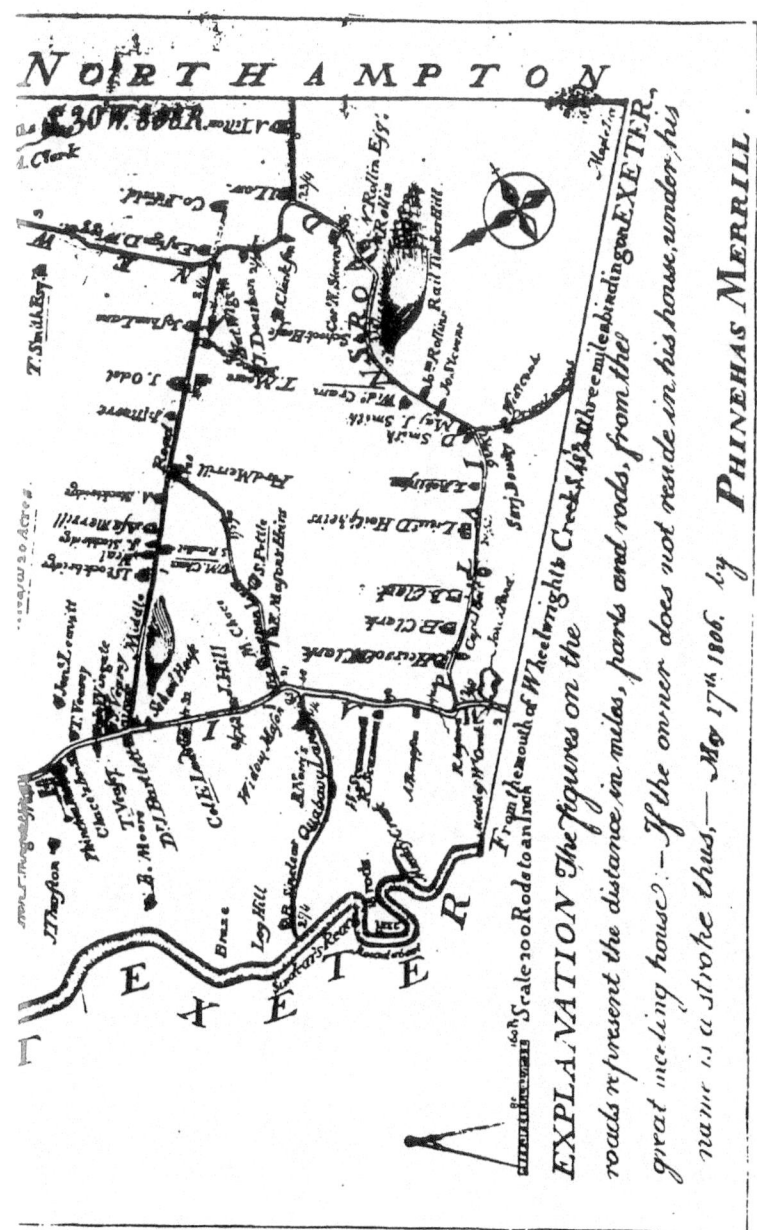

NH 1742 ESTATE TAX

The True Inventory take of the Polls and By order of the Genrell Court to the Present

Names	POLS	OXEN	COWS	3 YEAR OLD	2 YEAR OLD	1 YEAR OLD
George Wesey	2	0	4	2	3	0
Richard Calley	1	0	3	0	2	3
Joseph Baman	1	0	1	0	5	0
Ben^m Bannar	1	0	0	0	0	0
Jonathan Chase	2	0	2	2	2	3
Benamin Nerrs	1	4	3	0	2	5
Solomon Smith	2	0	0	0	0	0
John Hennford	1	0	2	0	2	0
Richard Sinkler	2	4	4	0	2	1
Jonathan Sibley	1	0	1	0	1	1
Willm Schaman	2	2	6	0	2	6
Mathew Tompsin	1	1	0	0	1	0
Matthew Tompson Junr	1	0	0	0	0	2
John Sped	2	0	2	0	0	2
Beny^m Jones	3	1	6	0	3	2
Richard Baman	1	0	1	0	0	0
John Colby	1	0	0	0	0	0

HORSES	SWINE	PLANTING	PASTURE	HOUSING
1	1	30	22	1
1	0	15	22	0
1	1	13	0	1
0	0	1	0	0
1	0	30	20	1
1	1	23	36	1
0	0	0	0	1
1	0	10	10	1
1	0	6	12	1
0	0	10	4	1
2	0	50	50	1
0	0	12	6	1
0	0	0	0	0
1	0	9	5	1
1	1	10	10	1
0	0	0	0	0
0	0	0	0	0

NH 1742 ESTATE TAX

Names	POLS	OXEN	COWS	3 YEAR OLD	2 YEAR OLD	1 YEAR OLD
John Meeds	2	0	2	0	0	3
Cap. Moore	1	0	3	2	2	2
Willm Moore	1	4	4	0	0	3
John Coper	1	0	4	0	2	3
Danied Stvens	1	0	3	2	0	0
Joseph Rolongs	1	2	4	0	2	4
Joshua Rolongs	1	0	3	0	1	2
Benj.^m Tayler	1	0	2	0	0	1
Edward Tayler	2	2	3	3	2	0

HORSES	SWINE	PLANTING	PASTURE	HOUSING
1	0	12	6	1
1	0	20	15	1
1	0	20	15	0
0	0	34	16	1
1	0	6	13	1
2	1	36	25	1
1	1	0	0	1
0	5	0	0	1
1	0	20	20	1

June 8th 1742

William Moore and George Veasy Junr Made Oth that the winthin is a true and exact List of all the Poles & Estates in Stratham in the Several Precenets that was allotted them to take according to order of the Gen^{ll} Assembly Last Sessions to the best of their understanding Sworn Before

Juner
Willm Moore Selet
man

NH 1742 ESTATE TAX

Names	POLS	OXEN	COWS	3 YEAR OLD	2 YEAR OLD	1 YEAR OLD
Jonathan Rolongs	1	2	2	0	3	2
Widdow Rolongs	0	0	0	0	0	0
Daveid Rolongs	1	0	1	1	0	1
Moses Rolings	1	0	0	0	0	1
Thomas Rolongs Junr	1	0	0	0	0	0
Thomas Rolongs	2	2	4	0	2	1
Calup Rolongs	1	2	4	0	1	3
Benj^m Taylar	1	2	4	0	2	1
Willm Chase	2	0	2	0	1	1
Joseph Smith	1	0	3	0	4	1
Josiah Smith	1	4	4	0	0	3
Joseph Larnes	2	2	4	0	0	2
John Wooddly	1	2	1	0	1	0
Joseph Horitt	2	2	3	0	1	1
Joseph Egley	1	2	3	0	0	4
Theopls Runlet	1	4	4	0	3	3
John Clark	1	4	4	0	2	3
Joseph Clark	1	0	0	0	0	0
Mr Miles Levitt	1	0	0	0	0	0

HORSES	SWINE	PLANTING	PASTURE	HOUSING
1	0	20	20	1
0	0	5	5	0
0	0	0	0	0
1	0	0	0	0
0	0	0	0	0
1	1	15	14	1
1	1	15	14	1
1	1	24	16	1
1	0	7	7	1
1	0	14	7	0
1	0	18	18	1
1	0	10	10	1
1	0	16	18	1
2	0	15	16	1
1	1	20	16	1
1	1	20	20	1
1	0	20	20	1
0	0	0	0	0
0	0	0	0	0

NH 1742 ESTATE TAX

Names	POLS	OXEN	COWS	3 YEAR OLD	2 YEAR OLD	1 YEAR OLD
Tusteen Wiggen	1	1	2	4	0	4
Wolter Wiggen	1	1	2	4	0	0
Joshua Neall	1	1	2	3	0	1
Joshua Kinston	1	1	0	1	0	0
Samuel Wiggen	1	1	0	1	0	1
Joseph Wiggen Junr	1	0	0	1	0	0
John Wiggen	1	1	2	3	0	1
James Kenston	1	1	0	3	0	0
Widdow Steven	0	1	0	1	0	1
Josiah Pasens	2	1	0	2	0	1
Josiah Pasens Junr	1	0	0	0	0	0
Cornet Wiggen	1	1	2	3	0	4
Samuel Piper Junr	1	1	2	1	0	2
Richard Crocket	1	1	0	1	0	0
Richard Young	2	1	0	1	0	0
John Wiggen Junr	1	0	0	0	0	0
William Burly	2	1	0	3	0	1
Samuel Piper	1	1	0	3	0	0
Josiah Piper	1	0	2	0	0	0

HORSES	SWINE	PLANTING	PASTURE	HOUSING
3	1	0	24	18
3	0	0	10	6
2	1	0	12	12
0	0	0	4	2
1	0	0	4	4
0	0	0	0	0
1	1	1	14	10
0	1	0	6	6
0	1	0	6	5
2	1	0	20	14
0	0	0	0	0
0	1	0	20	25
3	1	1	20	15
0	0	0	3	4
0	1	0	0	0
0	0	0	0	0
2	1	0	10	8
0	0	0	0	0
0	1	0	15	6

NH 1742 ESTATE TAX

Names	POLS	OXEN	COWS	3 YEAR OLD	2 YEAR OLD	1 YEAR OLD
Jonathan Piper	1	1	2	2	0	0
John Piper	1	1	0	5	0	0
John Sinkler	2	1	2	4	2	2
Isaac Fors	3	1	4	4	0	1
Ephraim Croket	1	1	0	2	0	0
Richard Croket Junr	1	0	0	1	0	0
Bengimon Juet	2	1	0	3	0	2
Timethy Mory	1	0	0	0	0	0
Nathaniel Peae	1	0	0	0	0	0
John Meldrum	1	0	0	0	0	0

June the 9th 1742

Joshua Pool made oath that the above is a true & exact List of all the Poles & Rateable Estates in that part of Stratham that was allotted him to take. according to the vote of the Gen⁰ Assembly Last Sesssions Sworn before according to the best of his Judgement

Samᵘ Gilman Justice of Peace

HORSES	SWINE	PLANTING	PASTURE	HOUSING
0	1	0	15	6
1	1	0	15	15
2	1	1	26	25
3	1	1	20	25
2	1	0	10	5
0	1	0	6	5
2	1	0	10	9
0	0	0	0	0
0	0	0	0	0
0	0	0	0	0

Names	POLS	OXEN	COWS	3 YEAR OLD	2 YEAR OLD	1 YEAR OLD
Jacob Low	1	1	2	2	0	2
Mr Samuell Green	1	1	0	0	0	0
Benjman Green	1	0	2	3	0	0
Joseph Meriel Junr	2	1	0	5	0	2
Mr Solmon Cotton	1	1	0	2	0	0
Widar Leavitt	0	1	0	1	0	0
Jeames Leavitt	1	1	0	1	0	0
Benjman Cotton	1	0	0	0	2	2
Jonathan Chase Junr	1	1	0	1	2	2
Mr Ambros	1	1	0	2	1	0
Benjam Leavitt	1	0	0	1	1	2
Mr Ephram Leavitt	1	1	2	3	0	1
Benjman Mason	2	1	0	1	0	0
Jeames Robnson	1	1	0	1	0	1
Ebenezer Folsom	1	1	0	2	0	0
Thomas Odel	1	1	0	1	2	0
Thomas Moor	1	1	0	4	2	2
Nathiel Piper	1	1	0	3	2	0

HORSES	SWINE	PLANTING	PASTURE	HOUSING
1	1	0	12	10
0	0	0	0	0
3	2	0	16	14
5	1	0	15	12
0	1	0	16	0
0	0	0	6	8
0	1	0	10	6
2	0	0	8	8
1	1	0	12	16
0	1	1	5	5
0	0	0	8	5
0	1	0	16	16
0	1	0	6	4
1	1	1	12	11
0	0	0	1	4
3	1	0	10	7
1	1	0	12	20
2	1	0	8	12

NH 1742 ESTATE TAX

Names	POLS	OXEN	COWS	3 YEAR OLD	2 YEAR OLD	1 YEAR OLD
Mr Joseph Merial	1	1	0	0	0	0
Enoch Meril	1	1	2	6	2	1
Mr Samuel Leavitt	1	0	0	0	0	0
Mr Joseph Jewet	1	1	0	4	2	3
Thomas Brier	2	1	2	2	0	0
Mr Thoplus Smith	0	1	0	1	0	2
Abram Morgan	1	1	0	2	0	0
Samell Veasay	1	1	0	4	0	4
Thomas Piper	1	1	2	4	0	1
Joseph Hoage	1	1	0	3	1	0
Nathan Hoage	1	1	0	3	1	0
Benjman Hoage	1	1	0	1	0	2
George Veasey Juner	2	1	2	4	0	0
Joseph Meriel 3Rd	1	0	0	0	0	0
Men That live out Town	30	15	14	47	9	23

Land in small bits 56

HORSES	SWINE	PLANTING	PASTURE	HOUSING
0	0	0	0	0
3	1	1	35	30
0	0	0	0	0
5	1	2	25	25
1	1	0	17	12
8	0	0	25	20
2	1	0	12	12
3	1	1	25	25
3	1	0	12	14
0	1	0	0	13
4	0	0	10	12
0	0	0	10	0
4	1	0	30	30
0	1	0	0	0
24	14	4	56	176

NH 1742 ESTATE TAX

Names	POLS	OXEN	COWS	3 YEAR OLD	2 YEAR OLD	1 YEAR OLD
Moses Leavitt Esqr	3	1	2	5	2	3
Mr Edward Fifield	1	1	2	3	1	2
Mr Thomas Veasey	1	1	0	2	0	0
Thomas Veasey Junr	1	0	2	1	0	2
Mr Davied Robison	1	1	0	6	0	1
Jonathan Fifield	1	0	2	1	0	2
Joseph Fifield	1	0	0	0	0	0
Mr Thomas Willson	0	0	0	0	0	0
Mr Jonathan Dearbon	2	1	2	5	2	3
Thomas Ranals	1	1	0	1	0	0
Mr Jonathan Clarck	2	1	0	2	2	2
Jonathan Clarck Junr	1	1	0	2	0	0
Echbod Clarck	1	0	0	0	0	0
Thomas Calay	1	0	0	2	0	0
Satchwel Rundlet	2	1	0	1	0	0
Satchel Clarck	2	1	0	3	2	1
John Rundlat	1	0	0	1	0	0

HORSES	SWINE	PLANTING	PASTURE	HOUSING
5	2	1	35	30
2	1	1	16	16
1	1	0	8	6
1	0	0	12	6
2	1	0	16	16
1	1	0	0	0
0	0	0	0	0
0	0	0	12	0
4	2	1	16	16
0	0	0	6	0
0	0	1	24	10
0	1	0	0	0
0	0	0	0	0
0	0	0	0	0
0	1	0	2	2
3	1	0	10	9
0	1	0	5	8

NH 1742 ESTATE TAX

Names	POLS	OXEN	COWS	3 YEAR OLD	2 YEAR OLD	1 YEAR OLD
John Stockbridge	1	1	0	1	1	0
Willyam Calay	1	1	0	1	0	0
Benjman Abot	1	0	0	0	0	0
Owen Ranals	1	1	2	2	0	0
John Thurston	1	1	2	3	0	2
Abram Stockbridge	1	1	0	2	0	4
Abram Tilton	2	1	0	0	3	1

HORSES	SWINE	PLANTING	PASTURE	HOUSING
2	0	0	8	8
0	0	0	6	2
0	0	0	4	2
0	1	0	12	15
2	0	1	14	10
0	1	0	14	8
1	0	0	14	12

NH 1742 ESTATE TAX

Names	POLS	OXEN	COWS	3 YEAR OLD	2 YEAR OLD	1 YEAR OLD
Ephraim Green	1	0	0	0	0	2
Joseph Robnson	1	0	0	1	0	0
Davied Haniford	1	1	0	1	0	0
Nathiell Leavit	1	0	0	0	0	0
John Purmot	2	1	0	1	0	0
Stephen Thurston	1	0	0	0	0	0
John Robnson	1	0	2	0	0	0
Samell Davice	1	0	0	0	0	0
Robert Morgin	1	0	0	1	0	0

HORSES	SWINE	PLANTING	PASTURE	HOUSING
0	0	0	0	0
0	0	0	0	0
0	0	0	0	0
0	0	0	0	0
0	0	0	0	0
0	0	0	0	0
0	0	0	0	0
0	0	0	0	0
1	0	0	0	0

a inveatery of a part of the town of Stratham

pools	19	in the
houses	14	
horses	11	year
oxen	14	1742
cows	31	
Three year olds	06	
Two year olds	22	
Swine	06	
planten and moen Land	124	akers
paster Land	133	akers
Jonathan weks paster Land	006	

    Taken by me Thomas French

June the 9th 1742 Thoms French made oath that the above is a true List of the Polls & Rateable Estats of that part of Stratham alloted him to take according to the vote of General Assembly made last Sessions according to the best of his Judgement Sworn before

    Sam" Gilman Justice of Peace

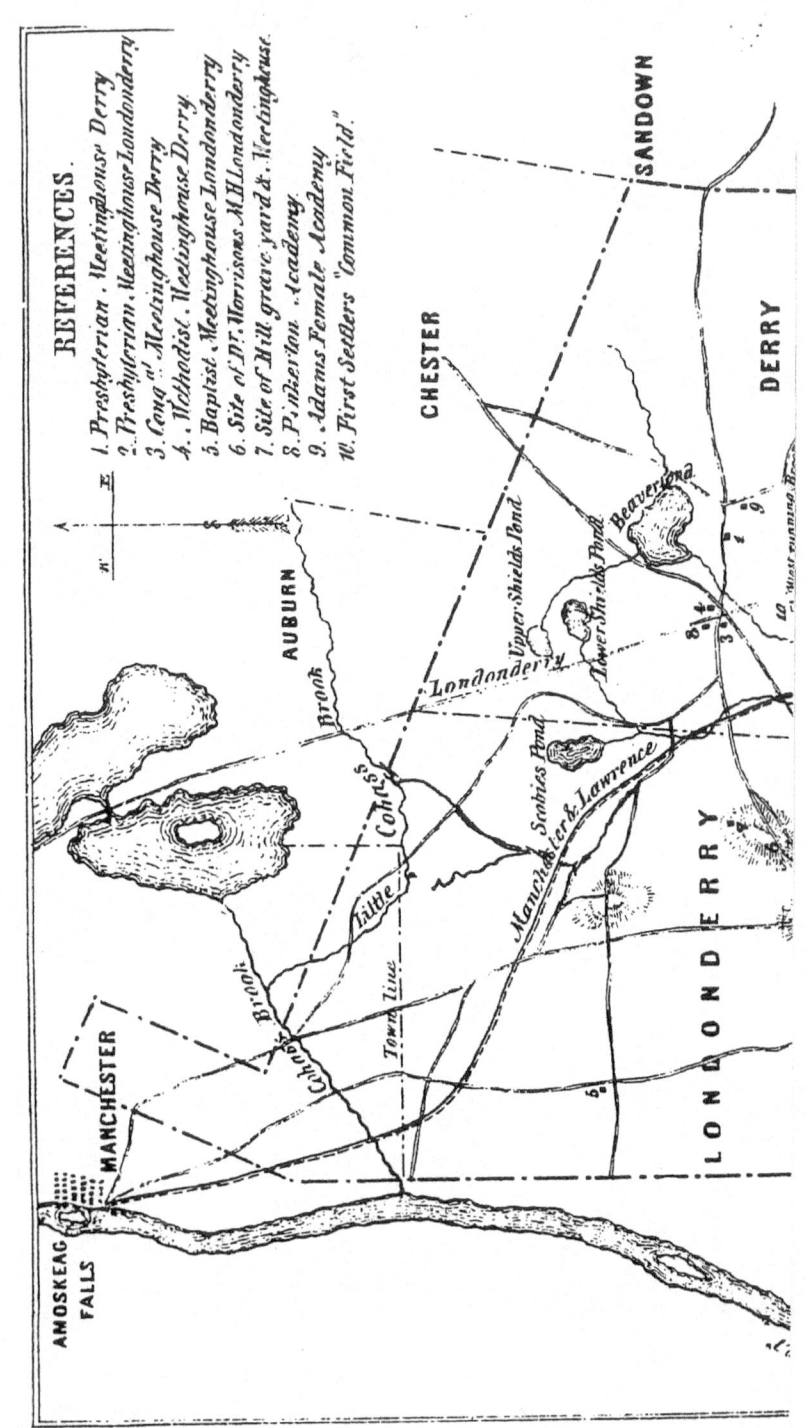

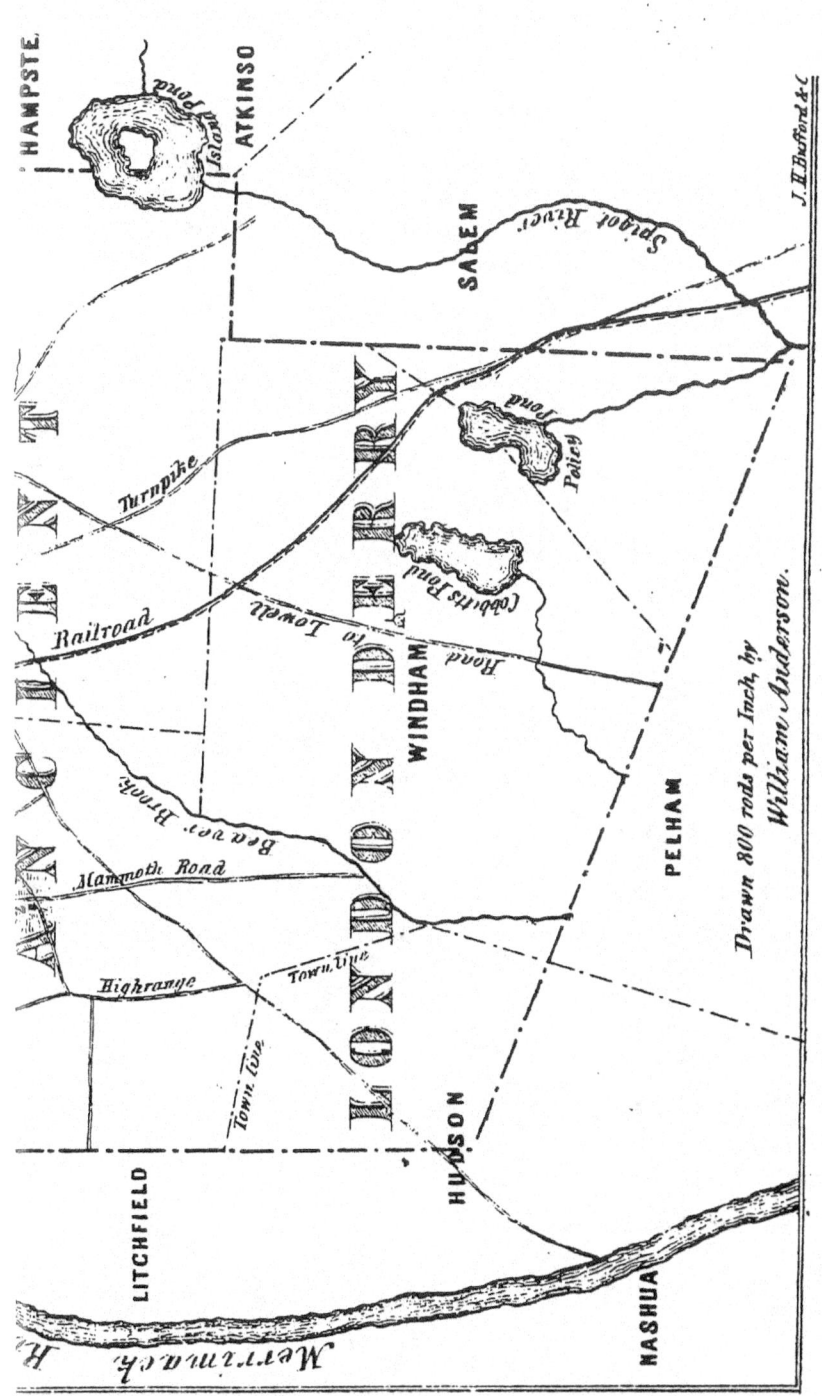

Windham April ye: 1: 1742
an Inventra of the pols and Reatable Esteats of Windham
All at Newhampshire

Names	POLS	HOUSES	PLANTING	MEDOW	MOWING	PASTURE
Nathaniel Hamphill	1	2	3	1	3	0
Robert Dinsmore	2	1	3	1	3	0
Robart Hopkin	1	1	1	0	0	0
William Jamison	1	1	3	0	½	0
Sam'll Morison	1	1	2	0	1	0
Tho° Morison	1	1	2	0	0	0
Robert park'er	1	0	1½	½	1	0
Alex'dr parke	1	1	5	1½	4	0
John stuart	1	1	2	0	0	0
John Kyle	1	1	0	0	0	0
William thom	1	1	1	0	0	0
James gilmore	2	2	3	0	3	0
Zekel Morison	1	0	1	0	0	0
John Vance	1	1	2	0	0	0

HORSES	OXEN	COWS	3 YEARS OLD	2 YEARS OLD	YEARLING	SWINE
1	0	7	2	3	1	0
1	2	4	2	2	0	0
1	0	2	0	0	0	0
1	0	4	0	0	1	0
1	2	3	0	0	0	0
1	0	2	0	2	1	0
0	4	1	0	1	2	0
1	2	4	0	2	3	0
1	0	2	0	0	0	0
1	0	2	0	0	0	0
0	0	2	0	0	0	1
1	4	4	0	2	0	1
0	2	0	0	0	0	0
0	0	1	0	1	1	0

All at Newhampshire

Names	POLS	HOUSES	PLANTING	MEDOW	MOWING	PASTURE
Halbert Morison	1	1	0	0	0	0
John Morron	1	1	1	0	0	0
Tho quigly	1	1	1	0	0	0
Alex^x Rikey	1	1	1	0	0	0
Jam^s Bell	1	1	1	0	0	0
William Bolton	1	1	3	0	3	0
Samuell McAdams	1	0	0	0	0	0
Sam^{ll} Armon	1	1	2	0	3	0
John Cochran	1	1	1	0	2	0
Joseph Waugh	1	1	3	1	1	0
Jam^s Dunlap	1	1	2	½	0	0
Jam^s Caldwall	1	1	1½	½	½	0
Jam^s Caldwall Jur	1	1	1½	0	½	0
Robart thomson	1	1	2	½	0	0
John Kyle	1	0	0	0	0	0
John Willson	1	0	1	½	0	0
John Armstrong	1	1	0	0	0	0
Alex^{dr} Dunlap	1	1	1	1	0	0

HORSES	OXEN	COWS	3 YEARS OLD	2 YEARS OLD	YEARLING	SWINE
0	0	0	0	0	2	0
1	0	2	0	0	0	0
1	0	2	0	0	0	0
0	0	1	0	0	1	0
1	0	1	0	0	0	0
1	2	4	0	1	0	0
0	0	0	0	0	0	0
0	2	1	0	0	0	0
1	2	1	0	0	0	0
1	2	4	0	0	0	0
1	2	3	0	0	0	0
0	1	2	0	0	1	0
1	1	2	0	1	0	0
1	0	1	1	0	0	0
0	0	1	0	0	0	0
0	0	0	0	1	0	0
0	0	2	0	0	0	0
0	0	2	0	0	0	0

All at Newhampshire

Names	POLS	HOUSES	PLANTING	MEDOW	MOWING	PASTURE
David gregg	1	2	4	1	2	0
William gregg	1	1	2	0	1	0
John Mccay	1	2	4	1	3	0
Heneray Campble	1	1	5	2	0	0
Sam" Campbele	1	0	0	0	0	0
Hugh graham	1	1	1	1	0	0
Thoˢ Campbel	1	1	0	0	0	0
James Smith	1	1	1	1	0	0
Arthar graham	1	1	1	0	½	0
John over	1	1	5	0	2	0
Oliver Sanders	1	1	3	6	0	0
Benjamin Cornen	1	1	1½	0	0	0
Sam" Sanders	1	0	0	0	0	0
Abenezer Woodberry	1	1	0	0	0	0
Nathanell Woodberry	1	1	1	0	0	0
Richard Ingerson	1	1	2	0	0	0
Robart Ellenwood	1	1	4	2	0	0
Timothy Sanders	1	0	0	0	0	0

HORSES	OXEN	COWS	3 YEARS OLD	2 YEARS OLD	YEARLING	SWINE
1	2	3	1	0	3	0
1	0	2	0	0	1	0
1	2	6	2	0	3	0
1	2	3	2	3	1	0
0	0	0	0	2	1	0
0	0	3	3	1	2	0
0	0	2	0	0	1	0
1	0	1	2	0	0	0
1	0	2	0	3	0	0
1	2	4	0	0	1	0
0	4	2	2	0	0	0
1	2	1	0	0	2	0
0	0	1	0	0	0	0
0	0	0	0	0	0	0
1	2	1	0	1	1	0
1	0	2	0	2	1	0
0	0	1	0	0	0	0
0	0	0	0	0	0	0

All at Newhampshire

Names	POLS	HOUSES	PLANTING	MEDOW	MOWING	PASTURE
John hall	1	1	1½	0	0	0
Jonnathan Woodbery	1	1	2	2	0	0
William Sanders	1	1	3	1	2	0
Hennery Sanders	2	1	6	0	3	3
Edward Bealy	1	1	0	0	0	0

HORSES	OXEN	COWS	3 YEARS OLD	2 YEARS OLD	YEARLING	SWINE
1	2	2	1	2	0	0
1	0	2	0	3	0	0
1	2	2	3	3	2	0
1	2	1	2	1	0	0
0	0	0	0	0	0	0

NH 1742 ESTATE LIST INDEX

ABBOTT
  Benjamin   Rumford   304
  Benjamin   Stratham   384
  Edward   Rumford   304
  George   Rumford   304
  Isaac   Rumford   304
  James   Rumford   304
  Nathaniel   Rumford   304

ADAMS
  Ephraim   Dunstable   2
  Henry   Dunstable   2
  James   Londonderry   188
  James   Londonderry   192
  Samuel   Durham   18
  Thomas   Dunstable   2
  William   Dunstable   10
  William   Londonderry   188
  Zachariah   Dunstable   2

ADDISON
  William   Londonderry   188

AITKEN
  Nathaniel   Londonderry   202
  James   Londonderry   202
  William   Londonderry   202

ALEXANDER
  James   Newington   256
  John   Londonderry   210
  Randall   Londonderry   210

ALLARD
  Henry   Rochester   294

ALLEN
  John   Rochester   290
  William   Rochester   292

AMAZEEN
  Christopher   New Castle   238
  Joseph   New Castle   246

AMBLER
  John   Rochester   292

AMBROSE
  Mr.   Stratham   378

AMES
  Daniel   Newmarket   266
  Nathaniel   Newmarket   266
  Simeon   Newmarket   266
  Stephen   Dunstable   10

ANDERSON
  Allan   Londonderry   196
  James   Londonderry   202
  James   Londonderry   212
  John   Londonderry   208
  John   Londonderry   212
  Samuel   Londonderry   214

ANDREWS
  John   Durham   30

ANNIS
  Abraham   Haverhill   140

ANTHONY
  Joseph   Litchfield   184

ARBUCKLE
  Widow   Londonderry   214

ARCHIBALD
  John   Londonderry   198
  Samuel   Londonderry   198
  Widow   Londonderry   188

ARMOUR
  Samuel   Methuen-Dracut   226
  Samuel   Windham   394

ARMSTRONG
  John   Windham   394

ASH
  Nathaniel   South Hampton   354

ASTON
  Abial   Methuen-Dracut   228

ATKINSON
  Joseph   Durham   30

ATWOOD
  John   Haverhill   134

AULD
  John   Dunstable   4

AYER
  James   Haverhill   136
  William   Haverhill   136

AYERS
  Christopher   Londonderry   204
  Ebenezer   Methuen-Dracut   228
  Edward   Newington   256
  James   Londonderry   214
  Peter   Methuen-Dracut   233
  Widow   Londonderry   204
  William   Londonderry   216

BAGLEY
  David   South Hampton   336
  Henry   South Hampton   354
  Jacob   Kingston   172
  Orlando   Kingston   170
  Orlando   Kingston   172
  Edward   Methuen-Dracut   226

BAILEY
  John   Methuen-Dracut   228
  Thomas   Methuen-Dracut   233

BAKER
  Benjamin   South Hampton   348
  Joseph   Durham   20

BALDWIN
  Henry   Nottingham   280
  Henry   Nottingham   281
  Thomas   Newington   254

BAMAN see PALMER

BANFIELD
  Capt.   South Hampton   361

BANKHEAD				Phinehas	Kingston	174
Hugh	Londonderry	221		Samuel	Hampton	62
BARBER				Samuel, Jr.	Hampton	62
John	Newmarket	272		Samuel, Jr.	Hampton	85
BARD				Sarah	Hampton	82
Simon	Methuen-Dracut	228		Simon	Kensington	152
BARKER				Simon	Kingston	168
Enoch	Hampton Falls	108		Stephen, Jr.	Hampton	62
Widow	Rumford	304		Theophilus	Hampton Falls	116
BARNARD				Theophilus	Hampton Falls	108
Moses	Londonderry	200		Thomas	Hampton	60
Samuel	South Hampton	346		BATSON		
Samuel, Jr.	South Hampton	342		John	New Castle	238
BARNET				BEAN		
John	Londonderry	206		Joseph	Kingston	162
BARR				BEARD		
Gabriel	Londonderry	192		John	Dunstable	10
James	Londonderry	200		BEATTIE		
Samuel	Londonderry	192		Edward	Windham	398
BARTER				William	Londonderry	221
Stephen	New Castle	242		BEHONEY		
BARTLETT				Gideon	Dunstable	6
Christopher	Haverhill	134		BELKNAP		
Gideon	South Hampton	336		Moses	Haverhill	126
John	South Hampton	342		BELL		
Jonathan	Haverhill	136		Benjamin	New Castle	242
Joseph	South Hampton	336		James	Windham	394
Josiah	South Hampton	354		John	Litchfield	182
Nathaniel	Haverhill	136		John	Londonderry	204
Seth	South Hampton	348		Joseph	Londonderry	206
BARTLEWAY				Mrs.	New Castle	242
John	South Hampton	348		Thomas	New Castle	238
BARTON				BENNETT		
Henry	Dunstable	10		Abraham	Durham	20
BATCHELDER				Abraham	Durham	28
Ebenezer	Kingston	166		Benjamin	Durham	20
Jeremiah	Kensington	152		Benjamin, Jr.	Durham	20
John	Hampton	62		Jeremiah	Hampton Falls	108
John	Hampton	82		Jeremiah	Hampton Falls	117
John	Hampton Falls	94		John	Newmarket	272
John	Hampton Falls	116		Thomas	Newmarket	272
John	Kensington	150		BERRY		
John	Kensington	154		Ebenezer	Rye	328
Jonathan	Hampton Falls	94		Joseph	Rochester	290
Joseph	Hampton	62		Jotham	Rye	320
Joseph	Hampton	82		Nathaniel	Rye	320
Joseph	Hampton Falls	96		Nehemiah	Rye	320
Joseph	Hampton Falls	116		Samuel	Rye	320
Josiah	Hampton Falls	98		Stephen	Rochester	290
Josiah	Hampton Falls	118		William	Rye	322
Josiah	Kingston	166		Zachariah	Rye	320
Nathan	Kingston	162		BICKFORD		
Nathaniel	Hampton Falls	96		Benjamin	Durham	36
Nathaniel	Kensington	146		Ebenezer	Newington	257
Phinehas	Kingston	166		Eleazer	Durham	26

Jethro	Newington	254		Robert	Dunstable	8
John	Durham	16	BLY			
John	Newington	256		James	Haverhill	124
John	Rochester	298	BOGLE			
Jonathan	Newington	256		David	Londonderry	204
Joseph	Durham	22	BOIES			
Lemuel	Newington	256		Ian	Litchfield	180
Lemuel	Newington	257		James	Londonderry	208
Lemuel	Newington	258		Joseph	Londonderry	208
Richard	Rochester	296		Robert	Londonderry	196
Thomas	Durham	18		Thomas	Londonderry	216
Thomas	Newington	254		Thomas	Londonderry	218
BLAGDON				Thomas	Londonderry	219
John	Rochester	296	BOLTON			
BLAIR				William	Windham	394
James	Londonderry	216	BONNER			
John	Litchfield	180		Patrick	Litchfield	184
John	Londonderry	216		William	Litchfield	182
BLAISDELL				William, Jr.	Litchfield	182
Jonathan	Kingston	170	BOYCE see BOIES			
Jonathan	Kingston	175	BOYD			
Lt.	Kingston	172		Arthur	Londonderry	190
Moses	Kingston	172		Samuel	Litchfield	184
Ralph	Kingston	170		Samuel	Londonderry	196
BLAKE				Thomas	Hampton Falls	108
Elisha	Kingston	166		Thomas	Londonderry	210
Hezekiah	Kensington	156	BOYNTON			
Israel	Hampton Falls	112		William	Kingston	170
Jedediah	Hampton Falls	110		William, Jr.	Kingston	172
Joseph	Hampton Falls	110	BRACKETT			
Joseph	Hampton Falls	117		John	Greenland	54
Joshua	Hampton Falls	98		Samuel	Newmarket	270
Moses	Kensington	156		Samuel	Rye	320
Moses	Kensington	158	BRADLEY			
Nathan	Hampton	62		Abraham	Rumford	304
Nathan	Hampton	83		Jeremiah	Rumford	304
Philemon	Kensington	146		Jonathan	Rumford	304
Samuel	Hampton Falls	98		Timothy	Rumford	304
Samuel	Hampton Falls	117	BRADSHAW			
Samuel	Kensington	146		John	Litchfield	182
Sarah	Hampton Falls	98	BRANSCOMBE			
Timothy	Hampton Falls	112		William	New Castle	240
Timothy, Jr.	Hampton Falls	110	BREWSTER			
BLANCHARD				Ebenezer	Rochester	294
Joseph	Dunstable	2	BRIMLEY			
Joseph	Litchfield	180		Robert	Londonderry	221
Thomas	Dunstable	2		William	Londonderry	220
William	Dunstable	8	BROWN			
BLODGETT				Abraham	Hampton	86
Benjamin	Litchfield	178		Abraham	Hampton Falls	98
BLOOD				Abraham	Kingston	164
Benjamin	Dunstable	10		Abraham	South Hampton	346
Elnathan	Dunstable	8		Abraham	South Hampton	360
Josiah	Dunstable	8		Ann	Kensington	154
Nathaniel	Dunstable	10		Benjamin	Kensington	152
				Benjamin	Kensington	158

Benjamin	Kingston	164		Joseph	Haverhill	138
Benjamin	South Hampton	346		BUNKER		
Benjamin	South Hampton	360		Clement	Durham	34
Enoch	South Hampton	354		James	Durham	34
Ephraim	South Hampton	344		Joseph	Durham	34
Ephraim	South Hampton	360		BURBANK		
Hugh	Londonderry	188		Samuel	Rumford	304
Jacob	Hampton Falls	102		BURKE		
Jacob	Kingston	164		Hersher	Portsmouth	286
Jeremiah	Hampton Falls	104		BURLEIGH		
John	Durham	40		Giles	Newmarket	268
John	Hampton Falls	92		Jacob	Newmarket	268
John	Hampton Falls	94		James	Newmarket	268
John	Hampton Falls	104		John	Newmarket	268
John	Hampton Falls	108		Joseph	Newmarket	268
John	Haverhill	136		Josiah	Newmarket	270
John	Londonderry	188		William	Newmarket	268
Jonathan	Kensington	148		William	Stratham	374
Jonathan	South Hampton	361		BURNHAM		
Joseph	Rye	326		James	Durham	28
Joshua	Hampton	62		John	Durham	18
Josiah	Dunstable	8		Joshua	Durham	40
Josiah	Kensington	154		Robert	Durham	18
Nehemiah	Kensington	152		Robert, Jr.	Durham	20
Nehemiah	Kingston	164		Samuel	Durham	20
Sam	South Hampton	348		BUSS		
Samuel	Dunstable	6		John	Durham	18
Samuel	Hampton	62		BUSWELL		
Samuel	Haverhill	136		Nathaniel	Hampton Falls	114
Samuel	Methuen-Dracut	232		Samuel	Kingston	164
Samuel	Rochester	294		William	Kingston	164
Samuel	Rye	326		William	South Hampton	360
Samuel	South Hampton	360		BUTLER		
Stephen	Hampton	62		John	Methuen-Dracut	230
Thomas	Hampton	62		John, Jr.	Methuen-Dracut	230
Thomas	Hampton Falls	100		Jonathan	Newington	256
Thomas	Kingston	164		Ralph	Hampton Falls	102
Thomas	Kingston	170		Samuel	Methuen-Dracut	230
Thomas	New Castle	248		BUTTERFIELD		
Thomas	South Hampton	361		Ephraim	Litchfield	182
Thomas, Jr.	Hampton	62		John	Dunstable	8
William	Durham	34		Josiah	Dunstable	4
Zac	Hampton	62		William	Litchfield	178
BROWNELL				BUZZELL		
Abraham	South Hampton	346		Isaac	Rochester	290
BRUCE				James	Rochester	292
Jonathan	Durham	38		CALDWELL		
William	Durham	40		Ephraim	Methuen-Dracut	232
BRYANT				James	Londonderry	188
Walter	Newmarket	270		James	Windham	394
BRYAR				James, Jr.	Windham	394
Thomas	Stratham	380		CALLEY		
BUCK				Richard	Stratham	366
Ebenezer	Methuen-Dracut	233		Thomas	Stratham	382
John	Dunstable	6		William	Stratham	384

NH 1742 ESTATE LIST INDEX

CAMPBELL				Thomas	Dunstable	4
David	Litchfield	184		William	Rochester	290
Henry	Windham	396		William	Rochester	298
Samuel	Windham	396		William	Rochester	300
Thomas	Londonderry	210		William	Rye	322
Thomas	Windham	396		CHAMBERS		
CANNEY				William	Londonderry	190
Thomas	Haverhill	134		CHANDLER		
CARD				David	Rumford	304
Edward	New Castle	248		John	Rumford	304
John	New Castle	240		Joseph	South Hampton	346
John, Jr.	New Castle	242		CHAPMAN		
Samuel	New Castle	244		Job	Hampton	62
Thomas	New Castle	244		John	Kensington	156
CARDER				Joseph	Hampton	62
Samuel	New Castle	242		Samuel	Newmarket	272
CARKIN				CHASE		
John	Litchfield	178		Abraham	Haverhill	136
CARLES				Charles	South Hampton	354
Ebenezer	Methuen-Dracut	232		Daniel	Hampton Falls	100
Jonathan	Methuen-Dracut	228		Daniel	Hampton Falls	117
CARLETON				Daniel	Rumford	304
Edward	Haverhill	132		Elihu	Hampton	82
Jeremiah	South Hampton	338		Elihu	Kensington	156
Jonathan	South Hampton	352		Francis	South Hampton	352
Moses	South Hampton	352		John	Hampton Falls	104
Richard	Haverhill	140		Jonathan	Hampton Falls	100
CARPENTER				Jonathan	Stratham	366
Robert	New Castle	248		Jonathan, Jr.	Stratham	378
CARR				William	Stratham	372
Ezekiel	Hampton Falls	100		CHESLEY		
John	Londonderry	210		George	Durham	32
John	Londonderry	220		Ichabod	Durham	36
Sanders	Hampton Falls	104		John	Durham	40
Sanders	Hampton Falls	117		Jonathan	Durham	34
Sanders	South Hampton	358		Joseph	Durham	28
Sanders	South Hampton	360		Joshua	Durham	34
Thomas	Litchfield	180		Lemuel	Durham	40
CARTER				Paul	Durham	38
Daniel	South Hampton	342		Philip	Durham	30
Ephraim	South Hampton	340		Samuel	Durham	40
Ezra	Rumford	304		Thomas	Durham	38
John, Jr.	Kingston	172		Thomas, Jr.	Durham	38
Thomas	Kingston	172		CHESWELL		
Thomas	South Hampton	336		Hopestill	Newmarket	270
CASS				CHOATE		
Amos	Hampton Falls	104		Samuel	Haverhill	124
Jonathan	Kensington	148		CHRISTIE		
Joseph	Hampton Falls	104		Peter	Londonderry	190
CATLIN				Thomas	Londonderry	190
Joseph	Durham	40		CILLEY		
CHALLIS				Benjamin	South Hampton	356
John	South Hampton	352		Benjamin	South Hampton	360
Philip	South Hampton	334		Samuel	South Hampton	356
CHAMBERLAIN				Thomas	Hampton Falls	106

Thomas	South Hampton	358	James	Londonderry	214
CLARK			John	Londonderry	208
Eli	Durham	32	John	Londonderry	210
George	Londonderry	216	John	Londonderry	216
Ichabod	Stratham	382	John	Londonderry	221
Isaac	Durham	40	John	Methuen-Dracut	226
Jacob	New Castle	246	John	Windham	394
James	Londonderry	200	Joseph	Londonderry	221
John	Londonderry	206	Ninian	Londonderry	202
John	New Castle	242	Peter	Londonderry	202
John	Stratham	372	Robert	Londonderry	194
Jonathan	Stratham	382	Samuel	Litchfield	180
Jonathan, Jr.	Stratham	382	Thomas	Londonderry	216
Joseph	New Castle	246	William	Londonderry	214
Joseph	Stratham	372	William, Jr.	Londonderry	202
Richard	Newmarket	262	**COKER**		
Robert	Londonderry	188	John	Stratham	368
Samuel	New Castle	242	**COLBATH**		
Satchel	Stratham	382	George	Newington	255
Solomon	Rochester	292	James	Newington	255
CLAY			**COLBURN**		
William	Durham	32	Aaron	Methuen-Dracut	232
CLEMENT			Abraham	Methuen-Dracut	232
Benjamin	Haverhill	124	Azery	Methuen-Dracut	232
John	Haverhill	124	Edward	Methuen-Dracut	232
Jonathan	Haverhill	122	Edward	Methuen-Dracut	233
Obediah	Haverhill	138	Ephraim	Methuen-Dracut	230
CLIFFORD			Henry	Methuen-Dracut	232
Israel	Hampton Falls	96	Jabez	Methuen-Dracut	232
John	Kingston	162	Jacob	Methuen-Dracut	232
John, Jr.	Kingston	162	John	Methuen-Dracut	230
Richard	Kingston	166	Jonathan	Haverhill	132
Samuel	Kensington	154	Moses	Methuen-Dracut	233
CLOUGH			Robert	Dunstable	10
Aaron	South Hampton	360	Robert	Methuen-Dracut	232
Benjamin	Kingston	164	Samuel	Methuen-Dracut	232
Caleb	Kingston	166	Timothy	Methuen-Dracut	232
Caleb	South Hampton	346	William	Dunstable	8
Daniel	Kingston	168	William	Methuen-Dracut	232
Ichabod	Kingston	162	Zacharias	Methuen-Dracut	232
Isaac	Methuen-Dracut	228	Zachary	Methuen-Dracut	230
Joshua	South Hampton	340	**COLBY**		
Josiah	Methuen-Dracut	228	Abraham	Rumford	304
Nathan	Kensington	150	David	South Hampton	334
Nathan	Kensington	150	Jacob	South Hampton	334
Theophilus	Kingston	170	John	Stratham	366
Thomas	South Hampton	360	Joseph	Haverhill	122
Zacheus	South Hampton	350	Lot	Rumford	304
CLYDE			Peter	South Hampton	354
Daniel	Londonderry	198	Rogers	South Hampton	334
COCHRANE			Sampson	Rumford	304
Andrew	Litchfield	178	Sampson	Rumford	312
Andrew	Londonderry	210	Zacheus	South Hampton	334
James	Londonderry	194	**COLCORD**		
James	Londonderry	210	Edward	Newmarket	266

Gideon	Newmarket	266	Jonathan	Londonderry	221
Jonathan	Newmarket	264	Joseph	Londonderry	221
Jonathan, Jr.	Newmarket	266	William	Londonderry	221
COLES	Hampton	82	CRAIG		
COLLINS			Alexander	Londonderry	208
Benjamin	South Hampton	358	David	Londonderry	194
Benjamin	South Hampton	360	John	Londonderry	204
Ebenezer	Kingston	162	John	Londonderry	206
Ebenezer	Kingston	174	William	Londonderry	216
John	South Hampton	356	CRAM		
John	South Hampton	360	Benjamin	Hampton Falls	92
Richard	South Hampton	344	Benjamin	Kensington	146
Samuel	South Hampton	358	John	Kensington	146
Tristram	South Hampton	358	Jonathan	Hampton Falls	94
Tristram	South Hampton	360	Thomas	Hampton Falls	104
William	South Hampton	344	Wadleigh	Kensington	156
COLMAN			CRATON		
Eleazer	Newington	254	John	Newmarket	270
Eleazer	Rochester	294	CRAWFORD		
Phinehas	Newington	255	Thomas	Haverhill	128
COLWELL			CRESSEY		
Alexander	Litchfield	178	Daniel	Methuen-Dracut	228
COMBS			CRITCHET		
Jonathan	Dunstable	4	Elias	Durham	28
CONNER			John	Durham	20
Joseph	Rye	316	CROCKETT		
CONNOR			Ephraim	Stratham	376
George	Kensington	150	John	Durham	38
CONVERSE			Richard	Stratham	374
Joshua	Litchfield	182	Richard, Jr.	Stratham	376
COOKSON			CROMBIE		
John	Methuen-Dracut	230	Hugh	Londonderry	218
COOPER			Hugh	Londonderry	219
John	Hampton Falls	94	John	Londonderry	216
COPP			CROMMETT		
David	Haverhill	130	John	Durham	28
Jonathan	Rochester	290	Joshua	Durham	20
Josiah	Haverhill	140	Philip	Durham	28
Moses	Haverhill	128	CROWN		
CORNEY			John	New Castle	246
John	New Castle	246	John	Newington	256
Nichols	New Castle	246	CUMMINGS		
CORNING			Isaac	Dunstable	2
Benjamin	Methuen-Dracut	226	Jerathniel	Dunstable	8
Benjamin	Windham	396	Jonathan	Litchfield	182
COTTON			Leonard	Litchfield	180
Benjamin	Stratham	378	Samuel	Dunstable	8
Solomon	Stratham	378	CUNNINGHAM		
COUSINS			Archibald	Londonderry	190
Samuel	Rochester	292	CURNOR		
COWEN			Samuel	Methuen-Dracut	224
Thomas	Dunstable	4	CURRELL		
COX			Gideon	Kensington	148
Charles	Londonderry	202	CURRIER		
Edward	Londonderry	221	Aaron	South Hampton	334

Benjamin	South Hampton	346	Joseph, Jr.	Durham	22
Henry	South Hampton	340	Joshua	Durham	40
Israel	South Hampton	348	Samuel	South Hampton	352
Jacob	South Hampton	348	Samuel	Stratham	386
Jeremiah	Kingston	170	Solomon	Durham	26
Jeremiah	Kingston	174	Thomas	South Hampton	354
John	Haverhill	132	William	Durham	22

DAVISON
John	Kingston	170
John	South Hampton	350	John	Londonderry	210
John, Jr.	Haverhill	140	Thomas	Londonderry	194
Jonathan	South Hampton	334

DEARBORN
Reuben	South Hampton	340	Henry	Hampton	58
Richard	South Hampton	334	Henry, Jr.	Hampton	78
Samuel	South Hampton	340	Jeremiah	Hampton	78

CLIFFORD
John	Hampton	87
John	Hampton Falls	96	John 4th	Hampton	78

DALTON
			Jonathan	Hampton	60
Samuel	Hampton	64	Jonathan	Hampton	82
Timothy	Hampton	78	Jonathan	Stratham	382

DAM
			Nathaniel	Kensington	156
John	Newington	254	Reuben	Hampton	60
John	Newington	255	Samuel	Hampton	78
Moses	Newington	255	Simon	Hampton	78
Richard	Newington	254	Thomas	Hampton	60
Zebulon	Rochester	294

DEERING
| | | |
| Clement | Rochester | 294 |

DANFORTH

DICKEY
| Jonathan | Dunstable | 10 | David | Londonderry | 214 |

DANIELS
			John	Londonderry	198
Eliphalet	Durham	16	Samuel	Londonderry	212
John	Durham	16	William	Londonderry	212
Reuben	Durham	16

DIMOND
| Samuel | Durham | 22 | Reuben | South Hampton | 342 |

DARLING
| | | | Reuben | South Hampton | 362 |
| Daniel | Kingston | 162 |

DINSMORE
| John | Kingston | 166 | David | Londonderry | 221 |
| John, Jr. | Kingston | 166 | Richard | Durham | 22 |

DARRACH
| | | | Robert | Windham | 392 |
| James | Londonderry | 220 |

DIX

DAVIS
| | | | Joel | Litchfield | 184 |
| Benjamin | Durham | 26 |

DOAK
| Daniel | Durham | 18 | James | Londonderry | 206 |
| David | Durham | 18 |

DOE
Ebenezer	Durham	26	Benjamin	Durham	22
Huldah	Hampton Falls	104	Daniel	Durham	26
Jabez	Dunstable	4	John	Durham	26
Jabez	Durham	22	Joseph	Durham	38
James	Durham	28	Nathaniel	Newmarket	270
James	Durham	30	Sampson	Newmarket	270
Jeremiah	Durham	40	Samuel	Newmarket	270
John	Durham	36

DOLBEAR
John	Haverhill	134	Israel	Rye	326
John	Newington	256	John	Rye	326
Joseph	Durham	22	Jonathan	Rye	326
Joseph	Methuen-Dracut	224

DORE
| Joseph 3rd | Durham | 40 |

Philip	Rochester	292	DOWST		
DOUGLAS			Ozem	Rye	326
James	Londonderry	220	Samuel	Rye	322
John	Londonderry	208	Solomon	Rye	322
Patrick	Londonderry	188	DRAKE		
DOW			Abraham, Jr.	Hampton	58
Abraham	Hampton Falls	102	Abraham.	Hampton	60
Benjamin	Hampton Falls	106	Nathaniel	Hampton	60
Benjamin	Newmarket	262	Robert	Hampton	74
Bildad	South Hampton	356	DRESSER		
Bildad	South Hampton	360	Jeremiah	Rumford	304
David	Hampton	62	DREW		
David	Methuen-Dracut	228	Benjamin	Durham	40
Ebenezer	Kensington	148	Elijah	Durham	20
Elihu	South Hampton	356	Francis	Durham	16
Eliphaz	South Hampton	356	John	Durham	16
Ezekiel	Kensington	150	Joseph	Durham	16
Jabez	Hampton	64	Thomas	Durham	16
Jeremiah	South Hampton	360	Thomas	Rochester	294
John	Haverhill	132	William	Durham	32
John	Kensington	154	DROWN		
John	South Hampton	346	Solomon	Rochester	296
John	South Hampton	360	DUDA see DUDY		
John, Sr.	Haverhill	140	DUDY		
Jonathan	Hampton	82	Joseph	Durham	28
Jonathan	Haverhill	136	Joseph, Jr.	Durham	20
Jonathan	Kensington	154	Samuel	Newmarket	272
Judah	South Hampton	356	DUNCAN		
Nathan	South Hampton	346	George	Londonderry	206
Nathaniel	Methuen-Dracut	228	John	Londonderry	206
Noah	South Hampton	356	William	Londonderry	208
Noah	South Hampton	360	DUNFREE		
Peter	Haverhill	138	Thomas	Londonderry	220
Philip	Kensington	154	DUNLAP		
Richard	Methuen-Dracut	228	Alexander	Windham	394
Samuel	Hampton	64	James	Windham	394
Samuel	South Hampton	360	DURGIN		
Simon	Hampton	64	Benjamin	Durham	16
Stephen	Haverhill	136	Benjamin, Jr.	Durham	22
Timothy	Haverhill	136	Frances	Newmarket	274
Widow	Rye	326	Francis	Durham	26
Winthrop	Hampton Falls	102	James	Durham	28
Winthrop	Hampton Falls	117	James, Jr.	Durham	28
DOWNING			John	Durham	26
Benjamin	New Castle	240	John	Newmarket	268
John	Newington	254	Jonathan	Durham	26
John	Newington	257	Joshua	Durham	30
John	Rochester	296	Trueworthy	Durham	28
John	Rochester	298	William	Durham	28
John	Rochester	300	William	Newmarket	264
Jonathan	Newington	254	DURHAM		
Joshua	Newington	254	John	Londonderry	202
Richard	Newington	254	DURRELL see DUDY		
DOWNS			DUSTIN		
Gershom	Rochester	290	John	Haverhill	136

EASTMAN
- Benjamin — South Hampton — 360
- Benjamin, Jr. — South Hampton — 360
- Ebenezer — Rumford — 306
- Ebenezer, Jr. — Rumford — 306
- Jeremiah — Kensington — 154
- John — South Hampton — 348
- John — South Hampton — 350
- John — South Hampton — 360
- Joseph — Kingston — 170
- Joseph — Rumford — 306
- Obediah — Rumford — 306
- Peter — Haverhill — 130
- Philip — Rumford — 306
- Roger — South Hampton — 334
- Thomas — Kingston — 170
- William — Haverhill — 134

EATON
- Benjamin — Dunstable — 2
- Ephraim — South Hampton — 356
- Ephraim — South Hampton — 360
- Henry — South Hampton — 360
- Jabez — South Hampton — 356
- Jabez — South Hampton — 360
- Jeremiah — Haverhill — 128
- John — South Hampton — 356
- John, Jr. — South Hampton — 356
- Jonathan — Haverhill — 132
- Samuel — Haverhill — 126
- Samuel — South Hampton — 360

EDGERLY
- John — Durham — 16
- Joseph — Durham — 16
- Joseph — Stratham — 372

ELKINS
- Henry — Rye — 324
- Jonathan — Hampton — 58
- Obadiah — Kingston — 162
- Thomas — Hampton — 74

ELLINGWOOD
- Robert — Methuen-Dracut — 226
- Robert — Windham — 396

ELLIOTT
- David — South Hampton — 336
- John — South Hampton — 334

ELLIS
- William — Rochester — 292

ELLISON
- Samuel — Londonderry — 194

ELY
- Nathaniel — Hampton Falls — 118

EMERSON
- Benjamin — Haverhill — 128
- David — Haverhill — 140
- Ephraim — Haverhill — 134
- Jonathan — Methuen-Dracut — 233
- Robert — Haverhill — 128
- Samuel — Durham — 32
- Stephen — Haverhill — 134
- Timothy — Durham — 30
- Timothy — Haverhill — 124
- Timothy — Methuen-Dracut — 233
- William — Durham — 22

EMERY
- Caleb — Haverhill — 138
- Humphrey — Haverhill — 122
- Jonathan — Haverhill — 124
- Joshua — Methuen-Dracut — 233

EMMONS
- Samuel — Kingston — 162
- Widow — Hampton — 82

ESTEY
- John — Londonderry — 221

EVANS
- John — South Hampton — 348
- John, Jr. — South Hampton — 360
- William — Kensington — 152

EWING
- James — Londonderry — 190

FABYAN
- John — Newington — 254
- Samuel — Newington — 255

FARLEY
- Benjamin — Dunstable — 8
- Joseph — Dunstable — 8
- Samuel — Dunstable — 8

FARNUM
- Barachias — Rumford — 306
- Ephraim — Rumford — 306
- James — Rumford — 306
- Joseph — Rumford — 306
- Zebediah — Rumford — 306

FARRINGTON
- Stephen — Rumford — 306

FARWELL
- Isaac — Dunstable — 2

FAVOUR
- Cutting — South Hampton — 336

FELCH
- Daniel — Hampton Falls — 106

FELLOWS
- Ebenezer — Kingston — 164
- Isaac — Kensington — 156

FERGUSON
- John — Methuen-Dracut — 230

FERRIN
- Jonathan — South Hampton — 334

FERSON
- James — Londonderry — 220

FIFIELD

NH 1742 ESTATE LIST INDEX

Edward	Kingston	168		Ephraim	Newmarket	270
Edward	Stratham	382		Ephraim	Newmarket	274
Henry	Hampton	72		Israel	Newmarket	274
Jeremiah	Hampton	68		Jeremiah	Newmarket	268
Jonathan	Hampton Falls	102		Jeremiah, Jr.	Newmarket	268
Jonathan	Hampton Falls	118		John	Newmarket	274
Jonathan	Stratham	382		William	Newmarket	268
Joseph	Stratham	382		William	Newmarket	274
Samuel	Hampton Falls	112		FOOTMAN		
FISKE				Francis	Durham	18
Jonathan	Newmarket	274		John	Durham	26
FITTS				FORD		
Richard	South Hampton	340		Robert	Haverhill	134
FLAGG				FOSS		
Eleazer	Dunstable	6		Henry	New Castle	246
FLANDERS				Hinkson	Rye	322
Asa	South Hampton	346		Isaac	Stratham	376
Jeremiah	South Hampton	342		John	New Castle	244
John	South Hampton	340		Joshua	Rye	320
Jonathan	South Hampton	344		Nathaniel	Rye	320
Joseph	South Hampton	340		Walllis	Rye	322
Philip	South Hampton	346		Zachariah	New Castle	240
Philip	South Hampton	360		FOST		
Philip, Jr.	South Hampton	346		Benjamin	Rochester	292
Samuel	South Hampton	346		FOSTER		
Stephen	South Hampton	344		Benjamin	Rumford	306
Thomas	South Hampton	360		David	Rumford	306
FLANDS				Joseph	Kingston	166
John	Londonderry	206		Obediah	Rumford	306
FLOOD				FOWLER		
Henry	South Hampton	354		Abner	South Hampton	344
John	Hampton Falls	108		David	South Hampton	356
John, Jr.	Hampton Falls	112		Jacob	South Hampton	344
Moses	Haverhill	124		Samuel	South Hampton	356
FOGG				FOX		
Abner	Hampton	72		Edward	Newmarket	272
Abner	Hampton	86		John	Newmarket	266
Daniel	Hampton	74		FREESE		
Enoch	Hampton	76		Jonathan	Hampton	72
James	Hampton	76		FRENCH		
James	Kensington	152		Benjamin	Kingston	166
Jeremiah	South Hampton	360		Daniel	South Hampton	340
John	Hampton	76		Ebenezer	South Hampton	340
Samuel	Hampton	84		Eliphalet	South Hampton	360
Seth	Hampton	72		Henry	South Hampton	340
Simon	Hampton Falls	100		John	Hampton Falls	100
Simon	Hampton Falls	117		John	Londonderry	188
FOLLANSBEE				Jonathan	Dunstable	4
Thomas	Haverhill	124		Joseph	Dunstable	2
FOLLETT				Joseph	South Hampton	340
Ichabod	Durham	36		Joshua	Kingston	164
John	Durham	40		Nicholas	Dunstable	12
FOLSOM				Sampson	Dunstable	2
Andrew	Newmarket	274		Samuel	Kingston	164
Ebenezer	Stratham	378		Samuel	South Hampton	346

Samuel	South Hampton	360	John	South Hampton	360
Samuel, Jr.	South Hampton	340	GILMAN		
Thomas	Stratham	388	Israel	Newmarket	276
Timothy	South Hampton	360	Joseph, Jr.	Newmarket	266
Widow	South Hampton	348	Joshua	Kensington	146
Widow	South Hampton	360	Samuel	Durham	24
FROST			Samuel	Durham	44
Andrew P.	New Castle	248	Samuel	Exeter	48
Madam	New Castle	238	Samuel	Exeter	50
Nathaniel	Durham	20	Samuel	Greenland	54
William	New Castle	240	Samuel	Hampton Falls	118
FULLER			Samuel	Kensington	151
Benoni	Hampton	58	Samuel	Methuen-Dracut	234
James	Rye	324	Samuel	Newington	258
Jeremiah	Rye	326	Samuel	Newmarket	276
John	Rye	326	Samuel	Nottingham	281
Joseph	Rye	326	Samuel	Portsmouth	287
Thomas	Hampton	82	Samuel	Rochester	300
Thomas	Hampton Falls	112	Samuel	Rye	330
FURBER			Samuel	South Hampton	362
Jethro	Newington	255	Samuel	Stratham	376
Moses	Newington	255	Samuel	Stratham	388
Nehemiah	Newington	255	GILMORE		
William	Newington	255	James	Londonderry	188
GAGE			James	Windham	392
Daniel	Methuen-Dracut	228	Robert	Londonderry	190
Josiah	Methuen-Dracut	230	Robert	Londonderry	194
GALE			Thomas	Methuen-Dracut	228
Jacob	Kingston	170	William	Londonderry	188
Jacob	Kingston	175	GIVEN		
GARLAND			John	Londonderry	204
John	Hampton	84	GLAZIER		
John	Rochester	292	Stephen	Durham	18
John	Rye	328	GLENDENNING		
John, Jr.	Rye	328	Andrew	Londonderry	200
Jonathan	Hampton	64	Archibald	Londonderry	200
Jonathan	Hampton	83	Archibald	Londonderry	220
Joseph	Hampton Falls	96	William	Londonderry	198
Peter	Hampton	58	GLIDDEN		
Peter	Hampton	85	Benjamin	Durham	30
GAULT			Joseph	Durham	30
William	Londonderry	221	GLOVER		
GEORGE			Richard	Durham	32
James	South Hampton	334	GLYNN		
GETCHELL			William	Dunstable	4
Nathaniel	Haverhill	138	GODFREY		
GILES			Isaac	Kingston	164
Daniel	Haverhill	136	James	Hampton	72
Ebenezer	Haverhill	128	John	Hampton	78
John	Methuen-Dracut	226	GOODWIN		
Joseph	Haverhill	122	David	South Hampton	334
Moses	Haverhill	122	James	Newmarket	272
Thomas	Londonderry	220	John	Haverhill	122
GILL			Nathan	South Hampton	338
Daniel	South Hampton	360	Richard	South Hampton	338

NH 1742 ESTATE LIST INDEX

Samuel	South Hampton	334		Jacob	Hampton Falls	98
GORDON				Jeremiah	Kensington	150
Michael	Londonderry	190		John	Hampton Falls	106
GORMAN				John	Kensington	146
John	Newmarket	272		Nathan	Hampton Falls	100
GOSS				Samuel	Stratham	378
Jethro	Rye	322		Sarah	Haverhill	130
Jonathan	Rye	328		GREENE		
Thomas	Rye	328		Robert	Haverhill	124
GOULD				GREGG		
Daniel	South Hampton	354		David	Windham	396
Joseph	South Hampton	342		Hugh	Londonderry	220
Nathan	South Hampton	346		James	Londonderry	214
GOVE				John	Londonderry	200
Ebenezer	Hampton Falls	100		Samuel	Londonderry	214
Ebenezer	Kensington	146		William	Londonderry	200
Edward	Hampton Falls	100		William	Windham	396
Edward	Hampton Falls	117		GRIFFIN		
Enoch	Hampton Falls	100		Eliphalet	Kingston	172
Enoch	Hampton Falls	118		Isaac	Kingston	166
Jeremiah	Hampton Falls	104		John	Kingston	170
John	Hampton Falls	100		Jonathan	Methuen-Dracut	233
Jonathan	Hampton Falls	100		Philip	Kensington	148
Jonathan	Hampton Falls	117		Theophilus	Kingston	170
Nathaniel	Hampton Falls	104		Theophilus, Jr.	Kingston	172
GRAHAM				Widow	South Hampton	348
Arthur	Windham	396		GRIFFITH		
Hugh	Windham	396		Gershom	Hampton	58
Samuel	Londonderry	212		Gershom	Hampton	83
GRANDY				GRIMES		
Clement	New Castle	242		Francis	Litchfield	180
GRANT				HADLEY		
Peter	New Castle	244		Benjamin	South Hampton	338
GRAVES				George	South Hampton	352
John	Kensington	152		John	South Hampton	352
GRAY				Joseph	South Hampton	338
Samuel	Rumford	306		Samuel	South Hampton	352
GREEK				Samuel	South Hampton	354
John	Newington	255		HAINES		
GREELEY				Thomas	Hampton	68
Andrew	South Hampton	360		HALE		
Jonathan	Kingston	164		Benjamin	New Castle	248
Jonathan	Kingston	166		Edmund	Haverhill	138
Joseph	Kingston	164		John	Londonderry	208
Joseph, Jr.	Kingston	164		Thomas	Haverhill	122
Philip	South Hampton	360		HALL		
GREEN				Ebenezer	Rumford	306
Abraham	Hampton Falls	102		Edward	Newmarket	262
Abraham	Hampton Falls	117		George	Rumford	306
Benjamin	Hampton Falls	102		James	Durham	32
Benjamin	South Hampton	361		James	Hampton Falls	108
Benjamin	Stratham	378		John	Methuen-Dracut	226
Bradbury	Hampton Falls	110		John	Windham	398
Ephraim	Stratham	386		Joseph	Newmarket	262
Henry	Hampton Falls	104		Joseph	Rumford	306

Thomas	Durham	32		HEALEY		
HAM				Nathaniel	Hampton Falls	98
Eleazer	Rochester	292		HEARD		
Reuben	Newington	257		John	Rochester	296
HAMBLY				Joseph	Rochester	290
Neil	Londonderry	220		HEATH		
HAMMETT				Bartholomew	Haverhill	138
John	Rochester	298		Benjamin	Haverhill	124
John, Jr.	Rochester	298		Caleb	Haverhill	128
HANCOCK				David	Haverhill	134
William	Haverhill	128		James	Haverhill	122
HANNAFORD				James	Haverhill	128
David	Stratham	386		John	Haverhill	124
John	Stratham	366		John, Jr.	Haverhill	124
HARDY				Joseph	Haverhill	134
Biley	Kingston	168		Josiah	Haverhill	126
John	Hampton Falls	110		Nathaniel	Haverhill	134
John	Kensington	150		Nehemiah	Haverhill	138
HARFORD				Richard	Haverhill	126
Stephen	Rochester	292		Samuel	Haverhill	136
HARRIMAN				Sargent	South Hampton	354
Abner	Haverhill	124		William	Haverhill	134
John	Haverhill	126		HEMPHILL		
Joseph	Haverhill	126		Nathaniel	Windham	392
Leonard	Haverhill	126		HILDRETH		
Leonard	Haverhill	138		Jacob	Litchfield	184
Samuel	Haverhill	126		HILL		
HARRIS				Eliphalet	Durham	38
Samuel	Hampton	82		Henry	Durham	36
Stephen	Dunstable	8		Nathaniel	Litchfield	178
HART				Samuel	Durham	36
Samuel	Portsmouth	286		Valentine	Durham	32
HARVELL				William	Durham	34
John	Litchfield	182		HILLIARD		
HARVEY				Benjamin	Hampton	82
Peter	New Castle	242		Benjamin	Hampton Falls	106
Robert	New Castle	248		Chase	Kensington	152
HARWOOD				James	Hampton	82
Thomas	Dunstable	2		Jonathan	Hampton Falls	94
HASKELL				Timothy	Hampton Falls	108
Abraham	Kensington	148		HILLS		
Job	Hampton Falls	104		Ezekiel	Litchfield	178
Job	Hampton Falls	117		Henry	Litchfield	178
HASSELL				Henry, Jr.	Litchfield	178
Benjamin	Litchfield	180		James	Litchfield	178
HAYES				HILTON		
Benjamin	Rochester	294		Joseph	Newmarket	262
James	Newmarket	274		Samuel	Hampton	62
John	Newmarket	274		William	Newmarket	264
HAZELTINE				Winthrop	Newmarket	262
Henry	Haverhill	138		HOAG		
Richard	Rumford	306		Benjamin	Stratham	380
HEALD				David	Durham	28
Joseph	Londonderry	210		John	Haverhill	130
Thomas	Dunstable	4		John	Newmarket	274

Jonathan	Hampton Falls	104		Michael	South Hampton	334
Jonathan	Newmarket	266		Philip	Haverhill	132
Joseph	Stratham	380		Stephen	Rumford	308
Moses	Hampton Falls	110		HUCHARDSON		
Nathan	Hampton Falls	108		John	Litchfield	182
Nathan	Stratham	380		HUCKINS		
Stephen	Hampton Falls	112		Joseph	Durham	32
HOBBS				Robert	Durham	32
Benjamin	Hampton	70		Thomas	Durham	36
Caleb	South Hampton	334		HUMPHREY		
Caleb, Jr.	South Hampton	334		William	Londonderry	192
James	Hampton	72		HUNKINS		
John	Hampton	72		John	Haverhill	128
Morris	Hampton	70		HUNT		
Morris	Hampton	85		Enoch	Dunstable	8
Nehemiah	Hampton	64		Nathan	South Hampton	338
Samuel	Hampton	74		Thomas	Hampton Falls	112
Stephen	Kensington	152		HUNTER		
HODSDON				David	Londonderry	202
Alexander, Jr.	Newington	255		John	Londonderry	188
Alexander	Newington	255		HUNTRESS		
Joseph	Rochester	298		Christopher	Newington	255
HOGG				John	Newington	255
Joseph	Londonderry	194		Samuel	Newington	255
Robert	Londonderry	219		William	Newington	256
Thomas	Londonderry	206		HUSTON		
William	Londonderry	190		David	Londonderry	196
HOLMES				John	Litchfield	182
Abraham	Londonderry	204		Samuel	Londonderry	196
Ephraim	Rye	326		HUTCHESON		
John	Londonderry	206		Jonathan	Kensington	148
Nathaniel	Londonderry	220		Timothy	Kensington	148
William	Londonderry	206		HUTCHINS		
HOPKINS				Jonathan	Haverhill	122
David	Londonderry	194		INGERSOLL		
John	Londonderry	198		Richard	Methuen-Dracut	226
Robert	Windham	392		Richard	Windham	396
HORITT				IRWIN		
Joseph	Stratham	372		Joseph	Haverhill	126
HORNE				JACK		
Ichabod	Rochester	290		Andrew	Londonderry	202
HORNER				JACKMAN		
Thomas	Londonderry	190		James	South Hampton	358
HOWARD				Moses	Haverhill	126
Jonathan	Litchfield	184		Samuel	South Hampton	338
HOYT				JACKSON	Hampton	86
Abner	Rumford	306		Benjamin	New Castle	246
Benjamin	South Hampton	358		Clement	Hampton	68
Benjamin	South Hampton	360		Clement	Hampton	83
Ephraim	Hampton Falls	106		Joseph	Durham	38
Ezekiel	South Hampton	344		Madam	New Castle	238
Jacob	Rumford	308		Samuel	Durham	40
Jacob	Rumford	312		William	Durham	32
John	Newington	255		William, Jr.	Durham	32
Jonathan	South Hampton	348		JAMES		

Benjamin	Hampton	60	Stephen	Haverhill	130
Benjamin	Kensington	152	Stephen, Sr.	Haverhill	122
Israel	Kensington	148	Thomas	South Hampton	338
JAMIESON			Timothy	Haverhill	130
Thomas	Londonderry	202	William	Dunstable	4
William	Windham	392	William	Haverhill	140
JELLISON			Zachariah	Haverhill	134
Thomas	Durham	42	**JONES**		
JENKINS			Benjamin	Durham	38
Benjamin	Durham	30	Benjamin	Stratham	366
John	Durham	16	Ebenezer	Durham	32
John	Durham	34	Ebenezer	Methuen-Dracut	233
Stephem	Durham	18	Jeremiah	New Castle	244
William	Durham	36	John	Durham	36
JENNESS			John	Rye	320
Capt.	Rye	316	Jonathan	South Hampton	350
Francis	Rye	326	Joseph	Durham	36
Hezekiah	Rye	322	Joseph	South Hampton	342
Job	Rye	316	Stephen	Durham	32
John	Rochester	294	Stephen	Durham	32
John	Rye	316	William	New Castle	238
Joshua	Rye	316	William, Jr.	New Castle	244
Mark	Rochester	296	**JORDAN**		
Richard	Hampton	84	Richard	New Castle	240
Richard	Rye	318	Stilman	New Castle	248
Richard, Jr.	Rye	324	**JOY**		
Richard, Tertius	Rye	324	Samuel	Durham	20
Widow	Rye	322	**JUDKINS**		
William	Rochester	296	Joseph	Newmarket	270
JEWELL			KARR see CARR		
David	Hampton	62	**KELLEY**		
David	Hampton	83	Abial	Methuen-Dracut	226
Jonathan	South Hampton	346	Daniel	South Hampton	354
Nathaniel	Dunstable	6	John	Durham	20
Thomas	Dunstable	6	Richard	Methuen-Dracut	224
JEWETT			**KELSO**		
Benjamin	Stratham	376	Alexander	Londonderry	190
Joseph	Stratham	380	William	Londonderry	190
JOHNSON			**KENDALL**		
Benj	Hampton	72	Allas	Litchfield	180
Cornelius	Haverhill	124	Christopher	Litchfield	180
Daniel	Haverhill	122	Daniel	Dunstable	8
Ebenezer	Greenland	54	Nathan	Litchfield	180
James	Hampton	66	**KENDRICK**		
James	Hampton	85	Benjamin	Kingston	172
James, Jr.	Hampton	66	**KENISTON**		
John	Hampton	72	James	Newmarket	274
Joseph	Durham	38	James	Stratham	374
Joseph	Hampton	66	John	Newmarket	274
Joseph	Hampton	85	Joshua	Stratham	374
Michael	Haverhill	128	Nathan	Newmarket	272
Obediah	Hampton	82	Waldron	New Castle	248
Obediah	Kensington	150	**KENNEY**		
Peter	Hampton	66	Huldah	Hampton Falls	108
Peter	Haverhill	130	Richard	Durham	38

KENT

John	Durham	16
John	Haverhill	138
Robert	Durham	16

KEZAR

George	Haverhill	130
John	Haverhill	130

KIDDER

Joseph	Litchfield	178

KILEY

John	Windham	392
John	Windham	394

KIMBALL

Abner	Methuen-Dracut	233
Abraham	Rumford	308
Benjamin	Haverhill	124
Benjamin	South Hampton	334
David	Rumford	308
Jonathan	Haverhill	128
Jonathan	South Hampton	334
Philip	Rumford	308
Richard	Methuen-Dracut	224
Samuel	Haverhill	134

KINCAID

Samuel	Londonderry	198

KNIGHT

John	Newington	256
John, Jr.	Newington	257
John, Jr.	Newington	258
Joshua	Haverhill	138
Nathaniel	Haverhill	122
Nicholas	Newington	255
Robert	Rochester	290

KNOWLES

Amos	Hampton	66
James	Rye	316
John	Rye	316
John, Jr.	Rye	316
Jonathan	Hampton	74
Simon	Hampton	70
Simon	Rye	322
Widow	Rye	328

KNOWLTON

Ebenezer	Hampton Falls	100
Ebenezer	Hampton Falls	117
Ebenezer	Kensington	156
Thomas	Kensington	156

KNOX

George	Londonderry	208

LADD

Daniel	Kingston	168
John	Kingston	170

LAMPREY

Benjamin Jr.	Hampton	66
John	Hampton	64
Morris	Hampton	66
Nathaniel	Hampton	66

LANE

John	Rye	324
Joshua	Hampton	58
Joshua	Hampton	83
Samuel	Hampton Falls	98
Samuel	Hampton Falls	117
Thomas	Hampton	66

LANGLEY

Job	Durham	38
John	Durham	36
Thomas	Durham	16

LANGMAID

Henry	New Castle	244
Samuel	New Castle	248
William	Rye	322

LARNES

Joseph	Stratham	372

LARY

William	New Castle	244

LASIN

John	New Castle	248

LASKEY

John	Durham	38

LEACH

John	New Castle	244

LEAR

Nathaniel	New Castle	244
Tobias	New Castle	242

LEATHERS

Abednego	Durham	36
Ebenezer	Durham	38
Edward	Durham	34
Ezekiel	Durham	26
Jonathan	Durham	38
Stephen	Durham	34
Thomas	Durham	32
William	Durham	30

LEAVITT

Amos	Hampton Falls	106
Benjamin	Stratham	378
Ephraim	Stratham	378
James	Hampton	74
James	Stratham	378
John	Hampton	72
Jonathan	Hampton	74
Jonathan	Hampton	85
Joseph	Kingston	168
Miles	Stratham	372
Moses	Hampton	70
Moses	Kingston	168
Moses	Stratham	382
Nathaniel	Stratham	386
Samuel	Hampton	72

Samuel	Hampton	83	LOVEWELL		
Samuel	Stratham	380	John	Dunstable	4
Thos.	Hampton Falls	96	Jonathan	Dunstable	4
Widow	Stratham	378	LOW		
LEIGHTON			Jacob	Stratham	378
John	Rochester	294	LOWELL		
Thomas	Newington	254	David	Methuen-Dracut	224
LENIERE			John	Methuen-Dracut	224
George	New Castle	240	John	Methuen-Dracut	224
LESLIE			LUBEN		
James	Londonderry	216	Elisha	New Castle	240
LIBBY			LUND		
Isaac	Rye	324	Ephraim	Dunstable	4
Jacob	Rye	324	Jonathan	Dunstable	2
John	Rye	324	Phinehas	Dunstable	4
Samuel	Rye	324	Thomas	Dunstable	2
LINDALL			William	Dunstable	4
James	Litchfield	180	William	Litchfield	182
LINDSAY			LUNT		
James	Londonderry	216	Henry	Kingston	168
LINN			LURVEY		
James	Londonderry	221	Stephen	Rumford	308
LITTLE			LYON		
Daniel	Haverhill	130	William	Rumford	308
George	Haverhill	128	MACAFEE		
George, Sr.	Haverhill	134	John	Rochester	294
Samuel	Haverhill	124	MACE		
Samuel	Haverhill	126	Andrew	Hampton	68
LITTLEHALE			Andrew	New Castle	244
John	Methuen-Dracut	230	Reuben	Haverhill	134
LOCKE			Reuben	New Castle	240
Edward	Kensington	146	MACK		
Eleazer	Rye	316	John	Londonderry	212
Elisha	Rye	316	William	Londonderry	221
Francis	Hampton	84	MAKER		
Francis	Rye	324	Tom	New Castle	244
James	Rochester	296	MARDEN		
James	Rye	316	Ebenezer	Rye	320
John	Rye	316	James	Rye	320
Jonathan	Rye	328	Jonathan	Rye	322
Joseph	Hampton	84	Samuel	Rye	320
Joseph	Rye	326	Stephen	Rye	320
Joseph, Jr.	Rye	326	William	Rye	320
Richard	Rye	316	William	Rye	322
Samuel	Hampton	66	MARSH		
Samuel	Kingston	162	Hezekiah	Newmarket	270
William	Rye	316	MARSTON		
William, Jr.	Rye	316	Benjamin	Hampton	58
LONGFELLOW			Caleb	Hampton	70
Jonathan	Hampton Falls	116	Caleb, Jr.	Hampton	70
LORD			Caleb, Jr.	Hampton	85
William	Durham	16	Daniel	Hampton	74
LOVERING			Ephraim	Hampton	74
John	Kensington	146	Ephraim	Hampton	83
John	Kingston	168	Ephraim	Hampton	87

Isaac	Hampton	78		John	Londonderry	220
Isaac	Newmarket	266		Richard	Londonderry	210
Jacob	Hampton	70		McCALLUM		
James	Newmarket	264		Alexander	Londonderry	204
Jeremiah	Hampton	68		McCLANAGHAN		
Jeremiah	Hampton	86		William	Londonderry	212
John	Hampton	70		McCLEARY		
Jonathan	Hampton	64		Thomas	Londonderry	221
Jonathan, Jr.	Hampton	72		McCLURG		
Joseph	Rye	326		John	Londonderry	204
Obediah	Hampton	68		McCONACHIE		
Reuben	Hampton	72		John	Londonderry	200
Samuel	Hampton	70		McCORMICK		
Thomas	Hampton	78		Archibald	Londonderry	206
Thomas	Hampton	82		McCURDY		
MARTIN				Archibald	Londonderry	196
Edward	New Castle	238		Charles	Londonderry	214
Edward, Jr.	New Castle	246		James	Londonderry	198
George	South Hampton	336		Robert	Londonderry	190
John	New Castle	240		McDONALD		
John	South Hampton	352		James	Dunstable	10
John, Jr.	New Castle	246		McDUFFEE		
John, Jr.	South Hampton	352		Daniel	Londonderry	192
Jonathan	New Castle	246		McEWEN		
Nathaniel	Londonderry	198		Robert	Litchfield	178
Robert	Londonderry	196		McFARLANE		
Robert	South Hampton	336		Nathan	Londonderry	192
William	Londonderry	198		Walter	Londonderry	192
MASON				McGREGOR		
Benjamin	Hampton	80		Daniel	Londonderry	220
Benjamin	Hampton	83		McINTOSH		
Benjamin	Stratham	378		Archibald	Londonderry	190
Isaac	Durham	20		McKAY		
John	Durham	30		John	Windham	396
John	Hampton	74		McKEEN		
Nat	Hampton	70		James	Londonderry	200
Peter	Durham	18		John	Litchfield	184
MASTON				John	Londonderry	200
Widow	Methuen-Dracut	230		Robert	Litchfield	178
MATTHEWS				Samuel	Londonderry	210
Abraham	Durham	16		McKILLOP		
Benjamin	Durham	20		David	Londonderry	220
Francis	Durham	18		McKNIGHT		
MATTOON				James	Litchfield	180
Richard	Newmarket	262		McMASTER		
Richard	Newmarket	277		William	Londonderry	190
MAXFIELD				McMULLEN		
Joseph	South Hampton	348		Daniel	Londonderry	214
Nathaniel	South Hampton	346		McMURPHY		
Nathaniel	South Hampton	360		Archibald	Londonderry	208
McADAM				John	Londonderry	218
Samuel	Windham	394		Widow	Londonderry	188
McALLISTER				McNEILL		
David	Londonderry	212		Alexander	Londonderry	196
William	Londonderry	212		Daniel	Rochester	294

William	Londonderry	214		John	Newmarket	264
McQUAID				MITCHELL		
James	Londonderry	204		David	New Castle	244
MEAD				George	Londonderry	200
John	Newmarket	268		James	Methuen-Dracut	233
John	Stratham	368		John	Londonderry	200
MEADER				Philip	Methuen-Dracut	233
Daniel	Durham	34		Samuel	Londonderry	200
John	Durham	38		MOFFATT		
Joseph	Durham	42		John	Portsmouth	286
Joseph, Jr.	Durham	34		MONTGOMERY		
Moses	Durham	42		Hugh	Londonderry	196
Nathaniel	Durham	30		Hugh	Londonderry	221
Nicholas	Durham	34		Robert	Londonderry	210
Samuel	Durham	40		MOODY		
MELCHER				Joshua	South Hampton	352
John	Kensington	156		Capt.	Stratham	368
Samuel	Hampton Falls	92		Hugh	Londonderry	212
Samuel	South Hampton	361		James	Londonderry	198
MELLDRUM				James	Londonderry	214
John	Stratham	376		John	Londonderry	188
MELVIN				Samuel	Litchfield	178
Jonathan	Dunstable	10		Thomas	Stratham	378
MERRILL				Widow	Londonderry	188
Abraham	Haverhill	126		Widow	Londonderry	198
Enoch	Stratham	380		William	Stratham	368
James	South Hampton	342		William	Stratham	370
John	Rumford	308		MORDENT		
Jonathan	Haverhill	126		William	New Castle	240
Joseph	South Hampton	342		MOREY		
Joseph	Stratham	380		Timothy	Stratham	376
Joseph 3rd	Stratham	380		MORGAN		
Joseph, Jr.	Stratham	378		Abraham	Stratham	380
Moses	South Hampton	361		Robert	Stratham	386
Nathaniel	Haverhill	128		Timothy	Hampton Falls	94
Nathaniel	South Hampton	342		MORRILL		
Stephen	South Hampton	361		Abner	South Hampton	340
Thomas	South Hampton	342		Abraham	South Hampton	336
MERRY				Abraham	South Hampton	361
Samuel	Rochester	298		Benjamin	Kingston	168
Samuel, Jr.	Rochester	298		Benjamin	South Hampton	348
MESSER				Benjamin	South Hampton	360
Nathaniel	Methuen-Dracut	233		Ezekiel	South Hampton	340
METCALF				Jacob	South Hampton	360
Joseph	Newmarket	264		John	South Hampton	340
MIGHILL				John	South Hampton	360
John	Newmarket	264		Joseph	South Hampton	342
Samuel	Newmarket	264		Nathaniel	South Hampton	342
Widow	Newmarket	264		Paul	South Hampton	340
MILLER				Paul	South Hampton	360
Archibald	Londonderry	190		Reuben	South Hampton	361
Benjamin	Newington	256		Samuel	South Hampton	342
James	Londonderry	200		Thomas	South Hampton	342
Samuel	Londonderry	200		William	South Hampton	348
MILLS				MORRISON		

NH 1742 ESTATE LIST INDEX 421

David	Londonderry	204		MUNSEY		
Ezekiel	Windham	392		John	Durham	36
Halbert	Londonderry	194		MURDER		
Halbert	Windham	394		Samuel	Dunstable	4
James	Londonderry	202		MURDOCK		
John	Londonderry	194		Samuel	Londonderry	216
Jonathan	Londonderry	220		William	Londonderry	216
Joseph	Londonderry	196		MUZZEY		
Robert	Londonderry	196		John	Haverhill	128
Samuel	Londonderry	196		Reuben	Kingston	162
Samuel	Londonderry	204		NAHOR		
Samuel	Londonderry	208		Hugh	Litchfield	184
Samuel	Windham	392		James	Litchfield	184
Thomas	Methuen-Dracut	233		NASON		
Thomas	Windham	392		Jonathan	Hampton Falls	98
MORROW				NAY		
James	Londonderry	206		John	Hampton	76
John	Windham	394		NEAL		
MORSE				Hubertus	Newmarket	266
Jacob	South Hampton	334		Joshua	Stratham	374
Peter	South Hampton	338		Richard	New Castle	240
MORTON				Samuel	Newmarket	266
Matthew	Hampton Falls	108		Walter	Newmarket	266
Matthew	Hampton Falls	116		William	New Castle	248
MOULTON				NESMITH		
Abraham	Kensington	158		James	Londonderry	200
Ben.	Hampton	82		NEVINS		
Benjamin	Hampton Falls	92		David	Dunstable	10
Daniel	Rye	316		Thomas	Dunstable	10
Edward	Hampton	72		William	Dunstable	10
Edward	Hampton	85		NEWMAN		
Eliz.	Hampton	68		John	Hampton	58
Ezekiel	Hampton	70		Thomas	Kingston	168
Hannah	Hampton	68		NEWMARCH		
Henry	Hampton	68		Joseph	New Castle	238
Henry	Hampton	83		NICHOLS		
Jacob	Hampton	74		George	Litchfield	182
James	Hampton	82		James	Londonderry	208
James	Hampton Falls	94		Robert	Litchfield	184
Jeremiah	Hampton	64		Widow	Kingston	172
John, Jr.	Hampton	66		William	Londonderry	194
John, Sr.	Hampton	66		NICKLE see NICHOLS		
Jonathan	Hampton	64		NIMOCK		
Joseph	Hampton	68		James	Londonderry	220
Joseph, Jr.	Hampton	70		NOBLE		
Josiah	Hampton	64		Lazarus	Durham	40
Robert	Hampton	76		NORRIS		
Samuel	Hampton	66		Benjamin	Stratham	366
Widow	Rye	324		NORTON		
William	Hampton	70		David	South Hampton	358
William	Hampton	72		Joseph	South Hampton	358
William	Hampton	85		NOYES		
Worthington	Hampton	72		James	Haverhill	138
MUGLADY				Simon	Kingston	168
John	Methuen-Dracut	230		Simon	Kingston	175

Sylvanus	Haverhill	126	Edmund	Haverhill	122
Timothy	Haverhill	124	Eliphalet	Haverhill	132
NUDD			Elisha	Hampton	72
Samuel	Hampton	66	Francis	Hampton	74
NUTT			Francis	Hampton	86
William	Londonderry	212	Jeremiah	Hampton	68
NUTTER			John	Hampton Falls	106
Anthony	Newington	256	John	Kensington	152
Hatevil	Newington	254	John	Methuen-Dracut	224
Hatevil	Newington	256	John	South Hampton	348
James	Newington	255	John	South Hampton	360
John	Newington	255	Jonathan	Hampton	66
Joseph	Durham	40	Jonathan	Haverhill	130
Matthias	Newington	257	Joseph	Hampton	74
Samuel	Newington	255	Joseph	Haverhill	132
NUTTING			Joseph	South Hampton	356
Daniel	Dunstable	12	Joseph, Jr.	South Hampton	360
O'SHAW			Joshua	Haverhill	132
James	New Castle	246	Moses	Haverhill	132
John	New Castle	238	Onesiphorus	Kingston	170
OBER			Onesiphorus	South Hampton	361
John	Methuen-Dracut	224	Samuel	Hampton	58
John	Methuen-Dracut	226	Samuel	Kensington	152
John	Methuen-Dracut	228	Solomon	Hampton	60
John	Methuen-Dracut	230	Theophilus	Kensington	154
John	Methuen-Dracut	234	Thomas	Hampton	60
John	Windham	396	Timothy	Haverhill	132
John, Jr.	Methuen-Dracut	226	PAINE		
ODELL			Henry	New Castle	238
Thomas	Stratham	378	John	New Castle	242
ODIORNE			John	Rye	318
Batha	New Castle	238	Philip	Rye	318
Benjamin	New Castle	248	William	Rye	322
John	New Castle	238	PALMER		
John	New Castle	242	Benjamin	Stratham	366
Nathaniel	New Castle	242	Christopher	Hampton	64
ORDWAY			Christopher	Rye	324
James	South Hampton	352	Edward	Kensington	146
Nathan	Kingston	162	James	Newmarket	272
ORNELD			John	Newmarket	272
Widow	South Hampton	361	Jonathan	Hampton	68
OSGOOD			Jonathan	Kensington	152
David	South Hampton	361	Joseph	Stratham	366
James	Rumford	308	Richard	Stratham	366
William	South Hampton	361	Samuel	Hampton	87
OTTERSON			Samuel, Jr.	Hampton	64
James	Londonderry	214	Samuel, Sr.	Hampton	64
PAGE			Stephen	Rye	324
Amos	South Hampton	346	William	Hampton	70
Benjamin	Kensington	146	William	Rye	324
Caleb	Haverhill	140	PARKER		
Caleb	Haverhill	142	Alexander	Litchfield	182
Christopher	Hampton	68	Alexander	Windham	392
Daniel	South Hampton	346	Benjamin	Dunstable	8
David	Hampton	66	Henry	Dunstable	2

Robert	Windham	392	Moses	Hampton	72
Samuel	Methuen-Dracut	228	Robert	Newmarket	268
Thomas	New Castle	240	Samuel	Durham	30
PARKES			Solomon	Rochester	296
Thomas	New Castle	240	Thomas	Rochester	294
PARSONS			PERRY		
Josiah	Stratham	374	Obediah	Haverhill	124
Josiah, Jr.	Stratham	374	PERVERE		
PATCH			Philip	Hampton Falls	110
Thomas	Dunstable	8	PETERS		
PATTEE			James	Rumford	308
Nathaniel	Haverhill	140	Obediah	Rumford	308
Peter	Haverhill	138	Seaborn	Rumford	308
Richard	Haverhill	140	PETTENGILL		
Seth	Haverhill	140	Benjamin	Haverhill	138
Susannah	Haverhill	140	PHILBRICK		
PATTERSON			Abner	Hampton Falls	104
James	Londonderry	212	Benjamin	Haverhill	130
Joseph	Newington	256	Eben	Hampton	84
Peter	Londonderry	212	Ebenezer	Rye	328
Samuel	Londonderry	190	Elias	Hampton	82
PAUL			Isaac	Hampton	64
Thomas	Haverhill	140	James	Rye	328
PEARSON			John	Hampton Falls	102
Jeremiah	Hampton Falls	100	John	Hampton Falls	117
PEASE			Jonathan	Hampton Falls	104
Nathaniel	Stratham	376	Joseph	Hampton	66
PEASLEE			Joseph	Hampton	84
Daniel	Methuen-Dracut	224	Joseph	Rye	324
David	South Hampton	352	Joses	Rye	324
Jacob	South Hampton	352	Nathan	Hampton	62
James	South Hampton	352	Nathan	Hampton	83
John	South Hampton	338	Thomas	Hampton Falls	102
John, Jr.	South Hampton	338	Thomas	Hampton Falls	118
Joseph	Methuen-Dracut	224	Zachariah	Hampton Falls	112
Joseph	South Hampton	352	PHILBROOK see PHILBRICK		
Moses	South Hampton	352	PHILLIPS		
Nathan	South Hampton	352	Amos	Dunstable	10
Samuel	South Hampton	352	PICKERING		
Widow	Methuen-Dracut	224	James	Newington	254
PEDRICK			James	Newington	257
Mary	New Castle	238	James	Newington	258
PEIRCE see PIERCE			John	Newington	256
PENDERGAST			Joshua	Newington	254
Dennis	Durham	20	Thomas	Newington	254
Stephen	Durham	20	PIERCE		
PERKINS			D.	Portsmouth	286
Benjamin	Hampton Falls	112	John	New Castle	244
Daniel	Hampton Falls	104	John	Rochester	296
Daniel	Hampton Falls	116	PIKE		
James	Kensington	158	Hugh	Haverhill	138
James	Rye	316	John	Haverhill	132
John	Newmarket	274	John	South Hampton	361
John, Sr.	Newmarket	268	Joseph	Kensington	154
Mary	Newmarket	268	Robert	Newmarket	264

Robert, Jr.	Newmarket	264		Samuel	Hampton Falls	117
Thomas	Durham	38		PRESON		
PINDER				Nathan	Newmarket	264
Benjamin	Durham	22		PROCTOR		
John	Newmarket	266		Moses	Dunstable	10
PINKERTON				Widow	Methuen-Dracut	232
John	Londonderry	208		PULSIFER		
PIPER				Jonathan	Kensington	148
John	Stratham	376		PURINTON		
Jonathan	Stratham	376		John	South Hampton	361
Josiah	Stratham	374		Joshua	Hampton Falls	106
Nathaniel	Stratham	378		Widow	Kensington	154
Samuel	Stratham	374		PURMORT		
Samuel, Jr.	Stratham	374		John	Stratham	386
Thomas	Stratham	380		PUTNEY		
PITMAN				Samuel	Rumford	308
John	Durham	36		William	Rumford	308
PLACE				QUIGLEY		
Eben	Rochester	290		Thomas	Windham	394
James	Rochester	296		QUIMBY		
Richard	Newington	256		Robert	Hampton Falls	98
Samuel	Newington	256		RAMSEY		
PLUMER				Hugh	Londonderry	216
Samuel	South Hampton	338		RAND		
POLLARD				Edmund	Hampton	68
John	Haverhill	136		Edmund	Hampton	85
Joseph	Litchfield	178		John	Rye	322
POOLE				Joshua	Rye	318
Joshua	Stratham	376		Joshua	Rye	322
POOR				Nathaniel	Rye	320
Daniel	Haverhill	132		Richard	Rye	316
POPE				Richard	Rye	322
Thomas	Haverhill	122		Thomas	Rye	318
POWERS				William	Rye	318
Ephraim	Litchfield	180		RANDALL		
Jonathan	Litchfield	180		John	New Castle	248
Peter	Dunstable	6		Nathaniel	Durham	30
PRESCOTT				William	Durham	36
Abraham	Kensington	148		RANKIN		
Benjamin	Hampton Falls	94		James	Litchfield	182
Benjamin	Kensington	148		Samuel	Londonderry	214
Ebenezer	Hampton Falls	96		RASIDE		
Edward	Kingston	166		Jonathan	Londonderry	221
Elisha	Hampton Falls	94		READ		
James	Hampton Falls	96		Robert	Litchfield	180
James	Hampton Falls	117		William	Litchfield	178
James	Kensington	148		REDMAN		
John	Hampton Falls	96		Joseph	Hampton	64
Jonathan	Hampton Falls	94		REID		
Jonathan	Kensington	154		James	Londonderry	198
Joseph	Hampton Falls	94		Matthew	Londonderry	198
Joshua	Kingston	166		RICE		
Joshua	Kingston	175		Joseph	New Castle	246
Nathaniel	Kensington	156		RICHARDS		
Samuel	Hampton Falls	94		Benjamin	Haverhill	122

	Jonathan, Jr.	Rochester	290	Benjamin	Rumford	312
	Joseph	Rochester	290	Ezra	Rumford	308
	Joseph, Jr.	Rochester	296	Nathaniel	Rumford	308
	Samuel	Rochester	290	Samuel	Rumford	308
RICHARDSON				ROLLINS		
	Benjamin	Dunstable	4	Caleb	Stratham	372
	Ebenezer	Methuen-Dracut	230	David	Stratham	372
	Ezekial	Methuen-Dracut	232	Edward	Newington	256
	Henry	Methuen-Dracut	230	James	Newington	254
	James	Methuen-Dracut	232	James	Newmarket	272
	Jonathan	Litchfield	184	Jonathan	Stratham	372
	Josiah	Litchfield	180	Joseph	Newington	255
	Robert	Litchfield	180	Joseph	Stratham	368
RING				Joseph, Jr.	Newington	257
	David	South Hampton	348	Joshua	Stratham	368
	Seth	Newington	254	Moses	Stratham	372
RITCHIE				Robert	Newmarket	272
	Alexander	Windham	394	Samuel	Newington	255
	John	Londonderry	196	Samuel	Newmarket	272
RITTERSUN				Samuel, Jr.	Newington	256
	William	Methuen-Dracut	230	Thomas	Stratham	372
ROBERTS				Thomas, Jr.	Stratham	372
	Daniel	Haverhill	132	Widow	Stratham	372
	Jonathan	Haverhill	136	ROWE		
	Samuel	Rochester	298	Abial	Methuen-Dracut	233
	Timothy	Rochester	294	Benjamin	Kensington	146
	Timothy	Rochester	300	Jonathan	Kensington	146
ROBERTSON				Joseph	Kensington	158
	John	Litchfield	178	Joseph	Kingston	168
	William	Londonderry	202	Moses	Kensington	156
ROBIE				Moses	Kingston	168
	Henry	Hampton Falls	100	Robert	Hampton Falls	96
	Ichabod	Hampton	82	Robert	Kensington	146
	Ichabod	Hampton Falls	98	Widow	Newington	256
	Ichabod	Hampton Falls	117	ROWELL		
	Isaac	Hampton Falls	110	Benoni	Methuen-Dracut	224
	Thomas	Hampton	70	Benoni, Jr.	Methuen-Dracut	224
ROBINSON				Daniel	Kingston	170
	David	Stratham	382	Elijah	South Hampton	340
	George	Londonderry	220	John	Methuen-Dracut	224
	James	Stratham	378	Josiah	Methuen-Dracut	224
	John	Stratham	386	Philip	Kingston	172
	Jonathan	Hampton	84	Samuel	Methuen-Dracut	224
	Joseph	Stratham	386	Thomas	South Hampton	340
ROBKIN				William	South Hampton	336
	Alexander	Londonderry	188	RUNDLETT		
ROGERS				John	Stratham	382
	Daniel	Durham	18	Satchel	Stratham	382
	Hugh	Londonderry	210	Theophilus	Stratham	372
	James	Londonderry	196	RUNNELLS		
	James	Rochester	294	Job	Durham	34
	James, Jr.	Rochester	294	John	Durham	36
	Samuel	New Castle	248	Owen	Stratham	384
ROLFE				Thomas	Stratham	382
	Benjamin	Rumford	308	RUSS		

John	Rumford	308	Timothy	Methuen-Dracut	226
RUSSELL			Timothy	Windham	396
Peter	Litchfield	180	William	Methuen-Dracut	226
William	Hampton Falls	106	William	Windham	398
William	Hampton Falls	117	**SARGENT**		
SALTER			Daniel	South Hampton	336
John	New Castle	240	David	South Hampton	354
SANBORN			John	South Hampton	352
Abigail	Hampton Falls	96	Nathaniel	Hampton	60
Abner	Hampton Falls	112	Nathaniel	Hampton	83
Abner	South Hampton	361	Nathaniel	New Castle	240
Abraham	Kensington	154	Philip	South Hampton	354
Benjamin	Hampton Falls	96	William	Newmarket	264
Caleb	Hampton Falls	110	William	South Hampton	336
Caleb	Hampton Falls	116	William, Jr.	South Hampton	354
Daniel	Hampton	78	**SAWYER**		
David	Kensington	148	Edmund	South Hampton	338
Ebenezer	Hampton	78	William	South Hampton	338
Ebenezer	Hampton	83	**SCALES**		
Ebenezer	Hampton Falls	110	Abraham	Durham	28
Ebenezer, Jr.	Hampton Falls	110	**SCAMMON**		
Enoch	Hampton	58	William	Stratham	366
Enoch	Hampton	86	**SCOBIE**		
Enoch	Hampton Falls	110	John	Londonderry	208
Ephraim	Hampton Falls	92	**SCOTT**		
Jabez	Hampton Falls	92	Joshua	Methuen-Dracut	233
James	Hampton	76	**SEARLES**		
James	Kensington	148	Daniel	Dunstable	2
John	Hampton	76	John	Dunstable	2
Jonathan	Hampton	76	Samuel	Dunstable	2
Jonathan, Jr.	Hampton	76	**SEAVEY**		
Joseph	Hampton Falls	96	Benjamin	Rye	318
Mephibosheth	Hampton	64	Benjamin, Jr.	Rye	318
Moses	Kensington	152	Henry	Rochester	298
Nathan	Hampton Falls	96	Henry	Rye	318
Reuben	Hampton	76	James	Rye	318
Reuben	Hampton Falls	96	Joseph	Rye	318
Richard	Hampton	74	Joseph, Jr.	Rye	318
Richard	Hampton	85	Samuel	Rye	326
Richard	Kensington	148	Samuel, Jr.	Rye	326
Richard	Kensington	150	Thomas	Rochester	296
Shubael	Hampton	58	William	Rye	316
Stephen	Hampton	78	William	Rye	318
Winthrop	Hampton	76	William, Jr.	Rye	318
SANDERS			William, Tertius	Rye	318
David	Haverhill	140	**SENTER**		
Henry	Methuen-Dracut	226	Mrs.	Londonderry	212
Henry	Windham	398	**SHATTUCK**		
John	Rye	320	William	Dunstable	10
Moses	South Hampton	354	**SHAW**		
Oliver	Methuen-Dracut	226	Benjamin	Hampton	82
Oliver	Windham	396	Caleb	Kensington	148
Roland	Rye	320	Ebenezer	Hampton Falls	110
Samuel	Methuen-Dracut	226	Ebenezer	Hampton Falls	116
Samuel	Windham	396	Edward	Hampton	58

Elihu	Kensington	156	SMITH			
Gideon	Hampton	64		Abraham	Kingston	162
John	Hampton	78		Benjamin	Durham	24
Joseph	Kensington	156		Benjamin	Durham	26
Joseph	Kensington	156		Benjamin	Hampton	60
Mary	Hampton Falls	108		Benjamin	Londonderry	220
Moses	Kensington	156		David	Hampton	84
Roger	Hampton	76		David	Rye	324
Samuel	Hampton Falls	110		Ebenezer	Durham	26
Samuel	Hampton Falls	116		Edward	Kensington	152
SHEAFE				Elias	South Hampton	361
Jacob	New Castle	246		Elisha	Hampton	58
Sampson	New Castle	238		Jabez	Hampton	66
SHEPARD				Jabez	Hampton	88
Israel	South Hampton	358		Jabez	Hampton Falls	106
Solomon	South Hampton	346		Jabez	Hampton Falls	116
William	Durham	26		Jacob	South Hampton	358
SHERBURNE				James	Durham	28
Henry, Jr.	Portsmouth	286		James	Londonderry	204
John	Hampton	60		James	Windham	396
John	Kensington	148		John	Durham	26
John	New Castle	238		John	Hampton	60
SHUTE				John	Londonderry	202
Jacob	Rumford	310		John, Jr.	Durham	26
SIAS				Joseph	Durham	28
John	Durham	36		Joseph	Newmarket	270
Joseph	Durham	36		Joseph	Stratham	372
Samuel	Durham	38		Josiah	Stratham	372
Solomon	Durham	32		Nathaniel	Haverhill	138
SIBLEY				Oliver	Kingston	168
Jonathan	Stratham	366		Philip	Hampton	58
SIMPSON				Reuben	Kensington	158
Capt.	New Castle	238		Reuben	Kingston	168
SINCLAIR				Richard	South Hampton	358
John	Stratham	376		Sam	South Hampton	360
Richard	Stratham	366		Samuel	Durham	28
SINKLER see SINCLAIR				Samuel	Durham	34
SKINNER				Samuel	Hampton	78
John	New Castle	242		Samuel	Haverhill	126
SLADE				Samuel	South Hampton	356
Arthur	Newmarket	262		Solomon	Stratham	366
SLEEPER				Stephen	Hampton	76
Benjamin	Kingston	168		Theophilus	Stratham	380
Ebenezer	Kingston	162		Thomas	Haverhill	132
Jedediah	Hampton Falls	112		Widow	South Hampton	358
John	Hampton	76		Widow	South Hampton	360
SMART				William	Kingston	162
Benjamin	Newmarket	274		William	South Hampton	361
Charles	Newmarket	274	SMYLIE			
John	Durham	30		Frances	Haverhill	136
Joseph	Newmarket	262		John	Haverhill	136
Richard	Newmarket	274	SNELL			
Robert	Newmarket	274		Thomas	Durham	40
Robert	Newmarket	276	SOUTHER			
Robert	Newmarket	277		Benjamin	Hampton	74

SPAULDING
Ebenezer	Litchfield	178
Stephen	Litchfield	178

SPEED
John	Stratham	366

SPENCER
Ebenezer	Durham	36

STANFORD
William	Hampton	68
William	Hampton	83

STANYAN
Jacob	Hampton Falls	112
James	Hampton Falls	112
John	Hampton Falls	112
John	Kensington	156
Joseph	Hampton Falls	112

STEARNS
Zachariah	Litchfield	182

STEELE
Ezekiel	Rumford	310
John	Londonderry	198
John	Londonderry	210
Thomas	Londonderry	194

STERLING
Hugh	Londonderry	220

STEVENS
Aaron	Rumford	308
Aaron	South Hampton	338
Benjamin	Haverhill	130
Daniel	Stratham	368
Ebenezer	Kingston	164
Hubbard	Durham	34
Jeremiah	South Hampton	361
John	Haverhill	130
John	New Castle	238
John	Newington	256
Jonathan	Haverhill	126
Jonathan	South Hampton	361
Jonathan, Jr.	Haverhill	128
Joseph	Haverhill	132
Joseph, Jr.	Haverhill	130
Moses	Haverhill	134
Nathan	Rumford	310
Nathaniel	Durham	22
Nehemiah	Haverhill	130
Otho	Haverhill	128
Patience	Kingston	168
Samuel	Haverhill	128
Samuel	Haverhill	130
Sarah	Haverhill	134
Thomas	South Hampton	338
Waite	Haverhill	130
Widow	Stratham	374
William	Haverhill	130

STEVENSON
Abraham	Durham	18
Joseph	Durham	18
Joseph, Jr.	Durham	22

STEWARD
Charles	Hampton Falls	102
Charles	Hampton Falls	118
Jonathan	Hampton Falls	102

STEWART
Charles	Londonderry	192
James	Londonderry	220
John	Londonderry	192
John	Londonderry	221
John	Windham	392
Widow	Londonderry	194

STICKNEY
Jeremiah	Rumford	310
Moses	Hampton Falls	100
Wade	Kensington	146

STILLSON
James	New Castle	242

STINSON
John	Londonderry	192

STOCKBRIDGE
Abraham	Stratham	384
John	Stratham	384

STOCKMAN
Robert	Kingston	166

STONE
Benjamin	Haverhill	134
Thomas	Haverhill	126

STRAW
David	South Hampton	354
John	South Hampton	338
Lawrence	South Hampton	342
Samuel	South Hampton	342
William	South Hampton	348

SWAIN
Caleb	Hampton Falls	98
Caleb	Hampton Falls	117
Elias	Hampton Falls	98
John	Hampton Falls	96

SWAN
Timothy	Methuen-Dracut	228

SWETT
Benjamin	Hampton Falls	108
Benjamin	Hampton Falls	116
Benjamin, Jr.	Hampton Falls	110
Benjamin, Jr.	Hampton Falls	116
Daniel	Hampton Falls	106
Daniel	Hampton Falls	116
David	Hampton Falls	106
Jonathan	Hampton Falls	106

TAGGART
James	Londonderry	204
John	Londonderry	206

NH 1742 ESTATE LIST INDEX

John	Londonderry	220
Neil	Londonderry	221
Patrick	Litchfield	180
TAPPAN		
James	Kingston	166
Widow	Hampton	68
TASH		
Jacob	Durham	22
TAYLOR		
Abraham	Dunstable	6
Abraham	Dunstable	12
Benjamin	Stratham	368
Benjamin	Stratham	372
Ebenezer	Litchfield	178
Edward	Stratham	368
John	Hampton	76
Joseph	Hampton	72
Matthew	Londonderry	194
Richard	Hampton	58
Richard	Hampton	85
Richard	Hampton	87
William	Litchfield	178
William	Newmarket	272
TEMPLE		
Christopher	Litchfield	182
Richard	Dunstable	6
TEMPLETON		
Adam	Rochester	296
THOMAS		
Benjamin	Hampton	78
Benjamin	Hampton	86
James	Hampton	78
Jonathan	Hampton	58
Jonathan	Hampton	83
Joseph	Durham	28
THOMPSON		
Andrew	Londonderry	210
James	Durham	38
James	Londonderry	194
James	Londonderry	196
John	Durham	32
John	Londonderry	212
Jonathan	Durham	36
Matthew	Stratham	366
Matthew, Jr.	Stratham	366
Peter	Kingston	170
Robert	Durham	34
Robert	Windham	394
Robert, Jr.	Durham	38
Samuel	Londonderry	212
William	Londonderry	196
William	Rochester	296
THOMS		
William	Windham	392
THORN		

James	South Hampton	361
THORNTON		
Ebenezer	Methuen-Dracut	232
THRESHER		
Joseph	Hampton Falls	102
Joseph	Hampton Falls	117
THURSTON		
John	Stratham	384
Stephen	Stratham	386
TIBBETTS		
Aaron	Rochester	292
Benjamin	Rochester	294
Edward	Rochester	296
Eliza.	Rochester	292
Ephraim	Rochester	292
Joseph	Rochester	292
Paul	Rochester	292
TILTON		
Abraham	Stratham	384
Jacob	Newmarket	264
Jethro	Hampton Falls	98
Jethro	Hampton Falls	116
Jethro	Hampton Falls	118
John	Hampton Falls	98
John	Kensington	152
Jonathan	Hampton Falls	94
Joseph	Hampton Falls	94
Joseph	Hampton Falls	116
Joseph	Kensington	154
Josiah	Kingston	166
Nathan	Hampton Falls	94
Nathan	Hampton Falls	116
Samuel	Hampton Falls	98
Sherburne	Kensington	152
TINKER		
Lewis	New Castle	244
TODD		
Andrew	Londonderry	204
Joseph	South Hampton	358
TOWLE		
Benjamin	Hampton	74
Caleb	Hampton	74
James	Hampton	70
Jeremiah	Hampton	76
Jeremiah	Hampton	83
John	Hampton	60
Jonathan	Rye	324
Joseph	Hampton	78
Joseph	South Hampton	342
Joseph, Jr.	Hampton	70
Joshua	Hampton	76
Philip	Hampton	68
Philip	Hampton	83
Thomas	South Hampton	354
Zachariah	Hampton	60

Zachariah	Hampton	85		Benjamin	New Castle	240
TOWNSEND				Joseph	Litchfield	182
Timothy	South Hampton	348		Phinehas	Litchfield	182
TREADWELL				URIN		
Charles	Hampton Falls	112		John	Rumford	310
John	Hampton Falls	102		Peter	Methuen-Dracut	228
John	Hampton Falls	117		USHER		
TREDICK				John	Litchfield	182
Henry	New Castle	244		VANCE		
TREFETHEN				David	Londonderry	196
Abraham	New Castle	246		John	Windham	392
Foster	New Castle	240		VARNUM		
Foster, Jr.	New Castle	246		James	Methuen-Dracut	230
Henry	New Castle	240		John	Methuen-Dracut	232
Henry, Jr.	New Castle	244		Joseph	Methuen-Dracut	232
James	New Castle	242		Samuel	Methuen-Dracut	230
John	New Castle	246		Thomas	Methuen-Dracut	232
Robertson	New Castle	246		VEASEY		
TRICKEY				George	Stratham	366
John	Rochester	292		George, Jr.	Stratham	370
Jonathan	Newington	256		George, Jr.	Stratham	380
TRUE				Samuel	Stratham	380
John	South Hampton	348		Thomas	Stratham	382
John	South Hampton	361		Thomas, Jr.	Stratham	382
William	South Hampton	361		VINCENT		
TRUMBLE				John	Newington	255
Judah	Rumford	310		John	Newington	256
TRUNDY				VIRGIN		
John	New Castle	242		Ebenezer	Rumford	310
TRUSSELL				WADLEIGH		
Moses	Haverhill	122		John	Stratham	372
TUCK				WAKEHAM		
Ebenezer	Hampton Falls	110		Caleb	Durham	18
Ebenezer	Hampton Falls	116		WALKER		
Edward	Kensington	146		Alexander	Londonderry	202
Ezra	South Hampton	336		Charles	Hampton	60
James	South Hampton	361		Edward	Newington	256
Jonathan	Hampton	58		Isaac, Jr.	Rumford	310
Jonathan	Hampton	86		Joseph	Rochester	296
Jonathan	Hampton	87		Timothy, Jr.	Rumford	310
Joseph	South Hampton	348		William	Rumford	310
Lemuel	Haverhill	122		WALLACE		
Nathaniel	Haverhill	136		James	Londonderry	214
William	Rye	320		John	Londonderry	194
TUCKER, see Tuck				John	Londonderry	202
TUCKERMAN				John	Londonderry	216
Jon	New Castle	240		Joseph	Londonderry	206
TUFTS				Robert	Londonderry	206
Henry	Newmarket	264		Thomas, Jr.	Londonderry	214
John	Londonderry	220		Thomas, Sr.	Londonderry	214
Thomas	Newmarket	264		WALLEN		
TWOMBLY				George	Newington	255
Samuel	Rochester	294		WALLIS		
UNDERWOOD				Deborah	New Castle	244
Aquila	Litchfield	182		Samuel	Rye	318

NH 1742 ESTATE LIST INDEX

WALTON
- Jonathan — South Hampton — 356
- Madam — New Castle — 238
- Samuel — South Hampton — 356
- Shadrach — Durham — 40

WARD
- Abel — Kensington — 154
- Noah — Hampton — 60
- Noah — Hampton — 85
- Shadrach — Kensington — 158
- Thomas — Hampton — 60

WATSON
- Jonathan — South Hampton — 334
- Nathaniel — Durham — 20
- Nathaniel — Newmarket — 270
- Samuel — Durham — 20
- Thomas — Rye — 318

WATTON
- John — Newington — 256

WATTS
- John — Haverhill — 140

WAUGH
- Joseph — Windham — 394

WEARE
- John — Kensington — 154
- Meshech — Hampton Falls — 114
- Meshech — Hampton Falls — 118
- Nathaniel — Hampton Falls — 106
- Nathaniel — Hampton Falls — 117
- Peter — Hampton Falls — 108
- Prudence — Hampton Falls — 108

WEBSTER
- Ebenezer — Kingston — 162
- Israel — Haverhill — 132
- Jeremiah — Kingston — 166
- John — Haverhill — 124
- John — Kingston — 162
- John — Rumford — 310
- John — South Hampton — 338
- Josiah — Rye — 322
- Thomas — Kingston — 162
- Thomas — Kingston — 175
- William — Haverhill — 132

WEDGWOOD
- John — Hampton — 70
- John — Newmarket — 264

WEED
- Capt. — New Castle — 238
- David — South Hampton — 342
- Orlando — South Hampton — 340
- Widow — South Hampton — 342

WEEKS
- Jonathan — Stratham — 388

WEIR
- Adam — Londonderry — 206
- John — Londonderry — 194

WELCH
- Jonathan — Durham — 34

WELLS
- Samuel — Rye — 326

WENTWORTH
- John — Rochester — 290
- Richard — Rochester — 290

WEST
- Edward — Rumford — 310
- Edward — Rumford — 312
- Nathaniel — Rumford — 310

WHEATON
- Ichabod — Newmarket — 268

WHEELER
- Benjamin — Haverhill — 140
- Jeremiah — South Hampton — 356
- Jonathan — Haverhill — 140
- Joseph — Durham — 16
- Peter — Dunstable — 10
- Stephen — Haverhill — 122

WHIDDEN
- James — Greenland — 54

WHITAKER
- Daniel — Haverhill — 132
- Jonathan — Haverhill — 138
- William — Haverhill — 140

WHITCHER
- Andrew — South Hampton — 336
- Timothy — South Hampton — 354
- William — Kingston — 170
- William — Kingston — 175

WHITE
- Henry — Litchfield — 184
- James — Haverhill — 126
- Nathan — New Castle — 238
- Nathaniel, Jr. — New Castle — 242
- Nicholas — Haverhill — 136
- Robert — New Castle — 246
- Solomon — New Castle — 246

WHITEHOUSE
- Pomfret — Durham — 26
- Samuel — Rochester — 290

WHITING
- Samuel — Dunstable — 4

WHITNEY
- Sylvanus — Dunstable — 6

WHITTEMORE
- David — Litchfield — 182

WIBIRD
- William — Hampton — 76

WIGGIN
- Andrew — Newmarket — 272
- Cornet — Stratham — 374
- John — Stratham — 374

John, Jr.	Stratham	374		Jonathan	Windham	398
Joseph, Jr.	Stratham	374		Nathaniel	Methuen-Dracut	226
Samuel	Stratham	374		Nathaniel	Windham	396
Tristram	Stratham	374		WOODMAN		
Walter	Stratham	374		Archelaus	Durham	30
WILLEY				Edward	Durham	32
John	Durham	22		John	Durham	30
John 3rd	Durham	22		Jonathan	Durham	30
John, Jr.	Durham	18		Jonathan, Jr.	Durham	30
Samuel	Durham	22		Joshua	Durham	28
Stephen	Durham	16		WOOLERICK		
Theodorus	Durham	18		Philip	Dunstable	10
Thomas	Durham	26		WORCESTER		
Thomas	Durham	40		Thomas	Methuen-Dracut	233
William	Durham	26		WORMWOOD		
WILLIAMS				Joseph	Durham	28
Edward	Hampton Falls	106		William	Durham	18
John	Durham	34		WORTH		
John	Durham	44		Joseph	Hampton Falls	102
John, Jr.	Durham	34		WORTHEN		
Joseph	Durham	30		Ezekiel	Kensington	154
Thomas	South Hampton	338		John	South Hampton	356
Walter	Hampton Falls	114		Samuel	Haverhill	126
WILMOT				Samuel, Jr.	Haverhill	128
Edward	Hampton	68		Thomas	Haverhill	138
WILSON				WRIGHT		
Benjamin	Londonderry	210		Joseph	Methuen-Dracut	228
Hugh	Londonderry	198		Josiah	Dunstable	8
James	Londonderry	200		Matthew	Londonderry	216
James	Londonderry	208		Robert	Methuen-Dracut	230
John	Londonderry	204		WYMAN		
John	Windham	394		Edward	Methuen-Dracut	230
John, Sr.	Londonderry	208		Joseph	Methuen-Dracut	228
Joseph	Litchfield	180		Thomas	Methuen-Dracut	230
Nathaniel	Londonderry	208		YEATON		
Thomas	Londonderry	198		John	New Castle	242
Thomas	Londonderry	216		Richard	New Castle	244
Thomas	Stratham	382		Samuel	New Castle	244
William	Londonderry	192		YORK		
WINGATE				Benjamin	Newmarket	268
Joshua	Hampton	78		Benjamin	Newmarket	272
Joshua, Jr.	Hampton	74		John	Durham	26
Joshua, Jr.	Hampton	85		John	Newmarket	270
WINTER				Joseph	Newmarket	268
Thomas	New Castle	242		Thomas	Durham	22
WOOD				YOUNG		
Joseph	Methuen-Dracut	230		Israel	Methuen-Dracut	224
WOODBRIDGE				John	Newmarket	270
Benjamin	South Hampton	354		Jonathan	Rochester	296
WOODBURN				Joseph	Hampton Falls	108
John	Londonderry	204		Richard	Stratham	374
WOODBURY				Thomas	Newmarket	270
Ebenezer	Methuen-Dracut	226		Thomas, Jr.	Newmarket	270
Ebenezer	Windham	396		---, Samuel	South Hampton	360
Jonathan	Methuen-Dracut	226				

www.ingramcontent.com/pod-product-compliance
Lightning Source LLC
Chambersburg PA
CBHW050325230426
43663CB00010B/1742